THE YOUTUBER JOURNEY

A Complete Guide to Pursuing a Creative Career Through YouTube®

BRADLEY BURKE

Published by Author Academy Elite
P.O. Box 43, Powell, OH 43035
www.AuthorAcademyElite.com

Paperback ISBN-13: 978-1-64085-180-1
Hardcover ISBN-13: 978-1-64085-181-8
Library of Congress Control Number: 2017919208

To the next generation of content creators.

Your journey starts today.

CONTENTS

That feeling of wanting to do more. The sense that the path you were told to take in life isn't for you. You realize something profound and break from the formula.

You think more and more about what you want to do and the creative endeavors that you want to explore. It's scary to think about, because you have to deviate from everything you may have been told. You begin to prep for the change, and you get to the edge and you don't know whether to jump or not. Will you be financially okay? What if things don't work out? You hesitate, but you jump anyways.

THE CARTOGRAPHER'S DISCOVERY   17

You land in an area that is new to you. Whether you eased your way into this journey or simply jumped in headfirst, you arrive at the same location. You don't know which path to take in this large world. You have feelings of what you want to do though, so you follow your gut and adapt along the way.

THE HERO'S DEFEAT   32

After creating you eventually get beat down. You imagined things would go differently. You believe you should be farther along than you actually are. Your rations are dwindling and you think about turning back. The thought of giving up crosses your mind, but you move forward regardless. One foot in front of the other. You conserve your rations and you adapt from your failures. In this giant world we are all looking for success, but we never know how close it is.

ADAPTING TO THE WILD   39

You gain a sense of traction and the growth is exciting. At this point you brainstorm how to make it grow. What next steps need to happen for this journey to continue? How can you expand what you're doing? How can you make it financially viable to make a living? You cast a big net to catch all kinds of different fish.

THE MATURITY OF TIME

You've found a really nice town that you enjoy and you set up
shop there. You've honed your craft through your journey and
you've really improved as a creative professional. This sense of
living works for you and you wouldn't mind being here for a
while. You've discovered a formula that is repeatable and you
may even have some people helping you at this point.

THE SECOND DEPARTURE

Your mind wanders from the safety of being comfortable. Things
might be going decently, but you begin to lose your spark. The
mundaneness of your formula begins to stale your creativity.
You remember why you started in the first place and decide to
begin moving again. Your friends join you as you wander back
out into the unknown. There's more stability this time around,
but you have yet to discover what you're looking for.

AT LAND'S END

You reach the edge of the world and you stare at the unknown
land before you. It's different than what you're used to, but the
challenge is welcoming. You've honed your craft enough to take

on a new challenge – to branch out creatively into a new avenue. To start from ground zero, but take all your experience with you.

TRAVELER'S NOTES

YOUTUBER STORIES

PREFACE

Welcome to the start of your YouTube journey. If you're reading this, you're probably interested in the life of an online content creator—and more specifically, being a YouTuber. The creative path of a YouTuber is quite the adventure and one I find myself loving day in and day out.

I grew up with my head always in the clouds. When I wasn't playing video games, I was lost in my sketch books doodling my favorite characters. Sometimes I felt like I didn't quite fit in with everyone else and I often hid my passions from the world. Looking back, I realize I shouldn't have hid who I truly was. If anything, I should have embraced my passions whole-heartedly and believed in myself.

I grew up believing in a cookie-cutter life path that consisted of getting good grades, going to college, getting a job that I would stay at until I retire, and during that process owning a house. Thinking that far into the future as a child is simply daunting. It's why no one can ever answer the question, "what do you want to do when you grow up," at the end of high school. We haven't gone out and experienced anything yet. We haven't learned from our failures in life to know what we are meant to do. So when we are presented with that plan, we just sort of agree and keep it in the back of our mind. That life plan is laid out to us as a form of guidance, but it is up to us to figure out what we will ultimately do with our lives. It certainly isn't for everyone, and I realized that after I had gone through almost the entirety of it.

YouTube was something that came out when I was in high school. While I messed around and made some videos with my friends, I never gave it much thought as a career path. But more than ever before it is full of amazing opportunities. When I grew up, people watched cable television for almost all their forms of entertainment. We grew accustomed to the people who were on tv and just accepted them for being there. I stopped watching tv five years ago. YouTube became my source of entertainment and I loved tuning into my favorite creators. I watched a lot of these creators start from ground zero and grow into what they are today. It was amazing to be a part of their journey, to see their ups and downs, their struggles and triumphs. There was a connection, one not found on television, that filled me with inspiration.

If you're like me, you've dabbled with the idea of pursuing YouTube yourself. Whether you're in high school, college, or even at your job—it may be a thought that has crossed your mind. If you did pursue it, what would you do? Gaming? Arts and crafts? Vlogging about your life? You might not even know what you want to do yet! And that's fine. There isn't a wrong answer. In this book, I'll be covering the creative journey, crafting it into a compass that will take you any direction you decide. It'll all be broken down, each narrative a degree on the dial leading you through the journey, helping you navigate your thoughts as you begin to create. If you're feeling nervous or afraid of starting, know you're not alone. Every creator you look up to was staring at a blank screen at some point, trying to figure out what to do. No one is confident when starting anything new, so just know even I felt the same things you'll be feeling. However, taking the first step is critical. Nothing can begin without it. By picking up this book, I know you've already given creating some thought. Don't lose sight of that! You'll never know what could have happened unless you let that creativity shine.

This book is broken down into three sections: The Grand Adventure, Traveler's Notes, and YouTuber Stories.

The Grand Adventure breaks down the entire process of starting your journey as a YouTuber, the hurdles you'll run into along the way, the decisions you have to make that define your path, balancing creating with other things in your life, and ultimately how you will evolve over time. Sound daunting? Don't worry, I'll be your guide!

The second section, Traveler's Notes, will be a topical guide to individual experiences and takeaways that I ran into on my journey. For those who have watched my vlogs before, you may be familiar with this. For those who haven't, think of it as small breakdowns of topics like dealing with hate online, creating your first video, tackling impostor syndrome, and much more. This section will be great reference material to return to once you encounter these on your journey as a YouTuber.

In the last section of the book, YouTuber Stories, I will be interviewing creators from all walks of life to share their experiences as YouTubers. This will include creators who animate, vlog, play games, craft, and many more. I believe it is super important to hear the stories of others when starting off. Any time I would feel down, I'd tune into the early videos of my favorite creators to remind myself about why I started making videos in the first place. Doing so would always bounce me back into a positive state of mind. I hope these stories both motivate and inspire you!

Well . . . that ends the introduction! I hope you'll enjoy the creative journey that lays before you. I've tailored it metaphorically to the idea of setting off on a grand quest in an unknown world, because that's exactly what creating feels like. So pack your bags, hold that compass tight, and let's dive into the world of being a YouTuber!

THE GRAND ADVENTURE

THE AWAKENING

That feeling of wanting to do more. The sense that the path you were told to take in life isn't for you. You realize something profound and break from the formula.

• • •

I had worked towards one goal my entire life: being successful. I didn't want to let down my parents, my friends, or anyone around me. I stuck by the books and did everything as instructed. Everything I was told and heard that would eventually lead to great things in life. I was an introvert by nature, and in my early years, I wasn't too popular in school. I studied, aimed for the highest grades, and then escaped into video games in my free time. Often times I felt like a shadow just sort of wandering through life. Life went on like that for a while, and throughout my entirety of high school I really had no idea what I wanted to do in life. Of course, I was scared to admit this, because everyone is supposed to have that figured out. You should know what you want to be when you grow up. You should know where you want to go for college. You should know everything that the older generation knows. This isn't the case though, and we often wander around questioning what we should really be doing. We haven't gone out and failed yet, nor have we had the opportunity to discover what we really enjoy. They are impossible questions to answer, and we beat ourselves down because we can't answer them. I didn't realize this until later on, so I stuck with what I was told and pushed on regardless.

The college years rolled by much faster than I thought they would, and thankfully while in college I discovered that I enjoyed video production. This was lucky because I actually was attending school for 3D animation, and the only reason for doing so was because I didn't know what to do. My older brother went for it, so I thought I might as well. I loved games, after all. Yet, stumbling upon the professional side of video in college really gave me a clearer direction. However, as I grew older I also began to lose my sense of wonder. The things I enjoyed as a child began to fade from my life and were replaced with the responsibilities of being older. Even though I didn't know that I would grow to question things, I still felt as if things were okay.

It wasn't long until I found myself at my first job and the feeling of excitement was overwhelming. I had finally made it. Everything I had always been told worked out for me somehow, and I managed to find myself making videos and animations for a pretty prestigious software company. I still had some huge student loans to tackle, but I couldn't have considered myself luckier. Prior to landing that job, I was scared that I wouldn't be able to find one. It's funny how your mind begins to drift after a while.

Two years into my job, I realized how stagnant things had become in my life. The stability was nice, but each and every day I found myself daydreaming more and more. I was always in my head thinking about the games I used to play and the stories I had invented over the years. During this time, I had watched my favorite creators blossom from the smallest of seeds into something noteworthy, and it was awesome to live vicariously through the videos they uploaded. YouTube had always been my jam—even since early high school. Back then I filmed silly videos with friends and we even created some while I was in college. To say I was obsessed with the platform was an understatement. While I was grinding away at my job, every day I would tune in to see what my favorite creators were doing. This filled me with inspiration to create, even if it was for the corporate animations I was doing that particular day.

But this year was different. This was the year I would start creating for myself again. I considered myself pretty good at video, and watching the content of others filled me with passion. I jumped back into YouTube, made a silly skit with my friends, and released it to the world. To my surprise, no one watched it. Even when I shared it online, it almost instantly got down voted or disliked. I was confused, but pressed on anyways. I would create some videos sparingly after work hours and put them online. Once again though, nothing had changed. No one had watched the videos, even when I specifically dialed them into things I thought people would be searching for. The added weight of YouTube on top of my full-time job was pretty brutal for me, especially coupled with the long drive I had home each day. With a grand sigh, I threw in the towel. This channel, which was actually the first iteration of SwankyBox, had come to a close before it was even given a chance to begin. Life went on, and I grew another two and a half years older.

I remember how my life was during these moments. I went to work every day, executed the same tasks, said hello to the same people, and then went home. My job wasn't bad by any means, and I was lucky to have it. But any spark I once had was gone. My favorite creators began to no longer inspire me, and in fact, they had the opposite effect. I was envious of what they had accomplished. They had grown so much over the years and I was still the same. The spark was gone from my eyes and my happiness for what I was doing in life was long gone. In many ways the world seemed sort of grey, and I retreated into my head more and more - still kicking around those dreams I once had. Why did this happen though? I did everything I was told to do, yet, I felt empty inside. I got good grades, I went to college, I got that job, I saved up at work and paid off my loans . . . and yet, I just sort of wandered through life. My drive for everything at work was next to zero and I couldn't wait to get away and daydream. It became my escape.

It wasn't until I took a trip to the middle of nowhere that I realized everything I had been working towards wasn't for me. I traveled out west to the state of Oklahoma and just wandered through the rolling fields reevaluating my life. Being disconnected from everything really helped, and only my passions bounced around in my brain. I credit this trip for really changing my outlook on things and it certainly was what they call a vision quest. For two weeks I explored the state with my significant other, and during this time my mind and heart did all the talking.

Why wasn't I creating? Why was I turning a blind eye on my passions?

It took a trip into isolation to really make me shed the layers of my mind and dial into what I really wanted. If I had continued with my normal day-to-day routines, I probably would have never had this self-discovery. By abandoning everything that normally filled my mind, all that was left was me. I wasn't thinking about the projects I had to do, the people I had to call back, or the check engine light that was on in my car. I quickly learned that this state of mental well-being was somewhere I would need to revisit in the future. It was the freest I had felt in a while. Plans for my passions came to life and I had a realization: I needed to leave my job.

The thought was an interesting one. I was always a very logical thinker, and even before diving into the logistics of what this would entail, I sort of beat myself up over waiting so long to take action. This realization that the path I was taught in life wasn't for me meant that everything I had worked towards was in the wrong direction. Excitement quickly turned to depression, but the more I thought about it, the more I began to reflect on everything that had happened in my life. Sure all my favorite creators were way farther ahead than me, but in the end that didn't matter. Everyone starts from somewhere, and although we feel insignificant at first, that's just part of the process. It certainly isn't a race. Everyone who came before me put one foot forward despite the doubt and I had to do the same. My entire life and what had happened in it was just as important as well. I realized the path I took in life wasn't a wasted effort at all, because if it hadn't happened I wouldn't have come to the realizations that I did. All of my experiences were factors in this and without them the drive to create I was feeling wouldn't be there. Sure I could have started five years ago, but what was important was that I started today.

HEEDING THE CALL

You think more and more about what you want to do and the creative endeavors that you want to explore. It's scary to think about, because you have to deviate from everything you may have been told. You begin to prep for the change, and you get to the edge and you don't know whether to jump or not. Will you be financially okay? What if things don't work out? You hesitate, but you jump anyways.

• • •

Planning to leave a job is quite the ordeal. Truthfully, this isn't a route that absolutely needs to be chosen either. You can always pursue your creative endeavors at your own pace on the side, but for me, I knew I had to dive in headfirst. Leaving your job is not something everyone can do, and if you are able to, it still requires a lot of planning. I had always been a saver though and I rarely splurged on anything. I cut corners on everything

I could: from meals to entertainment. My life was very simple, and I didn't have much in terms of costs. I lived in an apartment, drove a salvage car, and used the internet for all my entertainment purposes.

After I decided I was going to leave my job my spending became even less. Every dollar I could do without was set aside for my grand departure. I had to be stingy about what I was spending because longevity for my creativity was crucial for me. Time was my most important resource and I had to treat it as such. I drafted lists upon lists regarding what I needed to survive. I categorized all my expenses and determined what I would need to live each month while I created. Doing this helped me rationalize that this all wasn't as crazy as others would insist. In my eyes, it was worth the shot.

For the next few weeks all I could think about was how exciting all of this was, but also how scary it was as well. Giving up my job was like basically throwing away everything I had worked towards in life. What if things didn't work out? What if I tried to find another job later on down the line and couldn't land one? Was all of this worth the risk of my stability? These questions constantly racked my mind and made me ponder about the safety net of job security. I had been living on a shoestring budget for a while, but from this point forward it would be more cutthroat than ever before. Was I ready for this? Could I really make this work?

As strange as it may sound, I constantly paralleled my departure to the game Oregon Trail II. This was a game that came out in 1995 and it was one of the first games I had played on a PC. For those who haven't played it, you assume the role of a family moving out west for a new life during the 19th century. You embark on the Oregon trail and cover over 2,000 miles in your journey. When the game starts you have to buy a wagon, food, medicine, provisions, and anything else you may need. It was the ultimate pre-planning exercise for a kid and the sense of adventure was simply amazing.

When I was younger I spent so much time figuring out the best combinations for departing and how to make my budget go farther for what I needed. It's funny to think that a game I played over two decades ago was still burned into my mind. It certainly influenced my decisions during this process in real life. I wasn't charging forward with sixteen oxen and a hundred pounds of bacon, but I certainly did my best to determine what I needed in the long run to try to make this work.

Although I had no guidance for how all of this would unfold, if I had to do it all over, I probably wouldn't stray too far from the route taken. I played it pretty safe for the most part, and my ultimate goal was to survive for six months. If I hadn't made progress on my goal by then, I knew it was time to pack up and try to find another job. Even if I had been unsuccessful, I would have still tried. I would have tried harder than I ever had before, because living with regret would be far worse than falling flat on my face and failing. For the past few years I had put my passions on the shelf and lived vicariously through others as they pursued their creative endeavors. It was always just a half-baked thought on my end—a glorious "what if." This would be my one shot at making it work and thankfully my creative passions also offered an outlet for slight financial support as well. My funds wouldn't last forever, but because I taught myself tons of different creative skills, picking up projects along the way to stay afloat actually saved my trip altogether in the long run. I'll dive into that a bit later on to explain what I fully mean, but accounting for these one-off projects definitely made it on my big checklist before I departed.

Now, all of these thoughts are from the perspective of someone leaving a job. That may not be where you are coming from. For me, leaving my job was what I needed to kick myself into gear. Things will certainly be different if you have a family or a home to support. However, you can start creating at any point. Everyone's situation is different and the earlier you start, the easier it is in the long run. Sometimes I wonder what would have happened if I kept creating when I was in high school or even in college. Balancing making videos while going to school or even while holding a job. Making YouTube videos in conjunction with making videos at my old job didn't work because I was burned out of making videos by the time I got home. Any creativity for video I had was depleted because I had spent the day already making videos I wasn't passionate about.

However, if my job wasn't video production, I wonder how much creative energy I would have had by the time I got home. The outcome could have entirely been different, so really assess your situation and what makes sense for you. Create what you can with the time that is available. You can do multiple things at once and the only drawback is that your growth as a creator may be slower. But remember: it isn't a race, so go at your own pace!

All in all, it was about a month after I had my grand creative realization that everything I had been working towards was drawing nearer and nearer. The funny thing was I actually had what I considered to be a backwards experience. Most people would probably find the part where you let your boss know you were leaving to be the part where the reality check hits. After that conversation everything should be different since there isn't really an undo button. Once the chat is done, you return to your desk if all is well and you start your two-week countdown. In my case it was more so about three weeks until my last day, but the environment around you does change. It's a bit of an anxious feeling mixed with relief.

My reality bomb went off as my last day approached. I knew I wasn't saying goodbye forever, as I was still very good friends with my employer and the relationship we had would carry on long past my employment. But even with that thought rationalized in my head, from this point forward everything would be different. My life would be completely changed and I had no way to know what that would be like. For the hardcore planner like myself, the uncertainty of what lied ahead was quite the chaotic feeling.

On one hand you feel like you're sitting on the brink of greatness. On the other, your doubts are trying to break you down. You're on the edge of a giant cliff standing next to a bunch of people who are all ready to take the leap, but some of the people near you turn around and go home. You look around and notice you're the only one left and you doubt yourself for a second too. With a deep breath, you jump and leave everything behind as your traverse into a new land. From this day forward your adventure awaits and the world is your oyster.

THE CARTOGRAPHER'S DISCOVERY

You land in an area that is new to you. Whether you eased your way into this journey or simply jumped in headfirst, you arrive at the same location. You don't know which path to take in this large world. You have feelings of what you want to do though, so you follow your gut and adapt along the way.

• • •

The first morning after my departure was quite an interesting experience. I woke up, and for the first time ever, I had no idea what I was supposed to do. What was this feeling? It was as if the earth was standing still and I felt invisible to everything that was going on. In some ways I had a lingering feeling that I was supposed to be at work, or that I had to work tomorrow—but this wasn't the case at all. For the first time in a very long time I was living in the present moment. I could do anything I wanted to today even though it was a weekday. Not knowing what to do on my first morning, I decided to go on a walk.

Disconnecting from everything has always been important in my life. We get so caught up in technology and our daily routine that we forget to enjoy the present moment. Even prior to leaving my job, I would often go on long walks to clear my mind. This particular morning was no different. I went on a walk to discover myself, to think about the books I wanted to write, to ponder about dusting off my old YouTube channel, and to consider how I was going to chase my dreams. I had already done the leg work to get here and turning back now surely wasn't an option. But where does one start? Even if you have an idea of what you want to do, there's a myriad of ways to do it.

I prepared extensively for my departure, but truthfully, I still had no idea how I was going to make it all work. As I sat there staring at my logo that I hadn't looked at in two and a half years, I began to think about what went wrong last time. First and foremost, my original angle for my channel was based on something I saw others succeeding in and not necessarily something that was fully me. SwankyBox was based on skits, and being an introvert, it really wasn't a primary interest anymore. In the past it was fun to do with friends, but I don't think I ever thought about the longevity of what I was doing.

Secondly, the channel failed because it needed too many people involved in all the videos. I came from the world of filmmaking and corporate video where all of our shoots would involve a handful of people. I remember how many issues I had scheduling filming for my past videos since they had to take place after work hours. It was a nightmare. There was also the factor that I was operating on zero budget. People weren't exactly committed to the cause and that only made things more difficult. Considering these two things, this new iteration of SwankyBox had to be something I was truly passionate about and something I could execute myself. I thought long and hard about my passions, but they had been staring me right in the face the whole time.

Video games played a huge role in my childhood and I would often get lost in the worlds of games long after I had completed them. Instead of going outside to play, I would explore the digital lands within my television screen. I always wanted to travel and see the world as a kid, but we weren't the wealthiest of families so our trips were few and far between. To satisfy my sense of wonder, I turned to my collection of games that had tons of unique lands to explore. They were my pixel portals, imaginative places I felt so strongly about that they became topics for my earlier videos. Gaming played such a huge role in my life that it totally made sense to align my channel to it. It wouldn't be a traditional game-playing channel, but rather would be one rooted in analysis and nostalgia.

There's a high chance that, even though you want to pursue YouTube as a creator, you still may have no idea what you want to do. It's a tough choice because you want to do what you love, but ultimately it is best to boil it down to one thing. Gaming became that thing for me. It was a hobby I enjoyed as a kid and was something I really appreciated growing up. I had tons of ideas for other channels: traveling, motivational talks, cartoons, cats . . . I enjoyed all of these things and honestly could have probably made channels out of any of them. In terms of longevity and the people I wanted to be around though, I wanted to connect with people through gaming. Over the course of creating I managed to sprinkle in my other passions.

So if you're lost, make a list of your passions and choose from there. If you want to future-proof your choice, question whether you'll become bored with it in a few years. If the interest will fade, there's a better choice. At some point you might even become frustrated with your creative outlet if you drift from why you enjoyed it. YouTube will eventually become a job for you, and while the creative freedom is fun and exciting, sometimes it can also take toll on the passion it is aligned to. Just be wary of that!

Even though I had a direction I wanted to head in, the world around me was still completely new. The sense of starting off is much like taking on the role of a cartographer who has discovered a new land. Their role is to create a map of everything they discover and they draw it as they move along. There is no rule book for you to follow and there are no signs telling you the way. You have to map out your own destiny with every step you take. It's a daunting task because any direction you head in will ultimately define your journey. You can stray from your path later on, but your journey will always be influenced by what you did in the past. You are truly a free spirit who can do everything and anything. This journey you're mapping out is the same adventure any creator has to go on. We all start at ground zero. Your destiny is waiting for you out there in this unknown land and you take one step closer to it every day.

Stumbling Through Your First Videos

My first videos were a bit of a whirlwind. While I was super savvy behind the camera, I was absolutely awful in front of it. Not even joking. It was difficult for me to grasp the concept without stuttering or nervously locking up between sentences. Although people look at my videos today and compliment me on how high quality they are, it was definitely a learning process. I still don't think I'm even close to mastering speaking on camera today. Even for someone who did video professionally, online video for YouTube was completely different. Especially for someone who often instructed other people.

Taking your own advice, or more so directing your own advice to influence your behavior, requires time. To make things worse, I was using a manual focus camera with no way to focus it from far away. I remember using a five foot piece of wood stuck between two dumbbell weights to simulate where I was standing. I would focus on this piece of wood, move it out of the way, and hope that my face was in focus when I started to record. Definitely get something that auto-focuses. My laptop was propped up on a pile of boxes in my apartment's bedroom and this was my recording rig.

It's likely your biggest challenge will be understanding the process of making a video. Honestly, I sort of had it on easy mode because making videos was what I used to do for a job. I learned from some great teachers in college as well. It is incredibly important to spend the time learning everything you can about video. You won't start off as video guru, but you can certainly claim that title later on. Look into various editing programs to see what makes sense for your budget. My personal favorite is Adobe Premiere, but it certainly has a learning curve. It has more bells and whistles than you'll probably need, but there's no harm having all the extras. And with their subscription service, it's never been cheaper. At a later point in the book I'll walk you through software, equipment, and making videos in general. So don't sweat it!

When you first start creating, you don't need the biggest and the best gear. Tools and equipment allow you to increase the quality of what you do, but they don't define you. After all, a good photographer can still take an amazing photo with a cheap camera. Use what you can afford and check out accompanying tutorials. While YouTube is your creative platform it is also your free ticket to exploration. You can learn almost anything through it. There are user-created tutorials on recording video, capturing the best audio, saving your videos so they are optimized for YouTube playback, and so much more. YouTube even offers a Creative Academy that I highly recommend going through.

After taking time to dust off my channel and watch some tutorials on YouTube, I recorded my first video on nostalgic video game songs. I was so certain that gaming would be an easier avenue than the skits I did in the past, but it was still difficult. I spent about a week and a half on my first video as I flushed out the concept and bounced ideas off my brothers. I remember being super proud of the video and I was certain it would be a smash hit on YouTube. I was excited to release it to the world and I was curious to see if all nine of my subscribers would come back from the grave. My channel had been dead for almost three years.

Of course, this video did horribly as all first videos do. My dreams of the video smashing through 100,000 views turned to me hoping it would break fifty in a week. I tried my best to promote it through my various networks of friends. I hit up every blog I could think of and got a few responses back from writers thanking me for submitting the news tip, but ultimately no one shared it. I was definitely naive when it came to this sort of thing, and looking back at it makes me chuckle. I'm sure these writers got hundreds of messages a day from people like me and they were creative people themselves. They could choose to write about what they wanted to and that was their freedom. The drive to submit these videos was definitely spot on, but my expectations were also way too high. With anything you produce early on, it is always important to go the extra mile and spend more time sharing the work than what you spent on making it. Obviously don't spam places, but seek out others who may be interested in what you are producing. With a unique angle on your content, you might be surprised at how many people will enjoy it.

I was very number-aware as well—always shooting for a higher subscriber count and trying to gain as many views as possible. As time goes on you realize that, while these seem super important starting out, ultimately they aren't what you should have your eyes on. Value and ability can't be represented by a number and becoming obsessed with these things will only stress you out. On the flip side, you also want people to see the work you spent lots of time on, so this always pulls you back into the realm of comparing yourself to others. You get frustrated that another person's work performs better than yours in a social sense. You wonder why no one notices you. This happened to me very often and I always had to take a step back from the situation and think. Why was I creating to begin with? Was I creating solely because I wanted recognition, or was I creating to share my passion with the world?

If you simply want recognition you will find yourself failing right away because you are chasing after the wrong goal. Making a livelihood off what you do is important, but there is a time and a place for everything. Everyone's journey is different and the more you compare yourself to others, the worse your experience will be. You must stay focused on your own journey.

My second video was a colossal failure as well, or at least in my newbie eyes it was. My expectation for smashing 300,000 views on a video about forest songs in video games was definitely excessively high. People apparently don't care that much about digital trees. But hey, it was worth a shot. I saw plenty of other channels accomplish this feat, but I wasn't thinking about it from their perspective. I didn't understand the relationship between a fan and a creator yet, nor did I think about how long it took for these particular creators to hit these numbers on their videos. Our viewpoint is skewed upon starting because we instantly measure a person by their current standing. We don't think about the years and years this person spent building up a fan base to be where they are today. We see a video with 500,000 views and think that 500,000 people showed up on the upload date. While not impossible for a video to achieve this, most videos instead grow over time. Even if we think that channel's video is lower quality in comparison to ours, it is simply because we haven't given the whole situation proper thought. Jealously plays a role too. We fail to see the strong bond that was built and nurtured over time.

Eighty Percent Happiness

Your role as a cartographer is ultimately to figure out what you plan on doing with your life. It's such a daunting task and your first videos will be about self-discovery. They are probably going to be horrible, but you have to start somewhere. We all want to be perfectionists and have everything be amazing before we put it out to the world, but that is unrealistic. Nothing will ever be perfect. Toss perfectionism out the window. There will always be something you could have done better or differently.

That's precisely why you have to consider everything you do as a building block. It's like building this giant Lego statue and everything you do adds one block to the grand design. Your first blocks may not be the most glamorous, and perhaps you'll even use the random colored Legos that don't have any match to lay your first layer. However, they are just as important as any blocks that follow. Eventually you'll build upon these blocks and you won't see them anymore. That doesn't mean they weren't important for the foundation though. Take the time to make them the best they can be, but don't worry about their imperfections. The truth is, you would simply be slowing down your journey if you stopped to make everything its own masterpiece. This is incredibly important to be aware of.

If your happiness for a video was on a scale from 1 to 100 percent, aim for 80 percent happiness. I know you might be saying, "But SwankyBox! That's like shooting for a 'B'. Why not make it an 'A'?" The reason why you don't shoot for an "A" is simply because a "B" still hits the mark for what you were trying to accomplish. It is still a great video, and yes it could definitely be improved upon, but the time you spend trying to make it an "A" could have been going to your next video. Not to toot my own horn, but people often tell me the videos on my channel are decently high quality. They love the editing, animation, and overall attention to detail. I could certainly improve my voiceover, tweak my graphics, and ultimately make my videos flow better. Are those things my audience will for sure notice? Maybe. I produce documentary-like content, and if I took the time to polish everything to 99% happiness, I could have simply used that time to get halfway through my next video. You want your creative endeavors to be scalable, and that means maximizing your time is crucial.

Relationships

Over the next month I spent some time working on some different concepts for videos while also trying to learn as much as I could about content creation. I slowly began to understand things about YouTube that I didn't before, despite how well I knew the platform from a technical standpoint. My role as a cartographer was still only beginning and with each trial I learned something new. Every video I tried something different. I started to understand what drove someone to watch a particular video too.

Being adaptive on your journey as a creative is incredibly important. Same with understanding how your work influences others. For a YouTube gamer in particular, I quickly learned that there was sort of a golden triangle between YouTubers, video game designers, and journalists. Each of these entities greatly benefits from working with the other and it is important to understand this early on. For example, if I produce an analytical video on an indie game, that indie game may be discovered by new viewers who may have never known it existed. If I produce a video that fits well with the mission and direction of a blog, they can benefit by sharing my work. This was one of the most important things for me to grasp because it gave me viewership I would have never had otherwise.

I remember the feeling of having my first Zelda video covered by a blog as I frantically hit refresh to see what people thought about it. I poured my heart and soul into an analytical video about one of the Zelda video games and sent it out a few days before leaving for the weekend. This ended up being my first real breakthrough and it felt monumental. I realized this would be my shot at starting to gain traction because of the golden triangle relationship. A journalist can write whatever they want and doesn't need my input. That said, a journalist is always pursuing a scoop. Having that scoop waiting for you when you start work, needing only to give it a quick look to see if it clicks with you, may mean you have your first article already in the making.

This journalist saved time and can also make ad revenue as people visit their website to watch the video. A win-win situation. They gained an article and clicks, while I gained exposure to their audience. This way of thinking is important to understand when growing an online presence as you always want to be adaptive with your efforts. Simply tossing your videos online and crossing your fingers is a sure way to struggle as a creative. It can be a bit of a hassle, but you have to take your luck into your own hands sometimes. Snagging those first views is super difficult.

Even if you aren't interested in being a gaming YouTuber, this same relationship applies to all forms of creating. If what you make provides value to your viewer then it could very well be a great fit for other mediums that have similar goals. If you make an entertaining video reviewing cat toys, that video would be a great fit for a pet blog or a pet-focused website. If you practice yoga and meditation in your videos, then websites, Facebook pages, and other outlets that cover fitness may be interested in your content.

Always think about how your video can be used before starting it. If it is evergreen content it will always have a chance of being used in the future. Many people refer to a piece of content as "evergreen" if it never expires in usefulness. A video on exercising with your body weight would be evergreen because nothing ever makes the video irrelevant. Unless someone invents some magical way to reinvent fitness people will probably always find that video useful. However, if you created a video that focused on exercising with a specific fitness product and that product ceases production, then you may find that viewership on the video declines or even stops as it is no longer relatable.

I always aim to create this type of content because sometimes trending topics can burn you out. Trending or topical pieces of content are things people search for because that topic is currently the buzz. Think of a current news event and how attention dies down after the event passes. A grand opening would be topical because tons of people are curious about the approaching event. But weeks after it takes place, no one is really interested in it anymore. For me, chasing the next biggest thing always seems like I'm sacrificing my creativity for the sake of getting it out before anyone else. It's a great way to get viewership honestly, but at the same time, you will be at the whim of things out of your control. You have no idea if a game is going to randomly launch early or if a certain event is going to take place in our world. You pretty much have to drop everything you're doing and tackle that topic as soon as you can.

Striking a balance between topical and evergreen content is the most stable place to be, but if you can think of ways to make topical concepts evergreen, then you'll get the best of both worlds. People will always search for topical things. More searches means your relatable content has a greater chance of being discovered. On the flip side, if you make niche videos that people aren't likely to search for, then gaining traction and finding viewership will be way more difficult. It isn't impossible, but just be mindful of this.

After my first video was picked up by that blog, I started working on my next project. I was still trying to discover what I wanted to do with my channel, but

I figured I'd take the time to really tackle a concept that I know not many people were capable of. This is when I took two characters from opposing games and had them switch places. I outlined how each character would function in each other's world and highlighted scenarios in which these characters would have difficulties. What made this video was the editing I put into it. I made it look like the games had swapped characters and that the respective game engines simply adapted the other character's traits. I knew this was a concept no one had ever attempted before and it was pretty fun to make. However, it was definitely one of my most difficult videos and took a lot of time.

Upon release, the video hit instant success. While my channel didn't have the subscriber base to get people to see it, the blogs I wrote to loved the concept and in 24 hours the video had gained 28,000 views. This was monumental for my channel as it was another big step after my last Zelda video had been featured.

Seeing reactions across various social media outlets was such an awesome feeling. But, for as well as the video did, it still fell below my expectations. At this time in my creative journey I was still understanding the landscape around me and often times my perceptions of things were skewed. This smash hit of a video, which has well over half a million views today, only netted my channel about 200 subscribers at the time. Now, for a small channel, that is certainly a large amount of growth from one single video, but I knew if this video were on a larger channel it would have performed exponentially better. It would have hit a million views easily if it had the correct exposure and I let this cloud my judgement. I was being greedy.

This was at a time where I put content first and fan relationships second. It wouldn't be until later on when

I realized your relationship with your fans is the utmost important thing as a creator. How they perceive you and the connection you make with them is absolutely crucial. People want to feel connected and as if they are a part of something. As a creator, that's really what you should be aiming for. You want to establish a community. As a channel with only 5 – 6 videos though, I didn't understand why people weren't subscribing even when they enjoyed the video. It's because I hadn't spent enough time with them yet to make a connection. I was just a faceless voice behind a video and they didn't know who I was.

While the video was highly entertaining in their eyes, they simply carried on after viewing it, back out into the vast internet. Looking back, it's clear I was naive at the time. But, that's what growing is all about. This video was just a building block on the large statue I set out to build. There were different lessons that each block brought and I became wiser when I started to think about these concepts.

Perception and understanding others are the most valuable things you can learn as a creator. Take the time to understand why certain videos of yours resonate with people while other projects may not. Ask your audience questions and bounce ideas off them constantly. They'll appreciate you doing so, and you'll appreciate their candid advice.

I was beginning to understand the land around me at this point. It no longer felt as foreign to me and I had made a few friends who were on a similar journey. We shared laughs, discussed our failures, and supported each other when we would start to doubt ourselves. I had stumbled upon this group of creators on Reddit, and up until this point had spent many hours chatting with them. However, things change as time goes on.

People you were familiar with sometimes fade away. They packed up their bags and threw in the towel as a creator. This was always disheartening because it was like coming to a crossroad on a hike. You knew from this point forward you wouldn't be traveling together anymore, and you gave them a hug as they set off in a new direction in life.

As you departed you would think about chasing your dream even harder than before—for their sake. You would remember all the times they supported you and the late-night chats you had as fellow creators. You would still keep in touch when you could, but you had to keep moving forward even though their departure may have also filled you with doubt. Would you make it? Or would you be the one departing at the next crossroad? With one foot in front of the other, you press on across the land.

THE HERO'S DEFEAT

After creating you eventually get beat down. You imagined things would go differently. You believe you should be farther along than you actually are. Your rations are dwindling and you think about turning back. The thought of giving up crosses your mind, but you move forward regardless. One foot in front of the other. You conserve your rations and you adapt from your failures. In this giant world we are all looking for success, but we never know how close it is.

• • •

There comes a point during our adventure that things begin to look a little bleak. For me this actually occurred several times throughout my journey and each time I second guessed what I was doing with my life. The first of these events occurred after my two initial successes. Having landed my first two videos on a few gaming blogs, I felt like the world was my oyster. The future looked polished and bright for a moment before falling dull and bleak again. There was another monumental success that took place soon after that contributed to this feeling. You're probably wondering why a success would leave someone feeling defeated. It was more so the aftermath of the success that brought me down. After all, I have a tendency to overthink things.

Betrayed by Expectation

A few weeks after my second video was featured I stumbled upon an opportunity to film a creepy van. But this wasn't a typical van: It was a customized Nintendo 64 van my friend owned. I had worked with him consistently over the years as he owned a nonprofit I was very fond of and one day he showed me his newest endeavor. He had customized an old van into the ultimate retro-gaming dream machine. It was rusted and eerie looking on the outside, but simply spectacular on the inside. This van had three televisions, a Nintendo 64 mounted into the side of the van, controller ports wired to each seat in the back, and a backup cell phone tower battery for those extended gaming sessions.

We both knew this was one of the seven wonders of the world and my friend was aware that I was growing a gaming channel. He essentially gave me free reign to film the van to my liking and take as many photos as I wanted. He had a feeling Reddit in particular would really love the van and I agreed with him strongly. However, we knew that a video tour of the van probably wouldn't have the same results as a series of images would. Images were quicker to digest and share as the time commitment was minimal in comparison to a video. Since we both were always studying how people consumed and shared content, this was something we knew would have a better chance as a string of engaging images. So the plan became creating a string of images on Imgur that people would likely share around, but at the end of the post have a video link that went to my tour of the van hosted on my YouTube channel.

Prepping a post for Reddit is quite the interesting process. This was a post we knew would go viral prior to posting it, and we were certainly right. However, to get to that point, we had to consider what someone felt when they stumbled upon the link. The title of the post would be "So my friend has a creepy van . . ." and it would be shared in the gaming subreddit. The title itself is just interesting enough for someone to click it. They want to know what's up with this van and why it's being shared in the gaming subreddit. What's the twist? Is this a funny meme? Once you have their interest you of course have to meet or exceed their expectations. In order to do that we started with a standard photo of the van from the outside. The description for this explained how the paint was peeling off and it was a decently unpleasant sight. Following this image we completely flipped the viewpoint and showed the inside of the van and how amazing it was. People are always looking for that twist when consuming media and once you hit them with that twist you have them hooked. From this point forward, I highlighted the various cool features of the van, threw in some science stuff, and then closed it out with a link to the video.

Within 24 hours the post had received over two million views and 17,000 up votes on Reddit. Despite plans we were sure would make this a success, there's always an element of luck. You share something and if someone immediately down votes it you could be done as soon as you start. It's a lot like making a paper boat and setting it out to sail. You hope it will float but any moment it could simply capsize and sink.

On the flip side, Reddit doesn't take too kindly to self-promotion unless you truly deliver something special. While this series of images converted people over to watching the video, I really didn't benefit from the image post itself. It was just entertainment for the sake of entertainment. Out of two million people who viewed the post, only 33,000 people decided to watch the video. However, I was still excited that it worked. I mean, 33,000 people is a ton of people. Can you imagine that many people in a room? I'm not saying Reddit is a good place to spam your own work or anything. Sharing your pieces in specific subreddits is a great way to get new exposure, but make sure you aren't just using the platform for that. If Reddit was only self-promotion it would simply be awful. Part of its charm is that it's organically shared content and it can only exist in the way it does because of that. It keeps the experience much more genuine and relatable that way. Much like the gaming blogs I spoke about earlier, utilizing multiple outlets to gain traction is incredibly important when starting off.

Let's talk about why this event left me in a cesspool of emotion. The post was a success, but my expectation of how many people would watch the video was way off. Noticing a pattern here? I had my expectations too high based off the traction I was seeing on the Imgur post. Having super high expectations when you really have no previous data to base it off of is a surefire way to leave you feeling underwhelmed. But I had made it to the front page of Reddit! I was even inducted into their weird secret society subreddit that you can only get into once you've been on the front page. Before you ask—yes, that's a real thing. But if making it to the front page of Reddit wasn't enough, I don't know what else would be.

I remembered how Markiplier originally got his start by having one of his Amnesia gameplay videos shared on Reddit, but once again I was comparing his end game results to a starting point. If there's one thing I learned as a creator that I will consistently vouch for again and again, it is never to compare yourself to others. You will lose every time and it will make you feel awful. Someone else's journey and success are not your own. When you get there yourself everything will be different because everyone's path is different. Basing your expectations on someone who is not you will only burn you out and leave you discouraged. That's exactly why I felt the way I did. I was simply being greedy and not grateful. For as humble as people thought I was, I wasn't being humble at all.

Standing Up After Being Knocked Down

I was reflecting on my journey as a creator and the last nine months I had put into YouTube. I managed to stay afloat financially through some odd jobs, but it was surprising to know it had already been that long. I had some successes but my head was in the clouds. I was also pretty impatient, mainly because I had tried YouTube several times before in the past and it never worked out. I left everything behind for this, and if it didn't pan out, I'd have to throw in the towel again and give up on my dream. The feeling of this crushed me, and I'd try to muster up the courage to tell my significant other that everything was going to be okay. That I wasn't going to give up. That I would make it work.

Despite feeling like absolute garbage, which I had no reason to feel like at all, I pressed on. I felt beat down and I thought things would be different by this point. It had been nine whole months and what did I have to show for it? When people asked how YouTube was going, would I grit my teeth and tell them it was fine? I was plagued by these thoughts. But once again I thought about why I started in the first place. I had watched vlog after vlog by my favorite creators as they matured along their own journey. I also knew going in that this wouldn't be an easy task for me. It wasn't an easy task for anyone. The success you see in these channels is because they persistently pursued something they believed in until it eventually became reality. They adapted from each failure and pressed on regardless of how rough things got. They struck a balance so that they could scrape by and make it work while they figured everything out.

In this moment I felt lost, but it was only because I started to doubt my path. I felt confident in my ability as a creator, but the uncertainty of what was before me continuously made me hesitate.

The thing is, we never know how close we are to success. So many people turn around and head back the way they came right when they are on the brink of discovering it. It's like giving up at the moment you're about to find that deposit of gold while mining, or turning around while hiking when what you were looking for was simply over the next hill. While it is definitely a cookie-cutter Hollywood moment, it does happen in real life too.

Everyone has a breakthrough point as a creator and it is different for everyone. It could be gradual or it could be swift. But anyone who has found success can definitely think back to the moment where things changed for them. Where their fears began to fade and filling that space was hope. That moment was just around the corner for me, but at this point as a creative I had no idea it was.

The next month changed everything.

ADAPTING TO THE WILD

You gain a sense of traction and the growth is exciting. At this point you brainstorm how to make it grow. What next steps need to happen for this journey to continue? How can you expand what you're doing? How can you make it financially viable to make a living? You cast a big net to catch all kinds of different fish.

• • •

When we're out wandering in the wilderness for a while, forging our creative path step by step, we continually evolve as people. Every video and experience shapes who we are and the foreign feeling of the land begins to go away. We become comfortable with the idea of trying to make this work. However, when our breakthrough does come along and we begin to grow, there is another major shift waiting for us. We must now think about how we can scale up as a creator and truly make what we are doing worthwhile and sustainable.

After dwelling on the whole Nintendo 64 van incident, I really started to think about myself as a creator. What was I really good at? What did people who care about me say about me? A lot of people often told me I was very level-headed and openminded in my approaches to everything in life. The way I talked about things was interesting too. From my brother's perspective we always came up with the coolest strategies in games to thwart our opponents. These things were more than likely my strengths and up until this point I focused on topics I was very passionate about. I was making videos for me.

While you want to enjoy what you make you also want your audience to benefit from it. If your videos simply serve yourself then you will probably spin your tires for a while. You want what you do to resonate with people and make them want to come back for more. Focusing on older topics was very much the child in me speaking through my work. My videos on the Nintendo 64 era of gaming certainly showed that. But, why not try commenting on something different? Why not take a stab at a topic that was recent?

Up until this point I was ignoring modern gaming completely. I tuned in to watch and play things, but my voice was missing in this space. If I enjoyed something and found it interesting, why not expand my scope? The "Five Nights at Freddy's" series was something I was absolutely enthralled by. For those who may not know what this is, it is basically a game where you play as a security guard at night in a pizzeria. The animatronics, which are robotic animals similar to the ones at Chuck E Cheese's, come to life at night and try to hunt you down. Your role is to continually open and shut the doors next to you in the facility. All of this must be done while surveying the night through cameras operating on limited power. The animatronics will get you if your power runs out and you'll lose. The games were simple in nature and provided a style of gameplay that was unique. The internet was swept up in the lore and mystery behind the game. What was going on in this mysterious pizzeria? Why did the animatronics come to life?

Seeing how this game exploded online, I knew something similar to this would be a great way to gain traction. There were certain indie games that sparked curiosity in the player and that curiosity would turn to the internet to seek out answers. When "Undertale" came out in late 2015, which is an indie role-playing game, I got that same feeling from this game that I got from Five Nights at Freddy's. I had so many unanswered questions after I played it and I knew the online world would have these same questions. So I created a video based on one of my favorite characters in the game and crossed my fingers.

The video didn't do very well at all upon release, mainly because I only had a fan base of 600 people. On top of that, these 600 people subscribed to me for Nintendo 64 content. Not for videos on new indie titles. This was right when Undertale was starting to gain some mainstream traction in mid-October. Within a month this game would be all over the internet though.

I really took some time to analyze this game and came up with eight ideas right off the bat. There were so many mysteries left unresolved that I wanted to tackle. So many burning questions I needed to have answers for. Because I had thought about how the online world would react, and because I predicted the growth of the game, my video exploded. By the end of the month I had around 100,000 views on my first Undertale video.

I remember I was attending a gaming convention that weekend and I submitted a panel to host while I was there. They accepted the panel and I had prepared for presenting on Saturday night. Right before walking on stage to talk about Nintendo 64 mysteries, I refreshed my phone and I had hit 1000 subscribers. I was so excited I almost couldn't contain it. I will never forget that moment on stage.

What I learned from this moment was that foresight was one of the most important things to growing. Really take the time to understand what people are looking for online and deliver on that. If your ideas are nestled in the past, think of ways to put a modern spin on them to make them relevant again. Always ask for feedback and always be planning for the future.

As a gaming YouTuber it makes sense for me to look into what games are coming out in the months ahead. I mark them on my calendar and plan videos around them accordingly. If you reviewed TV shows on YouTube, you'd probably want to know when the latest season of episodes were being released. Same could be said about knowing when new products come out if you run a technology-based channel. This doesn't mean you can't build a following without dialing into future topics, but it can certainly help you stay relevant. Balancing between non-topical and topical concepts is a good place to be as your non-topical videos can serve as anchors on your channel while your topical ones bring in the new viewers.

Stabilizing Your Niche

For the next two months things really changed for the channel. By the turn of the year I was closing in on 30,000 subscribers and I honestly couldn't keep up with everything. Crazy to think how fast that growth came, right? I never would have predicted that. I continued to produce my mystery videos for Undertale and various other games, but one thing I didn't realize was that I was also digging my channel into a hole. After the turn of the year I was trying to be everything to everyone and it wasn't really working out.

I started a side series called Pixel Portals which explored those gaming lands I felt so strongly about from my childhood, but the bulk of the younger generation that was brought to the channel through my indie game videos didn't have a full grasp on nostalgia yet. Some of them never even had played a Nintendo 64 before, or only played it briefly. Beyond that, no one was actively searching for my super obscure videos. What had happened was I had developed two separate audiences on YouTube and they were conflicting with each other.

With YouTube in particular you have to be really careful with who you appeal to. My channel was sort of a mental dumping ground for me and I put up a wide variety of topics. However, not all viewers would like all of my topics. If they subscribed for one type of video, but aren't seeing that type of video anymore, they may not tune in to watch your content anymore. Think of it as having all your subscribers in a large room and you have them raise their hands as you call out things they may be interested in. If you break them all into different groups based on interests, and they appear to be too divided, it will actually harm you as a creator. Being niche in what you do is the easiest way to build a core audience, but at the same time, it can also drive you a bit crazy if you aren't truly passionate about it. Niche creators have the easiest time growing but they are bound to those types of videos.

If you run a YouTube channel about dogs and suddenly you start putting out videos about cats, while some of your audience may watch both, most won't. I'm a hardcore cat person and don't have a dog, so I would simply skip over your dog videos. The concept of dogs vs cats is simply metaphorical and really applies to different types of videos on your channel though. If you're bouncing between a ton of different types of videos but only release one video a week, a subscriber who subscribed may not see the content they like again for a month. However, this isn't the only thing to be wary of. YouTube keeps tabs on who shows up for each video and if they notice certain subscribers aren't watching they assume they aren't interested. YouTube may stop notifying these people that new videos are out.

This is what happened with SwankyBox. I was consistently delivering high quality weekly videos, but it took me forever to realize why viewership blew up from late 2015 to early 2016, but then steadily decreased over time. The YouTube algorithm played a role, but it certainly wasn't the biggest problem. It wouldn't be until much later on that I addressed this issue and I will cover it more thoroughly in a later chapter. My attempts to adapt up until that discovery were mostly in vain, but there were still many triumphs made.

Staying Financially Afloat

The land I had set off in over a year and a half ago was no longer as foreign to me. I was far away from where I started and I had developed plans on how I would proceed further. The fear of failing was replaced with a sense of confusion about how I could keep creating and make this worthwhile. On YouTube, your most immediate form of compensation is ad revenue. The feeling of getting paid for putting something online is pretty interesting, but it is also very unruly. It takes a lot of views to actually earn a decent living . . . and I mean a lot. Most creators align themselves to continually pumping out content faster and faster so that they can get more in return. While that may work for some creators, I'd advise against it. Work smarter, not harder.

I began to think of ways that I could become financially stable based off of creating. Ad revenue was certainly one way of doing so, but it should not be the only one. After you create for a while your channel evolves into a small business. It might be kind of weird to think of it that way, but the journey of being a YouTuber and starting a business are nearly similar enough to be called one in the same. It's important to branch out and think of new ways that you can stay afloat financially, whether it be selling merchandise, speaking at conventions, working with brands and sponsors, fan funding, or any other avenue. The more things you have in place, the easier it will be to get by.

Being a YouTuber is by no means a lucrative endeavor right off the bat. It has to be worked towards and it requires a ton of hours. By branching out with different ways to make money, you can make what you do have more value to you in the long run. I like to visualize it as a big river that several small rivers flow into. The big river is your financial well-being and it only has water in it because of all the small rivers that feed into it. All those small rivers are your different ways you make money as a creator and without them the big river wouldn't exist.

Conventions

At this point in my YouTube career I began to branch out into the convention space. There were tons of gaming and anime conventions around the country that could potentially benefit from what I had to offer. I developed several talks and presentations that I would do while at conventions pro-bono, filmed a few of them, and then used those to reach out to other conventions. After a while I started to get booked as an official convention guest and my time at that event was a paid opportunity. Conventions of all kinds exist, although not all of them do the similar type of programing that gaming conventions do.

That doesn't mean you can't also look into other ways a convention can be beneficial to you. If you're an illustrator or animator, a booth might be worth looking into where you can sell drawings. You could also sell merchandise there as well. Conventions were great for me because I was paid to talk about the games I loved. I also got to meet fans of my work and new people in general. People who attend your talks might not even know you exist as a creator. But if you are memorable to them in person, they will certainly remember that and seek you out online. Meeting someone in person leaves a totally different impression than online. It's much more powerful and is a great way to gain fans who truly love what you do as a creator.

On top of that, conventions typically have a lot of various companies at them. While you're enjoying your-self at the convention, take the time to say hello to all the various artists, sellers, companies, and other con-ventions' representatives that are there. You might feel uncomfortable going up and talking to random people, but it is certainly something to consider. If you don't know exactly what to say you can always inquire about what they do. Consider having some business cards made beforehand. You never know who you may run into and it could be mutually beneficial for both of you. Making creative friends is always a plus too. You start off as this lone entity navigating a world that's new to you, but over time you will see these people at other conventions and start to build relationships. Seeing a familiar face at a new convention makes it feel a little more home-like, but that only happens if you made the effort to say hello at a previous convention.

If you're super nervous about talking to people just know that most creators are feeling the same thing. Social anxiety can be overbearing and there's a high chance the person you're thinking about talking to may be socially anxious too. A lot of us are introverts who grew up on the internet not having to talk to people. So while you may feel like you're the odd one out, you're probably on the opposite side of the spectrum. It is very important to build relationships with others who are on similar paths because it makes our adventure easier. We feel like we're not going it alone because others are marching in the same direction. Talking to others at conventions has led to so many amazing opportunities for me, from being a guest at several other conventions to sponsorship opportunities. The most important thing, however, were the friends that I made. I treasure that the most out of anything and it all started by saying hello to a stranger.

Merchandise

Unless you're absolutely dominating it with views, merchandise and sponsors are another road you will cross on your journey. Let's start by talking about merchandise. Merchandise is a great way for you to develop a side income to continue creating while also giving your fans a way to support you. There are plenty of things you can do: Shirts, pins, stickers, hats, posters, etc. The thing about merchandise is there is a multitude of things you can sell and it doesn't have to be like everything else out there. Basic merchandise can of course cover clothing items, but what would really resonate with your audience? If you were a musician, what about selling your music? Selling special edition CD's with unique artwork at a convention booth? If you're an illustrator, what about selling signed prints? Or what about unique prints that can only be bought during a certain period of time?

Heck, perhaps your merchandise can even be a book, much like the one you're reading. You can shape your merchandise around who you are as a creator. My greatest selling point was my knowledge as an observer. I was often told I understood things about people and complicated concepts because I took my time with them. I may have not realized this unless other people told me, but it did make sense when I thought about it. So why not share that knowledge with the world? I always liked to write, so why not tie my merchandise to my writing? Videos will always be my main format as a YouTuber, but that doesn't mean I can't share my experiences through a book as well. This book for me was a big win because I could both inspire people to start creating and also support myself further as a creator. And I think that is really something important to take note of.

How can your creativity be showcased through your merchandise? Your fans will certainly want to support you when they can, but always think from their perspective. If you made shirts would they be something your fans would actually want to wear? Does it make sense given who your viewers are? Don't be afraid to ask them either! Throw out a poll in a video and see how they respond. Perhaps they will even submit ideas of their own that make sense to pursue. There's no shortage of websites you can partner with to help create these products, but just be mindful of what you're signing up for. Always read their terms and conditions to see if they are a good fit for you.

Sponsorships / Brand Deals

Sponsorships and brand deals are another large part of being a YouTuber. Most of the time these projects tend to be the ones that pay the most, since you are essentially being a marketing outlet for a company. They need to promote a product, they like what you do, and they will pay you to show your fans their product or offer your fans a deal. A lot of times fans can react negatively to these types of deals because they feel like the creator is "selling out." That frame of mind is definitely silly, but I can see why it is viewed that way too. If the creator has to compromise themselves in a way that makes them seem different than usual, or if they don't have creative freedom over how they work with the product, then it will probably not go so well.

Most of the issues with this are actually the brand's fault because they have very strict rules for the creator to go by. Sometimes a creator can't use specific words that may come across negative when associated with the product, or they have to act like they really enjoyed it. Any fan will see through such ruse right away. Most companies don't really understand how fans interact with YouTubers and they just run off of numbers. They don't realize how much more effective their promotion could be if they gave the YouTuber creative freedom to make something worthwhile. Instead, you are left with a YouTuber making a corporate pitch rather than something that makes sense for the audience.

As YouTubers we have something that a company can't get elsewhere—a relationship with our audience.

Our fans grew with us as we put out video after video. A relationship formed over time, and if this relationship is exploited by a company, the promotion will flop. Beyond that, a YouTuber has to be careful so they don't betray the trust of their audience. That is hard to earn back. Things on YouTube don't really work the same way they do as if you were running a commercial on television. There's an extra element to consider: The bond we all share.

So now that we have all that negativity out of the way, let's talk about the positives. For starters, not all brands are awful to work with. There are a lot out there that truly understand what we do as creators on YouTube and they realize how much more effective it is to work with us instead of just handing us instructions. These are brands you should treasure! You'll know right away who they are because they will actually care about you as a person. They won't hit you with an automated email talking about a product you and your audience have zero interest in. They'll actually have a conversation to see how you can both effectively work together.

Nothing is worse than a brand reaching out to you who has no idea what you do or if their product makes sense. These types of brands will try to make you do it for extremely cheap as well. While you may start off thinking uploading videos online doesn't have much value, it truly does. What you do has more value than any other advertising medium out there. You essentially built a community around shared interests and a personality. That's an advertiser's dream, and because modern commercials and advertisements are falling to the way side, you'll see a ton more brands working with video creators in the future.

People just tune out ads or skip them nowadays. However, if someone you enjoyed was part of the ad, you may consider actually watching it. Beyond that, knowing a company worked with a YouTuber as a way to support their creative endeavors may make you more willing to hear what they are about. This all comes down to the relationship between the YouTuber and their viewers.

Knowing how much to charge is always a big issue as well. If you've never been in the business world before, it is extremely hard to understand what you are worth as a creator. For the most part it is different for everyone and that is why you can't just Google it and get an answer right away. Same goes for how much you earn from advertisements on your videos. When you're figuring out a price and you have no frame of reference, consider the following things: How many views do I think this video will get? How often do people usually buy similar things online? How expensive is the product?

You may have none of these answers, but it doesn't mean you can't think about them from the perspective of the business. Let's say your video gets 25,000 views. That could be way higher or lower than what you get at this point on your journey, but let's use it as an example. That's 25,000 people. Can you imagine that many in a room listening to what you have to say? Now let's say the product you are offering is at the following prices: Free, $1, $5, and $20. The product could even be more expensive than that.

If the product is free, like say a phone app, then the company doesn't get money in return directly from someone signing up for the app through your link. However, they could make money off their app in different ways, including ads, in-app purchases, and so on. With nothing else to consider, they probably wouldn't earn a whole lot back immediately from working with you. It doesn't mean they won't in the long run, but that also means they might not have as much money to spend because the return on investment isn't immediate. More people may certainly be interested though because the product is free in some regards. You see this a lot with startup companies or new phone apps. A lot of lower-level sponsorships may fall into this category. Promotion is still promotion though.

For the other prices ($1, $5, and $20), each sale you make means they earn money back immediately. So let's say out of the 25,000 people who watched the video, 100 people were interested enough to purchase the product through a link the company provided. Again, that estimate could be high or low depending on your relationship with your audience, how much of a fit the product is for your channel, and how expensive the product is. That one hundred people brought back either $100, $500, or $2000 to the company. That means the company could technically have paid you 25% - 45% of that amount and still had it be a win for them. This depends on other operating costs too though. We have to factor in the cost of making the product, shipping it out, and the overhead cost of the employees. It gets a bit complicated.

However, there is fluctuation depending on how niche of a channel you have. Working with a brand who is only going to pay you $50 on a video that will get 25,000 views is obviously absurd. Don't do that. That's 25,000 people who came out to listen to you share your thoughts. If they ran advertisements themselves through social media they would be paying way beyond that to accrue such viewership. You would be doing yourself a disservice if you accepted that low amount. You'd also be damaging what YouTubers are worth to others as well, since the company will probably think it can charge everyone $50 from that point forward. I've talked to several companies who try to approach me saying that they've paid a certain amount in the past and that what I'm asking for is higher than what they normally do. Most of the time I just respectfully decline the offer, but it does suck to do so sometimes.

Basically what happened was someone didn't know what they were worth as a creator, undercharged, and then set the precedent for all creators from that point forward. The company definitely wins here because they don't have to pay as much and get huge returns on investments from people who don't know any better. Ultimately it devalues YouTubers and is hard to recover from. You typically encounter these types of companies when you're still a smaller entity on the platform, as everyone is trying to figure themselves out at that point. Some people accept the first sponsorship just because it is their first sponsorship and they want to learn from the opportunity. That's totally fine to do, but just know that the reason why they offered you what they did was probably because they've decreased the price every time. They get pretty sneaky!

If you're looking to get into booking sponsorships and brand deals, the best place to start is simply by asking. Companies will reach out to you over time, but by taking matters into your own hands you can speed up the process. What kinds of products make sense for your channel? Draft up an email saying who you are and why you want to work with them. Explain the benefit to working with you as well. I wouldn't make the email too long as reading super long emails can get tedious. Make the subject to your email engaging and include your value towards the top of the email. It's sort of like making a YouTube video. You want people to click on your email when it goes to their inbox. Your goal is to get them talking on the phone or through a video chat with you. Having that human interaction changes everything and makes the process easier. You can get a sense of who everyone is as a person that way. If it's a good fit, you may find yourself working with a brand you selected. Later down the line you might even partner with a manager who will take care of securing opportunities for you.

Negotiating / Contracts

Never feel guilty for asking for what you think you're worth. We all start off as "starving artists", but that doesn't mean we can't change that. Everyone still has bills to pay, and if you don't have them now you certainly will in the future. As creative people we have the ability to turn something mundane into something interesting and that is unquestionably a valuable skill.

The truth is there is no concrete formula or price you should use as a benchmark on what to charge for sponsorship and brand deals. It is different for everyone because we are all doing separate things and have distinct audiences. Success for some channels may be 100,000 subscribers where others could simply be 10,000. Some brands will do flat rates while others could do cost per view or add additional compensation based on the number of products sold. I've seen some even do viewership tiers, where if a video breaks a certain number of views in an allotted amount of time the payment increases.

Let's talk about cost per view though. Some creators may ask for one cent per view, whereas others could ask for ten or more. The rate typically fluctuates based on your anticipated viewership and how connected you are with your audience. It also depends on how you are integrating their brand. Is it just a shoutout or is it a fully branded video? This approach is different than the others I mentioned, but most marketers are used to doing this elsewhere.

If they were running targeted ads through Google or Facebook, they would be paying for people to see their ads and potentially click them. Every viewer and click is factored into how much they get charged. They typically are competing with other companies since ads are tied to search terms and by tracking interests. They could be paying anywhere from a cent per view to multiple cents. Sometimes this rate gets extremely high if there is a lot of competition for certain search terms. However, what we offer is more valuable than this. We aren't strangers on the street like traditional marketing. We have direct access to an audience we have a relationship with. Certainly don't undersell yourself!

There are tons of different approaches across the board, but just make sure to stick to your gut feeling when working with someone. On top of that, try to get half the payment up front before you start working on the video. Sometimes you'll do the work on your end but the company will avoid paying you if nothing is in writing. Even if it is in writing, they may try to wiggle their way out of it.

Contracts and all that business jazz are important because they can protect you. The company will typically send one to you, so be sure to look over the conditions and ask as many questions as you need before signing. You could even find out that everything looks great up until the point of signing the contract and that the contract itself is what breaks the deal. Don't feel pressured to sign anything you aren't comfortable with. I've walked away from several brands because their contracts were different than what we had covered. Never be afraid to walk away if your gut is telling you no!

Negotiating with conventions can be very similar as well. Know what you're getting into before signing a contract. Ask for what you think you're worth and negotiate with them to find something that works for both of you. Just be aware of what you will be doing at the convention. Will I have to be at a booth all day? If I'm doing panels or talks, how many am I giving and on what topics? Are there autograph sessions? Does the convention cover my meals, hotel, and transportation? Some conventions pay for appearance fees while smaller conventions do not. An appearance fee is basically how much they will pay you to come to the convention, do some panels, talk with attendees, and do guest signings. This is very notable in the entertainment side of things, as actors, voice actors, YouTubers, musicians, artists, and so on usually have an appearance fee. Some people sell merchandise while they are there, but they usually also get a flat rate too. If you talk to a convention about being a guest or speaker definitely ask them about these things.

Conventions usually base their guest bookings on several things: How much programming is this person providing? Will this creator bring fans to the convention who will buy tickets? How many tickets are predicted to be sold? Even if zero fans show up because of you, you're still there providing value to attendees who are there. If you're doing panels and other things as an official guest make sure you're getting paid for them in some way. That is part of your job after all and you shouldn't be working for free.

At the end of the day everything is negotiable. Whether it's a sponsorship, convention opportunity, or something entirely different. A lot of times if the company doesn't present a price they are expecting you to. If they accept your price right away, that means you may have underbid what they were expecting. Either that or you were right on the nose. Recovering from underbidding is near impossible because you would have to have a legitimate reason for charging more after you stated your price. It isn't impossible though. If they introduce more elements to the deal you can certainly interject and ask for more. Scope creep is something that can definitely happen too. This is essentially when the project's scope (its duration or what it is setting out to accomplish) becomes larger than what was originally pitched as the conversation evolves. Always keep in mind just how much involvement a particular project will require of you.

If you were to overbid, one of two things could happen: They could say the budget isn't that high and thank you for your time or they could ask you to reevaluate. If they drop you immediately that probably means they weren't too invested in you as a creator in the first place. Unless you asked for an absurd amount of money, that is. However, if they ask you to reevaluate, they could simply be opening the floor to negotiation. They want to pay as little as possible to get the most bang for their buck. If they can save money and still get results they will be happy. Beyond that, the bosses they report to will be happy. It usually means they don't want to lose you when they ask you to rethink what you're charging. It is like walking into a pawn shop and haggling back and forth. You may not be an expert at haggling, but you could give your friend a call who is an expert at haggling and he can come on down to take a look.

Jokes aside, don't fear the negotiation process and use it as a learning opportunity as well. Just because you negotiate something poorly the first time doesn't mean the experience won't help you next time you have to do it. You aren't going to hit a home run if you've never batted before, so treat it as a learning experience and use it to gain an understanding of the process.

Fan Funding and Teaching

The final element of making a livelihood as a creator is fan funding and teaching. Fan funding is essentially when your fans directly support your creative endeavors. This could be through support on Patreon, direct donations, subscription-based services, or chat opportunities.

Patreon is a great way to earn additional income while creating. Some creators can even count on it for almost the entirety of their earnings. Of course, this all really depends on how close you are with your fans and what value you provide. Sometimes Patreon can be treated as a tip jar, whereas other times people will get perks for becoming patrons. This could be behind-the-scenes content, personalized videos, direct chat access, artwork, shoutouts in videos, or a variety of other perks. You can get just as creative with these things as you can with your content.

However, be careful with what you're promising. Should you fail to deliver on what you say you'll give them, you'll no doubt ruin your relationship with them. Beyond that, if you're giving too much you will spend all your time fulfilling patron requests and won't be able to spend that time creating YouTube videos. It wouldn't make sense to do that, especially if you're not earning a lot from Patreon.

Direct donations are another great way to earn income too. Sometimes a creator will setup a Paypal account where fans can directly donate. This way the creator sees the most money out of the donation and it is instantly transferred. Other services like Patreon or in-app donations take percentages out of what is donated. Paypal will too if the money isn't within Paypal. Don't mistake the value of fan funding platforms though. Patreon and YouTube certainly have their perks in exchange for the fee that is collected.

Subscription-based services and chat opportunities are things that apply to YouTube and other streaming platforms. You can sponsor a creator through the platform itself and you can unlock perks by doing so. Whether by getting more access to live stream chats, special emoticons, or having a message reach the creator directly while streaming. You have the option to support creators monthly like this and they receive a certain percentage of what is earned.

Fan funding is a great outlet for getting additional income, though it can also be a bit unruly for creators. You never know if someone's payment is actually going to go through when they pledge it. You could be expecting to receive a certain amount of money at the end of the month but declined credit cards mean you receive far less than you were expecting. It can be very unpredictable much like advertisement earnings. Never put all your eggs in one basket because it could mean extreme frustration when payday comes.

Although this avenue isn't explored too often, you can always look into teaching others to make a living. That's pretty much what I'm doing with this book. Not only do I get to inspire the next generation of content creators, but it helps me make a living as a creator. I learned a ton of things while doing YouTube and all of that has value. If someone can spend a few bucks and get a jump start to creating themselves, it's a win-win situation for both of us. It doesn't even have to be about YouTube either. If you're an artist it could certainly be about how you make your art. If you are serious about it you could even set up a coaching group that you could charge people to be a part of. It'd be like paying for classes so they can learn firsthand from a master.

Yes, a master. You're sure to get amazing at your craft over time! These types of approaches involve learning a new skill set though and come with their own quirks. You may find yourself investing into additional programs, resources, and insurance to protect yourself. Everyone's journey is different and how you make a living from it can be just as creative as your actual YouTube channel. Take the time to brainstorm!

Over time you will continually adapt to the wild world of being an online content creator. Every success, failure, and interaction will shape who you are and your outlook on the future. Take the time to understand the things I talked about in this chapter and perhaps even do some research yourself. Expanding the scope of what you do beyond what you create is crucial to making your journey sustainable. Develop these different avenues so that you will have more wiggle room with your creative process. As you grow and things begin to pick up in pace, be open to adapting your content to meet the needs of your audience. Don't be afraid to experiment either. There isn't a strict formula to follow, so experiment to see what works and what doesn't. Sooner than later you may find yourself at the next stage on your journey.

THE MATURITY OF TIME

You've found a really nice town that you enjoy and you set up shop there. You've honed your craft through your journey and you've really improved as a creative professional. This sense of living works for you and you wouldn't mind being here for a while. You've discovered a formula that is repeatable and you may even have some people helping you at this point.

• • •

We continue to mature with each video we upload and every milestone we reach. Like any skill in life, the more you do it the more you become better at it. You become more efficient simply by doing. By failing. By getting up after you've fallen down. Eventually you'll figure out what works and what doesn't. You will realize what you need to do in order to grow, and when you look back at the person you were yesterday, you honestly may not recognize them. Your journey has made you grow in more ways than you could possibly imagine and you've arrived at a point where things feel safe. You aren't worrying as much because you have processes in place and for a moment you can finally rest. This feels like home.

It's weird when you reach this point because you realize you can relax a bit.

When we start our journey, we are constantly moving through an unknown land and trying to figure out things as we go. However, at some point we reach what we've been walking towards. We hit the goal we've been striving for and we slump back in our chairs to think about what has been accomplished. This hit me in a multitude of ways and I feel like it almost applies to several instances in my career as a YouTuber.

The first time it happened was when I broke one hundred thousand subscribers on my channel. My channel had exploded in growth initially after my first breakthrough, but then the process became a lot slower. It took me almost a year to hit one thousand subscribers and then almost one year after that point I was sitting at one hundred thousand. I was blessed to have had such a growth spurt, but in many ways it was because of continuous studying of the platform. I wanted to understand everything about this platform that, to some degree, held the fate of my dreams.

One hundred thousand. It's a number that makes you reflect. You're staring at your computer screen, but on the other side of that screen is one hundred thousand faces staring back. The feeling is indescribable, but it is one of peace. I had made it. I had proven to myself that this can work. All of the countless hours I put into my videos finally paid off.

I felt like I wanted to take a long nap. Things didn't have to be go-go-go-go-go anymore. I could stop and enjoy the things I had been neglecting in my life. Of course, what I was met with was an existential crisis as I had been ignoring things in my life. I became so YouTube-focused for a year that I didn't take the time to enjoy the little things.

I remember seeing my parents' pets while visiting one time and I couldn't fathom why they looked much older. I even argued with my parents that something was wrong with them. Nothing was wrong with them at all though. I had simply been stuck in a self-inflicted time vortex. During the week I'd research, write, record, edit, animate, and upload. I'd then rinse and repeat over and over again. Doing this for over a year straight when your videos typically took about 40 hours each to make certainly took a toll. However, now I began to have people assist me with some videos. I started to change my video process so they could be completed faster and so it wasn't so taxing on me. And for the first time in a long time I could shut off my mind.

Later on, the second instance of my profound realization took place when my channel passed one hundred videos. That alone was crazy to think about and I took some time to dwell on it. I could certainly get used to this feeling. It's a mix between a sense of accomplishment and excitement. SwankyBox could be something beyond just me. Those one hundred videos and one hundred thousand subscribers were my proof of concept for something bigger, and of course, that also meant bringing on some more people.

Expanding Your Team

At a certain point in your creative journey you may find yourself faced with the fact that you have reached your threshold of capability. One person can only do so much and in order to take further steps you will need to enlist the help of others. What you create will definitely influence how many people have to be involved. That is, assuming others aren't already involved. For myself, the video process for SwankyBox was a very long one. Having others helping out with editing videos was something that I certainly needed in order to grow. I still technically didn't have a solid team I was working with at the time of writing this book, but it was something I was piecing together. I found this endeavor to be exciting for a lot of different reasons and some of them might not be what you'd expect.

Obviously having people assist me with creating videos was a huge time save because the work could be split up across different people. However, one of my favorite parts of this process was actually bringing people on in a mentorship role too. Anyone who has ever worked with me knows that I want the experience to be beyond what a typical work relationship is. I want them to learn and be inspired themselves. Working with people who were still starting their creative journey was enjoyable for me because I felt like I could give them points and tips for their own journey. I felt like a trail guide telling people about the land around them because I had crossed through this same area a year ago. I could be the person I wish I had access to when I started to create myself. In return, I gained valuable experience too. You always learn something new with each encounter.

Giving back to other creatives feels extremely rewarding and passing on my story for others to grow from has always been something I wanted to do. I suppose that's why I wrote this book as well. Nothing would be more amazing than knowing someone started creating because they picked up a collection of my thoughts and felt inspired enough to give it a go. Or perhaps someone saw me at a convention and then a year later at that same convention, they approached me to tell me about what they've accomplished since we last met. I can't tell you how happy that would make me! (Hint: Extremely happy.)

With others helping out with the production of the channel's videos, I finally had time to think again. I had time to start brainstorming my future as a creator and what I wanted to accomplish. YouTube was my platform, but there were so many things I wanted to do. This sense of peace allowed me to contemplate these things with no urgency. I could go out, go sit at a park and ponder, and take walks again. I missed this part of myself, and indulging in these moments again allowed me to think of how I would grow over the year to come. When you allow your mind to be free you may find yourself thinking of fresh ideas. For over a year I was so focused on finishing videos only to then immediately switch gears and start the process over again.

I became an editing machine. And while I did feel like I had good video ideas, I don't think I ever granted my mind freedom. In some ways I was limiting my own potential from a brainstorming perspective. You make sacrifices to have a steady upload rate, but for the first time ever I had videos scheduled ahead of time. Sometimes multiple videos. It felt really good to feel ahead, to finally feel okay to relax. To abandon the feeling of catching up that so many creators operate on. I gave myself some time to enjoy this and really gather my thoughts.

Branching Out to New Projects

This was when I really started to branch out as a creator in ways outside of my normal uploads. With a little more free time, I explored live streaming so that people could get a better sense of who I was as a person. Normally on my channel I animated and used game footage to tell a story. I was a voice in the background and you never really saw my face. Being just a background voice on a video isn't something people typically feel connected with though. It was time to stop being just a narrator.

I'm a writer by nature so removing the script and forethought of who SwankyBox was online was super important for me to try. We often shape people's perception of ourselves by the videos we choose to upload, but they may never get a full sense of who we are as a person. We typically show our best photos, our best video takes, and essentially things we are comfortable with.

However, people in general are more than just that. Seeing someone in their rawest form was a completely different experience and unless you talked to me after presentations at conventions, that side of me was hidden from the world. Much to my surprise, people really loved my core personality. I was naturally nervous at first, but live streaming also had a sense of freedom with it too. The little things I worried about in my normal videos had no place here. I let myself go and purely became reactionary. I grew to really enjoy the experience minus a few streaming hiccups when I first started. To see the reactions of my fans in real time and answer their questions felt really awesome. It was something I looked forward to doing when I was able to and something I hope to continue to do in the future.

This is where the books came into play as well. This will surely not be the only book I write, and during this time of calmness I started writing besides just for my YouTube videos. I still have to finish the series of fantasy novels I started writing years ago as well. However, trying to write this book in the midst of all the chaos of chasing after a goal would have really made this book turn out dishonest to myself. My mind wouldn't have been as focused as it is now. It would be full of half-baked thoughts and probably wouldn't have gotten much attention.

To really tell my story I had to be free. During this time in your YouTube journey you may very well be going through a similar thing. The drive to succeed may die down a bit and your overall pace may be less than it was before. That's totally okay. Our journeys aren't meant to be a never-ending race where we can't slow down. Slowing down allows us to appreciate what we have and think about ways we can continue to make it grow. Perhaps this is really where you start thinking about your long-term solutions to things. Maybe you start creating a unique product or experience for your viewers that could specifically make your life easier in terms of financial worries. In addition, make it rewarding for those who buy into it. Or maybe this is where you do branch out and try experimenting with something, like I did with live streaming. You've hit a stride to some degree and things seem to be going well, so while things aren't crazy, it's probably a good idea to take this time to really think. To live a little again.

Of course, all good things come to an end. After a while of existing in this stride we realize that while the time wasn't wasted, we may have plateaued. It isn't something we regret, but it is something that definitely kicks us into overdrive. This town we've become accustomed to on our adventure has become a bit stale and it is time to pack up again. We look to the stars in the sky the night before we depart, and in the morning we set foot again into the great unknown.

THE SECOND DEPARTURE

Your mind wanders from the safety of being comfortable. Things might be going decently, but you begin to lose your spark. The mundaneness of your formula begins to stale your creativity. You remember why you started in the first place and decide to begin moving again. Your friends join you as you wander back out into the unknown. There's more stability this time around, but you have yet to discover what you're looking for.

• • •

As creatives I think we get stir crazy once we've been in one place too long. I believe that's why coffee shops are so appealing to a lot of people. It's a new environment that is different than what you are used to. I know with writing this book I often found myself sitting in coffee shops because I simply didn't feel inspired to write at my own desk sometimes. My desk was a place I usually did my video editing and it held a different feeling. When you work from where you live sometimes finding a creative drive can be difficult. I knew in order to properly execute this book I needed to go out somewhere and just write. I needed to be disconnected and focused on just sharing my story. The walks I often took helped refresh my mind before jumping back into my projects. However, while these methods typically help, there are some things that can't restore motivation when things are changing . . . And that is what started to happen with my channel.

Acknowledging Your Problems

My channel was beginning to die. Those who used to come and watch no longer came to watch. YouTube is constantly evolving as a platform and sometimes it can be difficult to understand how things happen. Was my audience getting older? Were they getting new responsibilities in their life that was preventing them from watching? Did the YouTube algorithm change? Or was the formula I established for myself not really working out anymore? The funny thing is people are usually horrible at taking their own advice and my channel was sort of a testament to that. This is where I resume the story I hinted at in the Adapting to the Wild chapter. SwankyBox was always a channel that had a potluck of videos on it. Whether you were looking for the latest gaming mystery, a video focused on nostalgia, or even motivational vlogs, it had it all. But because it had it all, that's exactly why it suffered. It wasn't niche at all. There were so many things working against the channel that in many ways it was like a burning ship. It would slowly sink over the years because its foundation was so scattered. I tried to be everything to everyone and that simply wasn't working. Now I know in one of the first chapters of this book I talked about how building a YouTube channel is similar to building a statue out of Legos. I also mentioned that your old, unpolished videos from the start would eventually be overshadowed once you solidified a direction for your channel. I only know this because I did this to the extreme.

The problem with my channel was that people came to it for a ton of different reasons. Those reasons were actually more important than the person who was creating those experiences. Because my channel typically put out four videos a month, and all those videos were on different styles of topics, people didn't tune in to watch every video. And to make things worse, YouTube keeps track of this too. Eventually it stops notifying people because it thinks the videos I'm putting out aren't interesting. However, the issue isn't that they weren't interesting, they just weren't what my audience wanted. Somewhere the people who would appreciate these videos existed, but they weren't here waiting with me. It's like ordering dinner at a restaurant and being served something completely different than what you were expecting. You'd probably refuse it and wonder why it was put in front of you. If they kept doing it over and over, you'd eventually stop coming to that restaurant.

My problem was that my channel was very, very broad without a focus. The topics were very deep and analytical, but they were presented in a way that also didn't let you get to know me as a person. People liked me of course, but I was stifling who I actually was by the way I made my videos. I was refusing to adapt when the whole world around me was changing and that is what put me in this predicament. By refusing to change and being blind to what was happening, I dug myself into a hole by slowly dividing my audience over the course of the year. My stubbornness got the best of me.

So I came to a crossroads. SwankyBox would either have to end as a channel or it would have to evolve. If it were to evolve, it would certainly take some time to do so. Recovering from all the damage I caused in the past with the YouTube algorithm and dividing my audience in general would take time to heal. It wasn't impossible, but it would certainly be difficult. While all of this may sound grim, it was actually kind of exciting. I'm the weird type of guy who gets excited when things get bleak because I like to rise up to the challenge and try to figure it out. I wouldn't have understood all these things about YouTube, what works on the platform, and ultimately the direction I wanted to head in without failing. By failing to meet my own expectations it sort of rekindled the spark inside of me to change what I was doing.

So what did I do? Well, starting off I put myself in all my videos. The real me—not just a voice. If there was a disconnect with my audience, I wanted to reconnect with them. I wanted everyone who came to the channel to know that I was a real person and not just a voice. Only a small fraction of your viewers actually tune in for live streams, so this was my answer to connecting with my audience even further. I also simplified the structure of my videos. I looked at my analytics to see when people stopped watching and addressed the problem areas of my videos. I took what I had established and broke it apart. I started tweaking things weekly to see what worked and what didn't.

I also simplified my scope. While I loved my nostalgic videos, I had to put them on hold for now. The same thing for my vlogs. Those videos may have a home in the future, but for now I needed to figure out how to make my channel work long term. I needed to be niche in what I did so people would know what to expect when they came to the channel. I needed to be known for being that quirky guy who analyzed games deeper than most. In order to do so I had to drop my walls and become more vulnerable. I had to let the real me be present, and I had to break away from the formula I became so accustomed to.

That is why this chapter is called The Second Departure. At some point in your creative career you could very well have this same experience. You may find success in what you do but it may not last forever. You have to be willing to change and adapt to stay fruitful in your efforts. Always be openminded enough to consider that there may be better ways to do things and to always vouch for working smarter. I think more YouTubers come to these same crossroads than we think. I see creators working through the exact problems I had. People who have been creating for a long time can recognize these things even if the channel is foreign to them. Things may seem bleak because everything you had been working towards was successful once and now it may not seem that way. It can be hard to pick yourself up and continue on but you have to do it.

Refining Your Formula

At this point you should really take a step back and analyze everything you are doing. Take a look at your videos and see which ones are performing the best. Why are they doing better than others? Was it the topic of the video? Was it how you delivered that particular video? There are tons of factors to consider and it would certainly be worth diving into your channel's analytics to see how things are going. If you compare your popular videos to your less popular ones, how do they differentiate? Are people watching the videos for a long time or are they leaving the video quickly? Understanding how your audience perceives what you create is super important. You want to place yourself in their shoes and truly understand how they experience your videos. At the end of the day what we do is truly a user experience test with our audience. We need their feedback outside of metrics too, so don't be afraid to ask.

By asking my audience questions I quickly learned the mistakes I was making. You'll be surprised to hear that things you may have not even thought of are deal breakers for those who are watching. It is a very fine balancing act you are working with. One of my issues was that I was giving away my conclusion near the start of my videos and then explaining why I thought this way. In my mind I always imagined that people would want to hear the reasons why I believed this about the topic, but people filled in the gaps themselves. When I would create video essays about specific topics I was shooting myself in the foot because of the order in which I presented my information. The content itself was fine, but how I delivered it actually made people stop watching the video early on.

Since everything on YouTube is defined by the number of minutes watched, I was essentially cutting the life span of my videos to a fourth of what they would normally be. If you have a ten-minute video but the perceived value of the video is achieved in the first two, your audience might not even stick around to get to the second half of the video that may have held amazing information as well.

When I was going through this, I was also worried that in some ways I was starting at ground zero. That whatever I changed would alienate my audience further from me. But the truth is, everything about creating is in a cycle. People come and people go. The fans you started with may not be the fans of today and that is okay. People may even say "I liked so-and-so better when they started" or "I miss the old so-and-so." However, you can't let that keep you rooted in the past.

Even if people come and go they still can remember who you are. What you've created still exists and the impact was still felt by people even if they don't stick around in the future. Who knows, perhaps they will start watching you again later down the line. Or maybe they'll be walking through a convention, see your name on the schedule, and then come meet you. Even if they stopped watching they will remember what they enjoyed. It will be like being reunited with an old friend you stopped talking to. No matter the amount of time that's passed, they can pick up right where they left off. When I started to think of things from my viewer's perspective things didn't seem so grim.

I set off on my next adventure. This time things would be a little more focused since I still had all the knowledge I had gained in the past. I was sort of hard on myself because this was something I could have addressed six months or a year ago. At the same time though, I started to think about the beginning of my journey. If I hadn't gone through every experience I had I may have never started creating in the first place. Every part of my life played a role in making me the person I am. This was no different. I may have been able to act on this months ago, but I didn't. And that's really the end of it. It is easy to discredit the time we spent "not doing something" but it is merely because we are judging that time incorrectly. We probably spent that time doing something we simply take for granted when in reality it was necessary for our development.

All that matters is that we are moving forward now. Today is the day that's important. Take a step back from everything you are doing and truly analyze things across the board. Improve on areas you've been neglecting and write out a list of things that you want to accomplish. Don't be afraid to act according to your fears. I know that may sound odd, but "second departures" can come in a ton of different forms.

If things are tough financially, know there is no shame in seeking out employment or supplemental work to get by if you are currently pursuing YouTube to your fullest. What you've built already doesn't go away. For the longest time while creating, I balanced YouTube with my own freelance client base. This was what I was referring to back in the Heeding the Call chapter. I took on odd creative jobs to stay afloat while I grew my channel. I made sure to teach myself enough basic things so that if someone needed help with social media, websites, graphic design, photography, or video, I could lend a hand. It was all part of my process because I knew the path to success wasn't too lucrative in a financial sense until you are established. If you play your cards right, all those hours you put in will pay off in the future, but until then you do what you have to do to survive. These little projects paid enough for me to scrape by while focusing on my YouTube channel.

If you simplify your process and decrease the time it takes to make videos it could be beneficial to pick up side work or a job. The money you make from working could also go towards bringing on someone to help you with your channel. That may not always be the case, but depending on time commitments it could help out. As long as you are taking steps on your journey, there is no set path we need to take in order to get there. Growing as a creator is a timely endeavor and does not need to be rushed. I left my job to pursue YouTube because I knew mentally I wouldn't be able to deal with doing both things. I needed to make it so failure wasn't an option. More power to you if you can manage to do both your job and YouTube at the same time. While you may not be able to give it your all, you may not have as many financial worries that way. When we start this journey, we go into it knowing that we are in it for the long haul. How we get there doesn't matter. We have to drop that ring into the volcano and we can't give up until we do so!

I didn't know what the future would hold for me at this point, but I suppose I never really did anyways. My channel would evolve and I would reinvent what I was doing. Little did I know my adventure was coming to one of my greatest landmarks ever . . .

I had reached Land's End.

AT LAND'S END

You reach the edge of the world and you stare at the unknown land before you. It's different than what you're used to, but the challenge is welcoming. You've honed your craft enough to take on a new challenge—to branch out creatively into a new avenue. To start from ground zero, but take all your experience with you.

• • •

The name of this chapter is dear to me for many reasons. The phrase "Land's End" has been something I've thought about since I heard the name as a kid. Truthfully, this name is totally stolen from an area in a video game I played when I was younger. Super Mario RPG: Legend of the Seven Stars was a game that I can never forget since it was one of my first grand digital adventures. When you're navigating through this world and trying to get your hero to the castle at the end of the game, you reach an area called Land's End. It's during the second half of your journey, this mountainous area that leads to a desert bordering an ocean by way of cliff. The only thing you can do is go up into the clouds.

It was appropriately named Land's End, because up until that point the game had you navigating the landscape along your journey. From that point forward, by way of land was no more. Everything beyond there was once again the unknown and you really had no idea how you would get from one place to the next. I've never been able to forget the name of this area or the lingering feeling it instilled in me. It's honestly the most fitting thing to call this last chapter because it symbolizes this part of the journey perfectly.

A New Creative Adventure

When I started doing YouTube again several years ago after leaving my job, I had no idea what I really wanted to do. I decided on gaming because my past was focused in it. Gaming was an escape for me and I had memories upon memories of it. It felt right to choose gaming as my path and it certainly worked out for me in the end. They say you should write what you know, so why not create from what you know as well?

Fast forward to today and I do not regret this path at all. I've made so many friends, shared so many life experiences, and had the opportunity to speak to millions of people about video games. Saying my life had changed would be an understatement. But the interesting thing about your YouTube journey is that you learn so much during it that could be reapplied if you ever choose to do it again. If you ever decided to start another channel from the ground up. That's exactly where my adventure led me.

Reaching "Land's End" for me was monumental because I had completely traversed the gaming landscape and learned all it had to offer. From new releases, to conventions, to working with blogs, brands, and other creators—I had explored every avenue of what gaming held. I analyzed stories within games, spoke with indie developers about how the indie game scene coincided with YouTubers and streamers, live streamed myself, attended forty to fifty conventions, and so much more. I loved every minute of it too and look forward to how gaming will grow in the future. But what it made me realize was that my passions weren't solely in gaming. I was passionate about a ton of different things and I felt it was time to start something new. Something different than what I had been doing before.

Something that involved cats.

Now that may be completely different than what you expected me to say, but for me it made perfect sense. My significant other and I wanted to start creating something together and we absolutely loved our cat. We loved her so much we got another one. I was always a huge fan of cats growing up and I will always treasure the time I spent with my family's pets as a kid. My gaming channel taught me everything I needed to know about YouTube as a platform and it was super exciting to align it to something different.

The feeling of starting a new channel from scratch after finding success with your first channel is quite interesting. I really don't know how to describe it honestly, but the thought of doing so filled me with inspiration. It certainly is the opposite of when you start your first channel. You no longer worry about the things you already experienced the first time around. When it is your first time, you have no idea what to expect and you can stress yourself out. However, once you've matured through your first journey, the second one feels stress-free.

Choosing to make a channel on pets, or more specifically cats, was a culmination of many things. For starters, I wanted to continue to branch out and make my creative lifestyle sustainable long term. I also wanted something I could work on with my significant other since she was just as creatively passionate as I was. We were both crazy cat people to some degree, so why not align that to a channel? But more so than that, no one was really doing the type of channel we were wanting to do. We quickly identified that there were plenty of opportunities for marketing cat toys and various pet products that could really make the experience fun.

We built a set for the show, created outfits, invested in some toys, and Cat Lab Toy Reviews was born. This channel would function just like that river metaphor I mentioned a few chapters back. It was another creative outlook that could bring in additional revenue long term and we could also use it to do a lot of good for the pet community. It is still in its infancy, but in the future, I think it would be amazing to align its efforts with pet support programs and the like. There would be nothing greater than making quirky cat analysis videos that support your well-being and also making the lives of other pets better through various causes.

We wanted to build something that would work well with pet product companies, nonprofits, and really any other medium involving cats. While working on this channel, SwankyBox would continue to grow as well. It would just make it so all my eggs weren't in one basket. My gaming channel would still be my pride and joy, but with someone else helping with my editing, the time I would have spent editing could be going towards building something else. I believe it is incredibly important to scale up what you are doing, and sometimes that involves other projects as well. My editor even has his own creative side projects going on.

In addition to this, I started helping out with other YouTube channels as well. One example is a channel my childhood friend started. While he didn't have an understanding of the YouTube platform, he loved the idea of making a living from creating. It was really cool talking him through the process and helping him understand what challenges awaited. I felt like an old sage passing down knowledge to the next generation. Coaching other people is certainly another way to make a living too, so don't ever discredit what you learn on your journey. You never know who may come knocking at your door seeking insight that you can offer. Whether it be about YouTube specifically or even about the passions you utilized to get to where you are today.

YouTube is Your Launching Point

When you reach Land's End your next move might not be another YouTube channel. It doesn't have to be creating something within the same area that you're already creating. Land's End could be deciding to write a book, to start working on artwork, or to even make a video game. It's simply the idea that your creativity is taking you to another outlet and you feel empowered to answer the call to try something else. I think as creative people we can become stifled if we do one thing for too long. Even if we love what we do, the idea of trying something else always seems appealing. I suppose it can be both a gift and a curse depending on how you look at it. I always considered it to be a gift because I've never regretted trying new things.

There's also the possibility that an opportunity will come along that will place you at Land's End immediately in your creative journey. You might not even be as far as you expect to be when opportunity could come knocking at your door. Creating your videos could lead to all kinds of jobs that may even fulfill your creativity further. A large channel may notice your work and may want to recruit you to help. A Website or company may be impressed and try to bring you on as well. It's important to remember that both of these things aren't abandoning what you set out to do. Your path has simply branched out into a different direction and, honestly, something like this could lead to more people discovering who you are. At the end of the day we want people to experience what we make and it doesn't hurt to have other outlets potentially passing viewers our way.

When I set out and left my job to pursue a life of creativity, I always thought about the things I wanted to do along the way. YouTube was merely the first step for me as a creative person. It was the platform I would use to connect with people as I continued throughout my life. There are several books I want to write as well and this was one of them. I still have a whole fantasy series I can't wait to dive into. Then there is the idea of making video games. When I was younger I actually spent most of my time building worlds through game-making programs and I know someday I'll return to that. I spent hundreds if not thousands of hours slowly designing a fantasy world that my characters would romp around in and the feeling of doing so was really magical. All of these things will be a lot easier now that I've taken the YouTube plunge.

Writing a book or making a game is very difficult when you don't have anyone to share it with. The act of creating them is the same, but the hardest part is finding people who share the same passions you do. If you have no one to read or play it, the majority of your time will be spent trying to convince people to do so. But if people become invested in who you are then it is a completely different story. If you bring joy or value to someone's life, not only will they tune in for your videos, but they will be interested in you as a person. There's a super high chance that whatever creative outlet you choose next at Land's End will be something they will be interested in as well. Whether you read this book because I inspired you somehow or you simply found it without knowing who I am, that is important to remember for when you reach this point in your journey.

Land's End may seem very intimidating, but it is no different than the jump we took way back at the beginning. Remember the reason why you started creating in the first place and walk confidently to the edge of the world. The land you're about to jump into will once again be different, but you are far wiser than you used to be. You are a seasoned veteran on YouTube and you can surely rise up to the challenges this next adventure will bring. Your next creative journey starts now, so jump into the unknown with confidence and march on across your newfound land. The possibilities are truly endless!

TRAVELER'S NOTES

TRAVELER'S NOTES
INTRODUCTION

I learned so many things throughout my journey as a YouTuber. Some of these things were psychological, others were in line with my craft, but all were lessons I wish I knew prior to starting. It would have saved me so much anxiety and stress if someone would have helped me along. I suppose that's why this section exists though. This is the SwankyBox mental dump of everything I encountered while creating.

I call them my traveler's notes. Learn from them so you don't have to stress out like I did!

The first part of the notes is specific to the craft of creating on YouTube. Everything that pertains to the creation process in a hands-on kind of way. From making your first videos, to equipment, thumbnails, fair use, branding, and the YouTube algorithm. There's a lot of stuff packed in. I hope you find it insightful!

The second section of the notes cover the mental aspects of being a content creator. The things people don't talk about or know how to actually articulate. Since I tend to analyze everything about life, I decided to document all the tough choices, interactions, and social barriers I encountered while creating. Hopefully this will shed some clarity about the terrain you're about to enter. You'll read about impostor syndrome, content thieves, how YouTube changes your life, burned bridges, and so much more. A lot of these notes will be good to be aware of before you encounter certain situations. They'll also be twice as helpful once you're in the midst of dealing with that particular situation.

WHAT IS MY SPECIALTY?

Deciding that you want to create on YouTube is really only the first step. The most difficult step by far is picking a direction that you want to move in. You may know that you want to create, but most people have no idea what they want to make. The problem isn't always that they are indecisive. It's just that they may see themselves being able to do multiple things.

Gaming made sense for me to pursue because I had an extensive history with it. However, I could have totally done so many different things. I love doing gaming documentaries, but I could also have done travel vlogs focused on forgotten places, anime and cartoon analysis, creepy stories about the mysteries of our world, or even a channel about cats. That last one in particular is one I actually decided to move forward with alongside my gaming channel.

Coming up with your specialty isn't supposed to be an easy choice. You're basically committing to something that you will spend tons of time building. There's a chance you could very well dislike it in the end. Sometimes things are better off hobbies and not job paths because you might become burned out of your passion. What you used to look forward to no longer inspires you, and it is now about simply getting it done. All of these are factors in deciding what we want to do.

Even though I knew I wanted to do gaming, I certainly didn't know what avenue in gaming I wanted to explore. Did I want to be a "Let's Player?" A game reviewer? A glitch / mod channel? A historian? Or an analysis channel? If you look across my channel you can see it took me a long time to figure this out. I knew my genre would be gaming so that at least pointed me in the right direction. But I could have done many different things, and believe that success could have been found in any of them. Hearing that might not make your decision any easier, but perhaps you can find comfort in knowing anything can become viable if spun in the right way.

I chose gaming because it didn't require me to go anywhere. I could do it from the comfort of my home and not have to leave. I also had a huge amount of knowledge about the subject because my childhood was spent in front of a tv screen while smashing buttons on a controller. As a writer they always tell you write what you know—so that's what I did. I also wanted my videos to be scalable in the future. If I was creating something that only I could make or edit, I would never have time for other things because my videos would consume my entire week.

Ask yourself the following questions about each thing you may be interested in and compare your answers:

Would I be happy doing this for a long time?

How many other people are doing this?

What personal twist could I add to this type of video to make it truly unique?

What brand or sponsorship opportunities could this particular creative path lead to?

When it comes to a point where I would want to branch out, would there be any sort of products that would make sense for my audience?

Will the type of videos I'm looking to make be sustainable long term?

You may have all of these answers or you may have none. However, thinking about them may eventually lead to something. People can certainly tell you what they think you're good at, but ultimately it is up to you to decide what works for you. No one knows what you're truly passionate about except for you. The only way to figure out what works and what doesn't is to experiment. You can always try something different if it doesn't feel right. When you're starting out it's the perfect time to have fun and try different things, because no one knows who you are yet. You aren't established in any area and it's quite possible you may start creating without having any idea about the path you want to take. That's entirely okay. Sometimes it takes us jumping in head first to discover what we're meant to do. You'll know when you find it, but until then, keep having fun!

YOUR BRAND
AND IDENTITY

There was one monumental issue I ran into way back when I started my YouTube channel the first time: What do I call myself? What do I want to be known as online? This is always a difficult choice to make. Whatever name you choose will forever define you from that point forward. You wouldn't want to have a super generic name, nor would you want something you wouldn't be happy with in the future.

Often times in the past people would create silly names on YouTube with a bunch of numbers after them and roll with that as an account. Your name could be "SillySam72" and that would be totally okay. However, as a creator, do you really want to have a legacy as SillySam72? Disclaimer: If a SillySam72 is reading this, I'm totally sorry! But if you gain a huge following over time I think you'd rather secure a name that doesn't have numbers after it. It sticks out a lot more and separates a brand you built from just an account you made. And that's where things get difficult . . .

Finding a name that isn't already taken can be a nightmare. SwankyBox certainly wasn't my first choice. I originally was CrapBox and then it was PartyBox. These names were because I wanted to have a container of some kind that was full of random things. The original plan for the channel was to do funny skits. Back when I started it in 2012 that seemed like a good direction for YouTube. On top of that, the channel had many people in the videos and it wasn't just me.

Even when I rebooted the channel in 2015 I still planned on other people being a part of it. My original identity was "2B" of SwankyBox. I adopted the actual name SwankyBox myself near the end of 2015 because it had become a solo endeavor. I think I dodged a bullet too since the video game "Nier Automata" came out in early 2017 which featured an android protagonist named 2B. There would definitely have been some search engine conflict if I still went by that identity!

The reason why I decided on SwankyBox for a channel name in general was because all the other names I tried before it were already taken. When you're coming up with your name, you want to secure all your social profiles associated with it. You'll want to register your Twitter, Facebook, Instagram, Twitch, Tumblr, and so on immediately after you find your name. Sometimes these may even define your name because you want something that is available. It is incredibly important you register all of these though. Why, you ask? Because if you don't, someone else will. It happened to me and it is a pain in the butt to deal with.

Registering a name first on a website doesn't fall under impersonation even if the name that is being stolen has an established following. They simply got the name first. If you try to complain that they are squatting on your name, chances are the social network you're complaining to will simply dismiss your case. The only way you can claim the name is if they are impersonating you or utilizing your copyrighted name or assets in their profile.

When you're thinking of a name, try to consider how people will search for it. If someone hears the name will they know how to spell it right off the bat? Hearing the name SwankyBox makes you just spell out the two words in your head. Most people can spell the words swanky and box. However, that's also a problem in itself. Something I didn't think of when making my name was that people would split the name up. The name is two words mashed together without a space. Together they are my identity, but separate they are just two words. I realized people started searching for "swanky box" more often than "SwankyBox."

I think this causes search engine issues sometimes because the words aren't unique to me. While they are easy to spell, there is still a choice that needs to be made when searching. Do I include a space or not? Beyond that, when I'm a guest at conventions it is always a coin flip whether my name will be written as SwankyBox or Swanky Box. Part of this may have been due to my Twitter handle including an underscore at the time since someone else already had the @swankybox name. Perhaps I'll be able to get it in the future, but who knows. My recommendation is to go with a name that won't cause an issue like this.

Ultimately your name is essentially an empty entity that you fill with creativity and personality. What you do with your name defines what your brand is. I had a logo made for my channel a long time ago, but what I realized is that I'm actually the brand. My face and knowledge defined what SwankyBox was. The logo actually came across as less personal because it was an entity and not a person. People would rather build a bond with an actual person than a logo that could represent anything.

Eventually you'll want to trademark and copyright your identity to protect yourself. This process is a bit boring and expensive, but it will save you a lot of hassle in the long run if something goes awry. You'll probably want to consult a legal counselor when you're going through this process to make sure you get everything set up properly. You'll more than likely find yourself establishing a small business in the process too.

Branding in general consists of many outlets. It's essentially what your channel looks like, how it is articulated, the colors it uses, its overall mission, etc. When you're first starting off, your brand will probably be very loose because it will be defined over time. You likely won't have a logo, a color palette you stick to for your channel, or a set style guide for how everything should work. Perhaps you may never have something like that. It can be extremely daunting especially if you're not an artist or don't have access to one.

When you start working with other brands and companies it will help to have these things in place. You will come off far more professional than others and it will let them know you are serious about what you do. I've gotten plenty of compliments for my branded elements when I'm negotiating with companies. I even send them branded proposals that are extra swanky. They feel safer tying their name to someone who took the time to orchestrate something rather than someone who simply threw everything together. Sometimes a first impression is all you get. Make sure you look snazzy! (Or, you know . . . Swanky!)

EQUIPMENT AND SOFTWARE

Choosing the right equipment and software can be just as daunting of a task as producing your first video. Just know that you don't have to have the best camera, microphone, software, and computer to start creating. So many people think they have to have the best of the best or people will look down upon them. This certainly isn't the case at all. Quality and ability will come with time. If you don't have the money to invest into better equipment that is totally fine. What matters is that you create with what you have.

Cameras

If you can't afford to get a camera, you can always use your phone or a webcam. The cameras that come in phones and laptops have certainly come a long way.

Some of the newer smart phones out there simply blow me away with their picture quality. It's honestly unreal. The crispness of the image makes me question my own camera that I use. Phones are great because you always have them on you too. If you're out and about and want to record a video, you can prop your phone up against something and film a vlog right on the spot. You could also just hold it as well.

If you're considering purchasing a camera though, definitely take your time choosing an appropriate one. One of my biggest hurdles was that I bought a DSLR camera years ago that wasn't autofocus. What that means is that the lens on my camera didn't focus on whatever it was looking at unless I manually did it. In order to get a clear picture, I had to dial in the camera myself, otherwise everything was blurry. When you're recording yourself, autofocus is a must. You would need extra tools in order to focus the camera properly without it. Trying to film myself was a pain in the butt because I had to guess and check my focus since I lacked the proper tools. No one wants blurry footage. An autofocus camera will save you so much trouble.

Besides autofocusing, you also need to look into how long a camera can record for. My DSLR in particular was only able to record for 11 minutes at a time before it stopped filming. I would have to redo my recordings if I forgot about that and went over the time limit. I could record more than 11 minutes total, but it needed to be divided into chunks on my SD card. Each time I'd have to start and stop the camera. I was using an older camera and this may not be an issue with the majority of cameras today, but it is still something to take note of.

My advice is to pick up a 1080p 60fps autofocus camcorder if you're new to the world of filming and have the money to do so. Ease of use simply outweighs the benefits that more complex models can give you. A seasoned videographer may argue with this stance, but we have to remember that your final output is a video on the web. Even if you get a higher quality camera, YouTube is going to compress your video anyways so that it can cut down the file size. Your quality is going to be diminished regardless and we also have to consider that many in your audience will be streaming the videos on their phone. This means they're watching a further compressed version of your video.

Compression takes place in order to shrink file sizes and make playback more manageable. When it is played back at a smaller resolution though it is hard to tell. Think about when you see images online that are small and sort of pixelated. They were compressed heavily to reduce their file size so that they can be loaded quickly on the web. This is what YouTube does to your videos except it tries its best to maintain your quality.

It may also be worth seeing if you can hook your camcorder up to a computer as well for live streaming. You could try to kill two birds with one stone if this is something you want to do in the future. However, you could always pick up a dedicated webcam later on. Autofocus DSLR's can certainly work in place of your camcorder, but there are a lot more components to them. You have to purchase lenses in addition to the camera.

If your camera runs on SD cards, make sure you're buying a card with a high enough speed. Some cards will have a little circle with a number in them. This is the speed class of the card. You will also see MB/s (megabytes per second) potentially on the card too. Look into reviews for your camera before purchasing to see which card is best for the job. Consider picking up more than one too. In this day and age, you'll probably encounter SDHC and SDXC cards since normal SD cards are sort of phased out in regards to modern cameras. More than likely the card you'll be seeking out will be labeled as SDHC.

To backtrack a bit, I mentioned that the camera you should pick up should be able to shoot video at 1080p and 60fps. Let me take a quick second to explain what that actually means. 1080p means that the resolution of the video is 1920 pixels by 1080 pixels wide. The "p" means progressive scan, whereas there is also 1080i which is interlaced. The 60fps part means "sixty frames per second" of video. Frames are essentially how many images the camera captures of video in one second. There's a whole world of specific metrics that professionals know the ins and outs of, but unless you're aiming to become a professional cinematographer, some of these things aren't attributes you should get hung up on. That doesn't mean they aren't important, but for what you are using them for it may not affect you much. I certainly had to learn all of them when I attended college for video. I recommend seeking out additional resources if you're interested in having a complete understanding of it all.

For what we need, 1080p 60fps is what to look out for. YouTube likes higher quality content that is set to sixty frames a second. It's trying to compete with television in some regards, so it's believed that it prefers videos that are similar.

Now that I touched on frame rates, I want to rewind once again to the start of this section. For those who are using a phone, it is worth knowing that phones don't record at a solid frame rate. Most record at a variable rate that is always changing. This means you could end up with audio or footage that could become out of sync when you try to play it back in certain video editors. Basically the program can't tell what the frame rate is and this is what causes this issue. This isn't always the case, but it definitely worth mentioning. If you notice that your voice isn't matched up with your mouth in your shots this may be what is happening. You may need to pick up a dedicated app for your phone to let you shoot at 60fps to bypass this issue.

The last thing I should mention about buying a camera is that you should really think about how you will be using it. Certain cameras come with a bracket on top that is called a hot shoe where you can mount external gear, such as small lights or microphones. It was originally used by photographers for their flash units, but since has gained a multitude of uses. The hot shoe secures mountable equipment on top of your camera so that you have one unit to work with when you're filming. Consider investing in a camera that has a hot shoe if you're going to be vlogging from places that aren't always your home. There are workarounds if your camera doesn't have one, but it will make things easier if it does.

Consider how far away the camera will be away from your face, too. If you have the wrong type of lens on your camera, it may be zoomed in too much or unable to focus properly up close. If you're going the DSLR route while walking and talking with your camera, you'll want a lens that is wider and has a smaller focal length. However, it is pretty tricky to nail this down because there's a lot of factors that go into it. If you plan on moving while vlogging with a DSLR, I highly recommend looking into tutorials for your specific camera. You'll want to search about things like sensor size and crop factor, the best wide lenses for handheld, and overall best supplemental gear setups for your particular camera model.

Microphones

The next thing you'll need to secure is something to record your audio. This can work in conjunction with your camera or it can be a separate unit altogether. There are a ton of different types to consider as well, so let's break them down a bit.

A cheap lavalier microphone will be something to look for if you're on a budget. A lavalier microphone is a microphone that clips to your shirt. The cheaper versions typically have a wire that runs from the mic to whatever it is plugged into. The more expensive variants are wireless. You can usually pick up a budget lavalier microphone for around $20 – $30. More expensive versions will yield higher quality, of course. You can plug your lavalier straight into your phone if you're using it to film video. This will give you much clearer audio than your phone speaker. Just make sure that before you purchase your mic it is capable of hooking up to what you will be using it with. Some older phones have 2.5mm jacks while newer ones use 3.5mm.

For a size comparison, most music headphones for personal use have a 3.5mm jack. That lavaliers I utilize fit into a 3.5mm jack. Certain products designed for cameras might not work for phones, while phone products may not work for cameras. There are adaptors that can fix this, but it may bring about an additional expense. Always read the reviews and finer details about the product before purchasing. Keep in mind that a lot of lavaliers also require some sort of power source too. Be sure to pick up the correct size of battery for your microphone. Some come with a single battery, but you will need to replace it after it runs out.

A USB-powered microphone is another choice. The only issue with choosing one of these is that you will have to have a computer or laptop nearby to record. If you have a designated filming area you plan on using, this can cause problems if it isn't near your computer. One such problem is filming on the go. Being tethered to a machine just won't work for that. At the time of writing this book, I use a USB-powered microphone because I like being able to save my audio files straight to my computer as I record them. I don't have to worry about running out of space on my SD cards and can let my audio run for the duration of my recording. There's no issues with the batteries dying during the middle of my filming process either. Nothing is worse than finishing filming only to realize your microphone ran out of power halfway through your session.

On the flip side, the portability of a wireless hand-held recorder has its perks. Not having to be at your computer certainly gives you more options of where to record. These do run on batteries, but this may be a great choice if the tradeoff of portability makes more sense for what you're creating. Some come with power cables too so you can just plug them into an outlet. Handheld audio units usually offer a lot of recording functionality that you would typically find in computer software.

Keep in mind that any audio you record that isn't directly linked to your footage will have to be matched up when you edit your video. You'll have your camera footage with its audio and you'll have your separate microphone with its higher quality audio. When you edit you will have to take both of these and line them up so your audio is timed correctly. This is something I'll go over thoroughly in my section about producing your first videos. If your audio feeds into your camera directly then they will be synced while recording. In that situation you won't have to worry about this.

The last type of microphone I'll be covering are shotgun microphones. These are microphones that are super sensitive in one direction. They have to be pointed directly at the source of the sound to pick up the audio. This can be helpful because it isolates your voice from background noise. A number of YouTubers who vlog use shotgun microphones mounted on their cameras. The metal bracket on the top of certain cameras is a place that you can mount your microphone. It's important to note that shotgun microphones require batteries in order to operate and do not normally run off the power of your camera. The ultimate form of portability is a camera with a mounted shotgun microphone. It doesn't require anything other than powering both on and recording. It delivers great visual and sound quality. Just know that the closer a shotgun microphone is to the source, the better quality you will get. If you want the best sound quality, you can use an external recorder for your shotgun microphone.

When you're choosing a microphone to use, there are a lot of things to consider. Will echoes be a problem? Is there any background noise you don't want to pick up? Microphones like lavaliers and shotgun mics can be helpful in situations where recording conditions aren't perfect.

If you do have a designated recording area, you may want to consider soundproofing it. You can mount sound absorbing tiles on your walls or cover them in thick blankets to absorb any echoing that may occur in the room. I record in a closet for my voiceovers and the clothes surrounding me work well!

For my USB mic that I run with my laptop, I typically have it decently close to my face just out of view from my camera. However, sometimes my laptop can become hot if I have too many things running. My internal fans click on and can be heard on the microphone. I also need to use a pop filter with my microphone because it is close to my face. Certain words pack more punch when they are said. Air from my mouth will hit the microphone and cause additional noise without one. Pop filters are simple devices that hook onto microphones to stop "popping noises" and I highly recommend getting one for desk-based units. With every microphone there are strengths and drawbacks.

In addition to the ones mentioned above, there are also XLR microphones that can be fed into mixers. People sometimes utilize these to get the best sound quality they can while doing things such as live streaming or podcasting. Usually these kinds of setups are a little more advanced, but they can be worth the time to learn if you have the finances. Take the time to consider what type of microphone makes the most sense for what you want to do before you buy.

Keep in mind this section really only scratches the surface of microphone knowledge. Microphones can be broken down further into dynamic and condenser categories. Dynamic microphones usually cost less, are more durable, and aren't as sensitive. Condenser microphones typically cost more, require a power source, and are more sensitive. Each has its benefits and drawbacks. A microphone that is omnidirectional records in all directions whereas a directional microphone has a far more narrow recording path. If you want to further your education on the subject, spend some time researching more in-depth topics online. You'll get a better idea about which microphone makes more sense for your recording area.

Lighting

Lighting for a video can make or break it. It doesn't matter how good your camera is: If your lighting is bad, your video will look bad. On the flip side, proper lighting can also make a cheaper camera look a lot better than it seemed out of the box. That's the power of lighting and why it is important to take it seriously.

Before diving into actual lights though, we need to talk about color temperatures. Not all lighting is the same and mixing the two may yield drastic results. Lights have a multitude of different temperatures and this can affect the way the light looks. Ever notice how some bulbs have an orange glow while others seem to be stark white or even slightly blue? This is because the color temperatures of the lights are different. Those on the lower end of the spectrum may seem warmer while those on the higher end may seem cooler. Lights can also be shined through objects to alter their color. In the professional film world these are called these "gels." But we don't have to get too crazy for our purpose. We just want to make sure we're properly illuminated and appealing on camera. Your lighting setup will change depending on what you're filming. If you're filming outside all the time during the day you may find yourself not needing lighting. Regardless though, let's go over some important lighting basics.

If you're planning on using multiple lights indoors make sure all the lights you're buying are the same color temperature. Usually you don't have to worry about this when you're buying a kit online that has multiple lights in it, but you do when you're looking for replacement bulbs for those lights. When you have a multi-light setup and lights have different color temperatures, those areas will be noticeably different color tones. You may realize one side of your face looks more orange or blue.

Your camera acts in accordance to what it thinks is absolute white. Depending on what it's set to will change the color it perceives. This is called white balance. You can't dial into an exact color temperature if there are conflicting ranges. Regardless of how you set it, one of the lights will be an outlier if they don't match. Take note of the bulbs you are putting into your lights to prevent this. Order spare lightbulbs that match the ones you have so that you don't run into this issue. Ideally you want your lighting to look as natural as possible since we want to come across as relatable. Unless there is a stylized reason you're trying to make your lighting look different, it's probably best to present yourself in the most approachable kind of lighting. Keep spare bulbs on hand because it's simply terrible having a light burn out while filming and not having a replacement!

Now let's talk about lighting setups. In a perfect scenario your best bet is to use multiple lights. I highly recommend looking up what a "three-point lighting system" is as you can mimic this if you have the space. You essentially have a powerful light in the front called your key light, a supplemental light on the side called a fill, and a light behind you called a hair or back light. This setup is three lights total. Most of us don't have a lot of room to do this in our homes. Some of us may simply be filming in our bedroom. That doesn't mean you can't learn from a three-point setup and use it to create your own.

The reason why a three-point is effective is because it gets rid of harsh shadows. If you have a light shining directly on you, you're probably going to have some shadows cast on your face. The fill light, or the light that is off to the side, is used to counteract those shadows

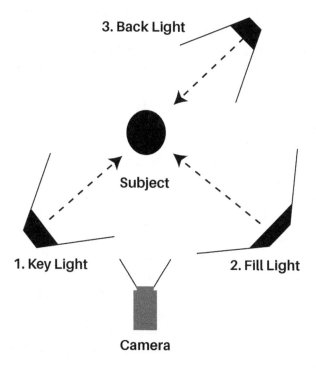

3. Back Light

Subject

1. Key Light

2. Fill Light

Camera

by adding in additional softer lighting. It's "filling in" the dark spaces. Finally, the light behind you illuminates your hair and your back. This is used to separate you from the background of the room you are in. If you watch any of my on-camera sections in my newer videos you'll be able to see what my hair light does for me. It lights up the back of my hair which is normally dark. This helps make it so my hair just doesn't fade into the black background. It sort of makes me pop out a bit and is a nice visual touch.

The biggest issue with a three-point lighting system is that it can be a pain to break down. If you don't have a spare room to keep the lights up all the time, that means every time you want to film you have to setup the lights again. It is honestly a pain in the butt, especially given how often you may want to record. Three-point lighting systems are ideal if you can leave them up, but if you cannot do so, I highly recommend looking into other options.

If you don't have the room or patience for a three-point lighting system you can always invest in a camera-mounted light or a ring light. A camera-mounted light is nice because it simply sits on top of your camera in the hot shoe mount. Usually these can be plugged into a wall or they can run on rechargeable batteries. These are great because they are extremely portable and easy to set up. If for some reason you were out and about vlogging in a dark place, a camera mounted light could do you wonders. You may need to get a supplemental mount for your camera though if you're using a shotgun microphone. If both are meant for the hot shoe bracket you'll have to choose and perhaps invest in a side arm for the other item. A lavalier microphone might spare you this issue.

A lot of stationary vloggers really like using ring lights because it provides balanced illumination for someone talking in front of a camera. The reason this occurs is because the light is a giant circle around the camera that shines in all directions. This prevents heavy shadows from forming on your face. However, this is only true if the ring light is close to eye level and is in front of you. They are designed to have the camera in the middle of them. When it's eye level it is shining from above and below which covers your face evenly. People typically use a hair / back light in combination with this to further separate themselves from the background.

Good lighting usually isn't cheap, but over the years it has gotten far cheaper than it has ever been before. The low-cost lights of today are actually great for YouTubers to use. We are typically just lighting ourselves in a simple environment, so we don't really need anything too powerful. Take the time to play around with lighting and certainly watch some tutorials online for setting up lights properly if you're unsure. Also remember that if lighting isn't in the budget, the sun can work wonders too. However, the sun can be a gamble depending on where your window is located and how bright it is outside. It could change because of clouds and it can be super bright and cast harsh shadows if you're in it directly. Lighting in general is just as important as your camera and without proper lighting your camera won't capture anything great. Keep that in mind!

Tripods and Monopods

Now that you have a camera you're going to need something to put it on. Fortunately for us we aren't producing the next Hollywood blockbuster. Obviously if you have aspirations of producing something that requires fine-tuning and steady control, then by all means invest in a more professional tripod. However, for most of us we're just looking for something to hold our camera. When you're picking out your tripod you want to make sure it is going to be able to withstand the weight of your camera. This probably won't be too big of an issue, but definitely take it into consideration. The heavier your tripod the less likely of it falling over if you accidentally bump into it. You wouldn't want it to fall over and damage your camera! Your best bet is to get a tripod that has a removable plate that you can screw onto the bottom of your camera. This way you can keep your tripod stationary and just pop your camera off if you need it elsewhere. The plate clicks into place on the tripod and will hold your camera there.

Consider how tall you need your tripod to be as well. If you're stuck in a room that doesn't have a lot of space, you might find yourself putting your tripod on top of a table. Make sure the minimum and maximum height makes sense for having the camera eye level. You want to be looking directly across from it.

What type of tripod do you want though? I personally would rather use a fluid head tripod over a ball head one. A fluid head tripod essentially allows you to rotate and tilt the camera with ease. It makes setting up your shot a bit easier even though we don't need to do any camera movements while we're filming ourselves. Majority of the time you'll probably just be doing static shots. Fluid head tripods work a lot better with heavier cameras as well.

A ball head tripod is a bit more finicky in my eyes. They are designed for portability and aren't meant to hold a lot of weight. I've also had trouble getting them set into place while filming. My issue is that the shot sometimes ends up being crooked slightly. Of course, that is just my personal opinion on the matter and other people may vouch for ball head tripods. They can be lighter and cheaper. They certainly aren't the worst thing to use by any means. If you plan on adding equipment to your camera in the future though, you may find that your ball head tripod struggles to hold up under increased weight.

You may find yourself using a monopod or some other handheld unit if you're going to be out and about while vlogging. When it comes to these units it is all about comfort and how securely they hold your camera. It's really a personal preference for what works best. You might be able to look into what your favorite vloggers use and pick up the same thing. Some units offer forms of stabilizing on the more expensive side of things. This isn't absolutely crucial, but it may be helpful if you don't have steady hands. You certainly don't want your shots to be too shaky!

Computer

This is the one section I'm really not going to give much advice on. The reason I say this is because a multitude of machines will work for basic editing. It honestly depends on what you are making and if you have money to invest into it. Start out using whatever you have available and see if it works for you. Consider upgrading parts if your machine is getting bogged down. There are a lot of amazing people online with tutorials about maximizing your machine and they can help you out a lot more than I can.

Personally, I have a Mac that I do all my video editing on and I acquired a PC later on that I use for my live streaming. I've always been a Mac guy since I started editing video in college, but since more games are available on PC, it was definitely something I needed to consider. My Macbook Pro has the perfect amount of processing power, RAM, and a nice graphics card. Was it a tad expensive? Yes. Could I still find a better machine for video? Of course. However, for what I'm doing I don't need an all-star machine. This one works just fine!

For the gamers out there, you're probably going to use your machine for both gaming and editing. A Mac probably isn't the best choice since not all games run on them.

Software

A lot of people always ask what software they should use when they create videos. Any editing program will probably suit your needs if you're starting out and are new to editing in general. You will want to find a timeline-based editing program that runs on your computer and also accepts your video format. A timeline editing program means it has a start and end point. You lay your video clips down in the desired order on a timeline. Trust me, it's actually a lot simpler to understand once you see one.

These first programs that you use will be for learning about editing in general. It's all about getting your hands dirty and just trying to figure it out. You'll be using them to get an idea for how videos are assembled and what components you need. Eventually you may branch out into audio editors, image editors, and possibly animation software if that tickles your fancy. There is no golden formula for quickly learning editing either so don't get frustrated if it takes some time for you to wrap your head around it. Start off by searching for free video editing programs and see if they work for you. There are also some really great free audio programs as well. Seek out tutorials specific to your program to help you out with them.

When you get further along in your journey you may want to seek out more professional-grade software. I'm a huge fan of the Adobe Creative Cloud. It's a service that I can subscribe to monthly and I get all the programs I could ever need. The best part about it is that all these programs integrate seamlessly. I can drag and drop from my animation program to my video editing program and it auto updates in my video editor whenever I tweak my animation. This goes for audio editing as well.

When I create a video I typically utilize Adobe Premiere Pro, After Effects, Photoshop, Audition, and sometimes Illustrator if I need to make specific graphics.

Premiere Pro is by far my favorite video editor I have ever used and it is my main hub for creating my videos. I animate in Adobe After Effects, use Photoshop and Illustrator to handle all my image needs, and refine my voiceover audio in Audition. For a lot of you that may be overkill for what you want to do. You may find yourself just working in Premiere and using Photoshop for your images. Basic animations can be done in Premiere and you can edit your audio as well. You certainly won't have as much control, but it is pretty nice that Adobe's video editor has these capabilities.

There is no right or wrong answer when it comes to software. I'm not sponsored in any way by Adobe at the time of writing this book, but I certainly love their products. (Pssst, if you're listening Adobe, we should talk!) Honestly though, you can have just as much success with simple videos as you can with highly edited ones. Your software is just a tool you use to showcase your personality in the best way possible while also supporting your message. Great editing is time-intensive and sometimes a quick simple video can fit the bill. Experiment and see what works for you. Find creators whose editing style you like and figure out what you like about it the most. Take the time to watch tutorials on YouTube as well so you can learn new things.

Jump in and give your software of choice a try. You'll learn so much by just messing around, and once you have an idea about how it works, a tutorial can take you to the next level.

PRODUCING VIDEOS

Creating your first videos is often the most daunting task involved with making a YouTube channel. Where do you start? What should the video be about? Will people like it? These questions will continue to wrack your brain during the process and that's entirely okay. This feeling is absolutely normal because you haven't done this before. It's new territory, but I'm here to guide you through it!

Planning Your Idea

This first step in the video process is thinking about what you want to create. If you've decided on a direction you want to go in for your channel this will be easier. If not, get thinking! And maybe revisit the "What is my Specialty?" section to help you get a better understanding. Ideas for videos often come from everyday life or just browsing around on the internet. Look up other channels that inspire you and see what type of content they deliver. What is it about their content that brings people to it? What value does it provide the person who shows up to watch it? Sometimes the value is simply entertainment, but other times the viewer will learn something.

It may also be worthwhile to have an idea of what people are searching for as well. As a creator you don't always have to cater to what people are searching for, but it can give you an added boost out of relevance. Pop open a private web browser and head over to YouTube and just start typing things into the search bar. Before you hit enter, YouTube will autofill the remainder of what you are typing based on what people are searching for. The most popular things will show up at the top while the less popular things will appear at the bottom. You can use this to help you gauge what may make a good video topic as well. I recommend a private browser so that the results will not be skewed by previous searches. You can also look into Google Trends for more ideas.

Once you have a few thoughts floating around your head about what you'd like to produce, you now need to write it out. Writing your idea helps shape the direction of your video a lot better. For some people this is writing a full script. Others may only use bullet points. It really depends on what you're trying to create. Writing a script may be better if it is incredibly important to nail a ton of details. If you only need guidelines for speaking off the cuff, then go the bullet point route. Either way, doing this will increase the chances that you won't forget something important when it is time to record.

Consider who you may be speaking to as well when you are trying to figure out what to say. What would your ideal fan be like? What value are they getting in the video? If there is some sort of payoff in the video consider saying it closer to the end. You wouldn't want someone to stop watching a video because they got everything they needed right at the beginning. You want to keep them around as long as possible so that they have time to connect with you as a person. Make the video worth their while regardless of how long they stay though. It doesn't do you any good to waste someone's time by not delivering what you're promising. They'll certainly leave.

At the start of your video consider adding something that will grab their attention. Make it something thought-provoking or engaging. Throughout the video build on that until you close out in the end. There's a formula you will learn as you create more videos. If you tune into your favorite creators time and time again, chances are you really like the way they deliver their content. Try to break down their process and learn from it.

Once you have your idea written out, the next step is to think about what you need to accomplish it. I typically make a shot list because the videos I create have a lot of components to them. A shot list is a list outlining what the person will see during each part of the video. I break it down by each sentence spoken. My videos usually include gameplay, game cinematics, images, animation, clips of me talking to the camera, and a splash screen at the end. Perhaps showcasing a certain image during a part of your narration makes sense. Maybe a specific video clip would support what you're saying. All of these things are listed out beforehand so I can get a better idea of what I'm trying to make. After listing or sketching all of these out, I can then go into the next phase of creation.

I will say that my shot lists became very loose as time went on because I knew I could improvise things. Once I started creating regularly and hit my stride, I could then get away with not having to list everything out. I knew what I needed. However, if you ever plan on working with an editor later down the line it is a good practice to get into. They surely can't read your mind so you will need to help them understand what you're going for in the video. A shot list is a great tool for guiding them through the edit.

Gathering Your Assets

It is time to start gathering all your assets now that you've finished preplanning. The first thing I do in the process is record my message. This may be filming your on-camera spoken parts, recording your whole voiceover, or perhaps a mix of both. I like to get this recorded first since it guides all the other parts into place. When you begin editing, this is the content that makes up the first layer to the video. It contains your raw message and all your other assets are used to spruce it up.

Recording

Filming can be a little odd if you're not used to it. Speaking to a camera and not another person is something that takes time to become comfortable with. You may find yourself coming off as robotic or different than you normally do because it is generally uncomfortable when you start off. You're super worried about your on-camera appearance and whether or not you are speaking clearly. This fear will fade with practice. Remember that you can always edit sentences together. I don't advise trying to do this mid-sentence unless there is a natural pause, but jump cutting is totally acceptable. A jump cut is when you cut between takes in your footage without introducing other footage. You basically cut back to different sentences from the same footage of you talking to the camera. We'll talk about that in greater detail when we get to the video creation part of the process though.

I strongly advise to get multiple clips of everything you need to say so you have some options when it comes to editing. You may find that the way you said something didn't work too well or maybe there was an audio hiccup that makes the clip unusable. You don't want to have only one take of something, only to find it has an error that can't be fixed. I've had microphone interference, weird noises I couldn't get rid of with editing, and slurring of words mid-sentence which made it hard to understand what I was saying. You may not use all of your additional takes, but it creates a safety net so you don't have to go back to the recording process again. Being efficient with your time as a creator is something you'll want to practice as you learn the craft.

Audio recording for voiceovers is a tad easier than video since you only have to worry about speaking into a microphone. The drawback to this is that you have to figure out visuals for everything you say. You don't have the luxury of cutting to a clip of you on camera. Try to break your recording into multiple sections if you're reading from a script. I typically do two reads of each part of my script so that I can make sure I have backup audio clips if something doesn't work out. I also redo specific sentences I had trouble with just to be extra careful. If you're going off the cuff and just talking, I still recommend tackling the video in its entirety at least twice so you have options to choose from. Perhaps your delivery in one take will be better than the other. You can mix and match to get the best of both worlds.

Tips to Follow

Whether you're recording video or just audio, there are some things you should take note of. For starters, know that when you start recording you will be less emotive than when you are in the middle of recording. Once you get into the swing of things mid-recording, you will be warmed up and able to articulate things better. It might be good to go back to the beginning of your video again at this point and redo the intro. The reason I say this is because in a lot of my earlier videos, the beginning would come off as dry whereas towards the end I would be more emotive due to being warmed up. I wasn't fully in the mood when I started my video and it was apparent. However, people encounter that part first so by redoing it I was able to ensure that it felt more alive than my first read through.

Make sure you stay super hydrated during your recording day as well. The less hydrated you are the more difficulties you will have with your audio. You may find yourself shouting due to being dehydrated and your mouth will make more clicking and popping noises. This is because there isn't enough moisture in your mouth and the insides are sticking together. Sounds a tad gross, right? Drinking lots of water is important the day of recording. Bring room temperature water with you during the recording as well. Cold water will tighten your throat and affect your performance overall. In addition to this, just know that whatever you eat prior to recording will also play a role in your audio quality. Avoid dairy products if you can because they will create problems within your mouth and throat, such as a feeling of mucous buildup that could lead to more clicking and popping noises.

When I first started recording audio I botched a lot of my recordings because I was a repeat offender of these things. By the end of my recording I was shouting because my throat was so dry and I had coughed many times to clear it. If you do have to clear your throat, just know a forceful cough is going to damage your vocal range. I know this may be a lot to take in but do consider these things prior to recording. If you follow these steps now they will become second nature to you when you have to record. A great foundation for recording will save you a lot of hassle in the long run!

Lastly, it's important to prep your recordings for use later. What do I mean by that exactly? You want to optimize your recordings so that when you get to editing you can execute things faster and improve your audio quality. Whenever you start recording a new file remain silent for about 5 to 10 seconds. You always want to record the tone of the room you are in because more than likely you aren't in an ideal soundproof room. Recording the natural hum of your room will allow you to run a scan later in certain software to remove it from your audio. Think of it as you telling your software to listen to this background noise, search for it, and then remove it when you hear it. This will make your audio sound a lot clearer. If you need to increase your volume, now your background noise won't increase with it.

If you're recording audio and video separately, I recommend clapping on camera. You ever see those white boards they use on movie sets that they clap before rolling the camera? They use those because it lists out the scene, what take of the scene it is, and because they can use the loud clapping sound to align all their audio. Let's say you are recording on a camera that has a low-quality microphone on it. However, you are recording high quality audio on a separate mic not connected to the camera. This gives you two audio files to work with. The one connected to your camera footage and the one recorded on your separate mic. You will want to use your high-quality audio to replace the low-quality audio on the camera. When it comes to editing you will need to align these audio tracks so that when your lips move on screen your words match it. By recording on both devices and clapping, you will see a visible straight line in the waveform of your audio tracks. A waveform is a graphical representation of audio where you can see the highs and lows of it. This clap will be extremely loud and last for only a split second, but you can use that to match up your audio. You just look for the super loud sound on each file and align them in your video editing program. Of course, you won't have to do this if your camera is also recording your high-quality audio. In cases where the camera does not record audio, you can sync up the clapping sound in your recorded audio file with the exact frame that the clap makes contact.

Supplemental Assets

Now that you have the foundation recorded for your video it is time to get all the supplemental content you'll need to create it. This could come in the form of additional footage, images, supporting graphics, music, and animations. This is why having a shot list ahead of time can be super helpful. If you create a video without preplanning things you'll find yourself constantly being drawn away from the editing process to acquire the things you need. Wouldn't it be much better to have these resources gathered so you aren't constantly interrupted? Now for things like animation, music, and supporting graphics you may find that you can't do them without a rough cut of the video. However, if you take the time to find supporting images and shoot any supplemental footage you need, you will be more efficient in the long run.

In order to animate you will need any images and graphics already created too. Identify what these are and acquire them. Be careful with just pulling random images from Google though. A lot of photos and images are copyrighted to their creator. Just because you found it through searching doesn't mean it is yours to take. I'm not saying every person will hunt you down for using images found online, but if it is a specific photograph or work of art you may find someone angrily knocking at your door. Protect yourself and the artist: Exercise fair use and citation. I have a chapter on it and it's one I recommend to double-up on.

Organization

Try to organize your assets accordingly as you gather them. I create a new folder for each video I'm doing. Of course, I'm only creating one video a week usually. If you're doing multiple you may find yourself organizing things differently. I create separate folders for my audio, images, and video. My video editing and animation software files sit in my root folder but I suppose you could create a place for them too. My audio folder is broken down into voiceover and music, whereas my video folder is broken down into the following categories: Filmed, Captured, Reference, and Scrap. I put all the footage of myself talking to the camera in the "Filmed" folder. All my game footage goes into "Captured." Any material I refer to or cite goes into my "Reference" folder. And last, any footage I've used before in other projects ends up in the "Scrap" folder.

The reason this scrap folder exists is because when I'm done with a video I back it up onto a hard drive. Often times I don't revisit the project anymore, but in case I do, it is nice to have it for reference. There have been times when I wanted to copy specific sections of a video and use them for newer ones, and having a backup was extremely helpful. However, this scrap folder is something I delete before backing up my footage. The footage already exists on my hard drive so there isn't any point in copying it over again and eating up additional space. This is a system I just sort of created as time went on, and perhaps you'll find yourself coming up with your own.

Creation

It is time to create now that you have all the pieces of the puzzle. The thing about creating is that there isn't a formula for how all your pieces need to be laid out. That's the beauty of it. The end result would be different each time even if everyone had the same assets. It's how you use everything you gathered to create something personal to you. You may not have even had many assets to gather depending on the videos you planned on making. Let's get into the nitty gritty of creating.

Cutting Together Your Base Video

The first step is putting together your rough cut of a video. This either means stringing all your talking points together, editing your voiceover so it is coherent, or putting all your vlogging clips in the right order. You'll do this by taking your raw video and audio files and cutting out the sections you want to use within your editing software. These sections are then placed on a timeline or sequence. This blank slate, which might be called something besides timeline or sequence depending on the programs, has a start and end point. You normally will want to select 1080p 60fps for your sequence / timeline settings. Your timeline can sometimes automatically conform to your video clips in certain software. That means it will adjust your timeline to fit the settings your video was actually shot in.

On your timeline you will place your clips in the order you want them to be seen as time goes on. This is editing. As editors we manipulate media to get the desired message we want out of it. We cut out the bad parts and we string together the good ones.

As a side note, everything mentioned beyond this point will be different depending on what software you use. I'm outlining the best process to get the highest quality out of your recordings. However, these may also be things you might not do when starting out. I thought it was still important for creating a guide that covers all aspects though. Just know that you can always skip ahead if some of these things seem super confusing. You'll know where to look later when you want to refine your process.

Optimizing Your Audio

When I start my editing process I normally begin with audio. Remember how I told you about recording your room tone for 5 – 10 seconds? This is when I go into my audio program, highlight that part of the audio, and tell it to keep track of this (called a noise print). I then highlight all my audio and tell it to remove it. If for some reason my refrigerator is humming in the background of my recording I can use this to remove that sound from my audio.

After this, I then go through and find all the good takes I want to use. Since my work is script-based, it is pretty easy to follow. I sometimes find two separate clips that both accomplish what I want and I have to choose between the two. I then string these clips together after I get them all cut out. I make sure I edit out any breathing noises or distracting sounds like clicking. I also normalize my audio and run a compressor on it. You can do this with your video clip audio too, but the process may be a bit longer. You want to make sure your audio is loud enough to be heard, but not loud enough to be distracting. Audio volume is measured in decibels (DB) and it is best to aim between -12 and -6 DB.

Normalizing will make your audio quieter or louder without you having to change the volume on your computer. A compressor is something you run on your audio to make it sound more even throughout. Most people start off talking loudly but get quieter as they continue on in their sentences. A compressor can be used to create a balance between the highs and lows for an easier listening experience.

Audio is certainly a confusing topic and one that took me the longest to grasp. If everything I just said confused you, that's normal. Look up tutorials for your particular software as I'm sure someone else has the same questions you do. The principles described above will be confusing at first until you see them in action. However, they will yield some pretty awesome effects when done correctly. Your audio will sound better than it ever could without them. Audio by far is one of the most important parts of a video, so take the time to make sure you do it right!

Jump Cuts and Transitions

One thing that I do when I'm editing things together is jump cut. This was something I briefly touched on in the previous section. "Jump cutting" is essentially cutting videos together to optimize time and delivery. The process looks jumpy because you are constantly cutting back to the same footage, stringing together all the best takes. I jump cut because, when I'm talking, I tend to trail off and take long deep breaths between sentences. Over the span of a video my breaths could honestly add up to 30 or 45 seconds. Not only is it important to mute the audio from these loud breaths, but for me in particular I feel it is equally important to speed up my rate in which I deliver information. I'm not increasing the speed of my footage to sound like a chipmunk though. I just cut my breaths out because they are so lengthy.

When I find a clip I want to use, I cut the video right before my audio waveform appears. This makes it so that once it transitions over to the next clip I'm talking right away. If you don't do this it may look odd. You'd go from the silence after your last sentence to the silence before your next. The power of a jump cut is eliminating this gap so that once your next shot appears you are immediately talking. You can leave some space at the end of your last shot to buffer the next, but in order for jump cutting to work effectively it is important that the clip you cut to immediately starts with talking. Try to get it down to a window of 1 – 3 frames. If you're just editing audio without video then you have some more buffer room for your voiceover. I would still advise tightening up your audio tracks by removing some of the time between breaths.

With your base video and audio edited, you now have the core part of your video. This is the backbone to your

YouTube video. If you're doing a simple vlog, you may be close to being done! However, this is normally where the fun begins. You have your message in video form but how can you spruce it up? If you wrote out a shot list, this is where you will go back and plug in all your assets you gathered. You can sprinkle in your supplemental footage, images, music, and other media. When you are cutting between supplemental footage and images, think about the most appealing way to introduce them. How your assets are introduced are called transitions in editing. Sometimes it makes sense to just fade them on, whereas maybe it might be flashier to have them slide in. It could simply be a raw cut as well.

All of these things change the mood of whoever is watching. Something quick could re-engage a viewer positively whereas something too extreme could distract or confuse them. The idea is to introduce your assets in a way that support the mood of your video. You don't want your video to be entirely relaxing because someone may simply stop watching. However, you also don't want to turn people away by being too over-the-top. There is a happy medium in-between that you want to aim for. Make your video engaging enough for them to continue watching and make sure nothing that you introduce is meant to detour that. You want your video to look like you spent time on it so they can appreciate it for its quality. However, you can also over-edit something to the point that the entire video is distracting. Sometimes less is more.

One thing I do with my images, animations, and supplemental footage that I add is put a slow zoom on it. If you have a static image sitting on screen it can get boring if nothing happens to it, especially if it is taking up the entire screen. The image and footage become more interesting by adding a slow zoom or subtle movement to it. This is called the "Ken Burns" effect. It is named after a pretty famous documentarian who used these slow zooms quite frequently. I highly recommend searching about this online so you can get a clearer idea.

Keyframes

A lot of editing software utilizes things called keyframes to keep track of effects and movement. Keyframes tell the software that at a specific frame this effect should be set to a particular value. That value could be an objects position, transparency, how big it is, etc. Keyframes can get more complicated than that, but they essentially hold values for specific traits. Your software will then transition from one keyframe to the next during the time between them. This could cause an image to move across the screen from one point to another. It could also make your audio fade to silence.

Keyframes will be important when you are sprucing up your video with additional assets. Even if your current software lacks them you will encounter them sometime in the future. Explaining the quirks and full uses of keyframes through text is a bit complicated though. Tutorials are probably your answer if you want to understand animation and how to spruce up things on a case-by-case basis. Play around and get a feel for how they work. Even just using the basic functions with keyframes can yield great results!

Balancing Music and Spoken Word

If you are planning on using music in your video make sure it doesn't compete with your voice too much. One of the biggest issues that creators have when adding music to their videos is setting the correct volume. If your music is too quiet it doesn't do you any good, and if it is too loud it ruins the message of your video.

So how do you find a happy medium? First and foremost, music has a wide variety of quiet and loud sections. That means at certain parts it could be too quiet, too loud, or just right. It may be wise to run a compressor on your music track so that it is even in volume. That may make musicians reading this frown. However, if someone is talking over music, the constantly changing levels can get distracting. A soundtrack that is uniform in volume is probably best unless there is purpose behind your music becoming louder in your video. You can always keyframe specific parts later on to make it louder as well. Remember, we want to aim for between -12 and -6 DB for your voice.

Now that you have a music track with steady levels, the rest is more or less guess and check. The trick to getting your music level right is to test it on various output devices. How does it sound coming out of your computer speakers? How about normal, everyday earbuds? If you have the time you could even render out a quick version and play it through a cell phone speaker. All three of these are going to sound different. You may hear the music more clearly on the headphones and not so much on others. However, what you're looking for is a middle ground. Could you still make out all the spoken words? Were you able to hear the music in all three? Eventually through tweaking you can find an audio range that will satisfy all these platforms. It's important to remember how people will most commonly watch your videos. You want to cater to those devices so that your voice and music sound good together on all of them.

Color Correction and Enhancements

When I'm almost done making my video I go through and color correct the footage. Color correcting is tweaking what the video looks like so I can make it look better. Typically I brighten my on-camera footage so that I'm not as dark. You may find yourself altering the color tones of your shot, making your footage look sharper, or a multitude of other things. I do this last so that if I have any intense effects, it won't bog down my computer when I'm piecing together my video. You can usually toggle effects on and off to prevent this, but for my workflow doing it last usually made the most sense for me.

There's a ton you can do with color correcting and enhancements in general. Trying to explain all of them here would honestly be a nightmare. I recommend looking up tutorials on enhancing footage for your specific problems. If your footage looks to dark, look up ways to brighten the footage in a way that makes it look more natural. If your footage is red, blue, or green tinted, check out how to color correct your footage to make it look more balanced. Need something to look a tad crisper? Sharpening can help you out. However, what you can do varies on the software you have.

Your Closing

The last part of the video production process is your closing. This could be an image splash screen or you just delivering your final thoughts. This is normally where you want to tell your audience to do something. In the marketing world we refer to this as a "call to action." At this point you may suggest subscribing, commenting, or to have them check out other videos on your channel.

Design this section with this in mind so that you have room to show videos on screen too. When we get to the upload phase of the video you will be placing clickable buttons within your YouTube video. As it stands now, you can place these within 20 seconds of the end of your video. Try to keep the ending of your video as clean as possible. You wouldn't want a video to load over your face when you're still talking. Having as much open space as possible is ideal. I recommend looking up the end screens of your favorite creators to see how they do it.

Thumbnails

There is one part of the video-making process that doesn't really fit into any particular order. This is making your thumbnail. I highly recommend reading the chapter on "The Power of Thumbnails" to get a greater understanding of them. You'll want to secure an image editing program where you can work with various layers.

A typical thumbnail consists of a background, subject, and supporting text. You may find yourself not using text or that your subject and background are combined. Different types of thumbnails make sense for different videos subjects. I personally use text on mine to support my video's title, but it certainly isn't a requirement. Take screenshots of a lot of thumbnails that you like from creators who are similar to you. List out the things you like about them and what you don't. Then design your thumbnails as a hodgepodge of all the good things. Just be sure not to overdo it! Thumbnails are an art form in themselves so don't be frustrated if your first ones don't turn out good. My first ones were awful. The way I designed them actually made them look like advertisements on certain mobile devices. I wasn't aware of this until my audience pointed it out.

Since then I've continually tweaked them. Practice makes perfect after all!

Delivery

You're almost done! It's time to encode now that your video is at a point where you're comfortable with it. You will never 100% be satisfied with a video, so don't spend too much time fretting over it not being perfect. We all grow with every video we release. What you will want to do now is export your compiled video timeline into an actual video. This process is called encoding. You may hear others refer to it as rendering as well. When you start this process you will have to select specific settings to export your video to. Unfortunately, it is going to be different for every piece of software so definitely look up a tutorial if you can't find your specific settings.

Encoding

YouTube seems to like the mp4 video handle the best. If you can export your file as a 1920 x 1080 mp4 video, you will be in the clear. You may be presented with something called H.264—be sure to select that. It's one of the most common video compression formats (a codec). If you are able to choose something called a bitrate, make sure it is set between 12 – 16 Mbps (megabits per second). If your software doesn't list it as megabits, that is equivalent to 12,000 – 16,000 Bps. In layman's terms, bitrate is how much data is being written and transferred. It will determine the overall quality of your video file. The higher the bitrate, the higher the file size. YouTube is automatically going to compress your video's bitrate down to around 12 Mbps anyways for standard 1080p 60fps content, or at least this is what it says according to their current online guides. If you have the option to choose your bitrate I suggest opting for in-between that number range. If you want to maximize your quality, you can go a bit higher.

You'll want to also select "variable" instead of "constant" if given the option. Variable bitrate (VBR) allows your bitrate to fluctuate. It will increase during more intense parts of the video and lower when things are less complicated on screen. This allows lower file size. Constant bitrate (CBR) keeps your video encoded to one bitrate value without flexibility. With a higher value CBR, this will mean less intense parts of your video will still be held to a higher bitrate than they actually need. You will end up with a larger file. Variable bitrate is best for YouTube creators overall for video files.

Once you're done picking out your settings it is now time to encode your video. The length of this process will vary depending on the power of your machine and the complexity of your video. It could take twenty minutes or a few hours. I typically leave my computer alone when it is rendering because I've had issues in the past where my computer has overheated. I would be doing too many other things on the laptop during the process and it would freeze up. If you do work on a laptop I highly recommend picking up a cooling pad for it. If your computer overheats while encoding you may find your computer locking up or restarting. Your render is ruined at this point and you'll have to start over. You'll end up with a video file assuming everything goes well.

Uploading to YouTube

At this point I begin to upload my video to YouTube and I set it to private in the upload window. This will ensure the video won't go live as soon as it is uploaded. I watch the video to ensure there aren't any mistakes or glitches during this process. If I find a mistake I absolutely have to fix, I cancel the upload and go back to my video editing program. I then fix the issue and render the video again. If it is a small fix, sometimes I import my erroneous render in my video editor and simply patch up the mistake. I then render the video out and the process is faster because there isn't as much compiling that needs to be done. This can save render time when exporting the video again.

It is now time to fill out all the information for your video—assuming the video you're uploading doesn't have any mistakes. I highly recommend looking at the examples included in the chapter on "The Algorithm and Metadata" for the best way to do this. You need to fill out your title, description, and tags accordingly. You will also want to head to the bottom of your upload window to import the thumbnail you created for the video. In the Advanced Settings tab at the top of the screen you will want to select your video category too. If you're choosing gaming be sure to select the name of the game. If this video includes a paid product endorsement, you'll need to notify YouTube by checking the "content declaration" box at the bottom of Advanced Settings.

Some of the information in this upload window can be automated ahead of time if you change your default upload preferences within your Creator Studio's Channel section. This will make it so that certain settings are always selected when you upload. Once you get the hang of uploading I recommend popping over to there and filling in your default settings. It will save you a lot of time for every future upload.

Prepping for Release

The upload window is really only the start of the uploading process. Before releasing your video, you should head over to your Video Manager so that you can finish the process. When you're editing your video in this window you will see a lot more options. We'll walk through each of these step by step.

Let's start with "end screens" first. End screens are clickable regions you can apply to the end of your videos. YouTube has a couple template options that you can use to set these up. These can include video links, playlist links, a subscribe button, and approved external links. You are able to add up to four elements within the last twenty seconds of your video. Obviously if it is your first video you may not have anything to add yet. However, you can always come back to change these. I recommend adding at least the subscribe button and a video link. You could even set your video link to be your most recent upload or have YouTube recommend a video for them. Don't worry: YouTube will only recommend your own videos. This recommendation is based off of their own watch history and can be a pretty good way to personalize the ending for that particular viewer.

In addition to end screens we have another similar feature called "cards." These are small drop-down messages that pop up while people are watching your video. They can pretty much do the same things as end screens except they can occur at any point during the video. You can have up to five cards as well, although I recommend using two or three. Cards have to be manually selected but they can include custom messaging whereas majority of end screens cannot. Try to space them out in your video where they make sense. It may be wise to hit someone with a card when they are three-quarters or so through your video, or if you refer to another video specifically. If it leads them to watching another one of your videos then it has done its job.

The next part of the upload process is "subtitles / closed captioning (CC)." This is where you can caption your video so it can be read while being watched. I usually turn these on by default when watching any video. Making your video more accessible for translation will help you reach a wider audience. You never know if someone in your audience is hearing-impaired either. If you wrote a script for your video it is actually a really simply process. You just identify what language your video is in, choose transcribe and auto-sync from the menu, and then paste your script. YouTube will automatically go through your script and subtitle your video after a few minutes. This process is usually quick, but sometimes it can take a while. You can then review and publish your subtitles if everything looks good.

I highly recommend doing this if you have a written script because it only takes a moment to do so. Plus, I have a strong feeling that subtitles and captions play a role in letting YouTube know what your video is about. It's basically telling them word for word what the video contains. If I were a robot trying to make sense of human interactions taking place in a video, a written script would certainly help me do so. I strongly believe it aids in video discovery—although don't quote me on that. That is just based on my own experiences. Regardless, I think it makes sense to consider a global audience. Perhaps in the future your audience may even subtitle your videos for you. YouTubers can have some pretty swell fans!

If your channel has passed the view threshold for enabling monetization, I recommend enabling it and checking into your video settings. This is where you can select the types of ads that can appear on your videos. Not the actual ads themselves, but the types and categories they fall into. Things like overlay ads, sponsored cards, skippable video ads, etc. If you have a video that is longer than ten minutes you can even put ads in the middle and at the end. While these additional ads aren't required, having at least one ad on your video will likely let it perform better. YouTube wants to make money when it can, so it will certainly promote monetized videos over ones that aren't. Hosting videos isn't cheap, you know!

Releasing Your Video

With all of these things done we have now reached that pinnacle moment. It's time to release our video to the world! Or at least schedule it for release. If it is your first couple videos you will notice that nothing really happens when you make your video public. No one will show up because you don't have an audience yet. However, remember the things I talked about in the first section of this book. Starting out is incredibly difficult and you need to gain your viewership from elsewhere.

After you release your video, think of ways you can get viewership by reaching out to specific people who may enjoy it. Never spam people, but spend time looking into places where you could potentially share it with like-minded individuals. Seek out video review forums or subreddits where you can have your video reviewed as you review other creators' work. You'll still get viewership out of it and it can help you improve. You might even find some communities or topical apps that could grant initial viewership as well. It takes a long time to gain traction, but eventually it becomes exponential. Don't give up and always adapt if something isn't working!

THE POWER OF THUMBNAILS

Thumbnails are often not viewed as the most important part of a video, but they are exceptionally powerful. You can have the best video in the world, yet if no one clicks the thumbnail, it's all for nothing. The hard part is that even if you make something you think looks great it can still be counterproductive to people's perception of the video. If you don't understand proper thumbnail layout, color theories, and how a person reacts to them, you may make something you think is good when in reality it may not be. So, let's spend some time to really understand the concept of what makes a great thumbnail.

First and foremost, they are called thumbnails for a reason. They are small. You may be designing your thumbnail 1280 x 720 or 1920 x 1080 pixels wide, but we really need to think about how people are actually seeing the thumbnails. In this day and age, most people are watching videos on their mobile devices. I don't know about you, but I have a pretty small phone screen. The smaller the phone, the smaller the thumbnail appears. It's only going to be a fraction of your screen's width, so that means it needs to still get the same impression and message across despite what size it is. If a person can't read your text on your thumbnail or if they can't make out what your image is, there's a high chance they won't bother to watch your video. It already looks unappealing, so they assume the video is going to be unappealing as well. It's a harsh world out there!

What makes a good thumbnail? A clear image that showcases one thing. Single-focus thumbnails are good because they only have the person looking for one thing in particular besides text. This doesn't mean you can't pull off multiple focal points in your thumbnail, but just know if you do it improperly it will harm you. Text that is large, bold, and contrasted with the background is a great addition as well. Remember to check if you can read it on your small phone screen. I prefer placing text on my thumbnails even though some people do not because it allows you to feed more information to someone at a glance.

When you're scrolling through YouTube videos on your phone, you don't get to see the entire video's title if it is too long. Your thumbnail text is a great second chance to pitch something interesting. Besides text, think about what sort of image makes the most sense to showcase. If you're a vlogger, perhaps most of your thumbnails may consist of your face. People typically are drawn to other human's faces. We almost always look at people's eyes right away. The benefit to this is that your thumbnails will look cohesive because you are your own brand. On the flip side, some people may find those thumbnails unappealing after a while since they may all look the same. If you have a recurring image in your thumbnails, like your face for instance, it will be important to make them all look distinct as well.

Change up the color, the orientation, and the text to make it feel fresh. If you're talking about a specific thing, it would probably make sense to show what you're talking about too. If I'm reviewing a video game, it may make sense to showcase a video game character. If I'm reviewing a new phone, showing the phone in the thumbnail will probably make sense. Make sure whatever is being shown on the thumbnail is also separated from the background. When images get small, it tends to become more difficult to determine the edges of what we are looking at. Add a drop shadow or color stroke around your specific object if you cut it out in an imaging editing program. Then place it over a visibly contrasting background. You may find that your thumbnail pops out and is easy to see if you do this.

Keep in mind that YouTube typically shows the duration of your video over the bottom right corner of your thumbnail when people are browsing videos. If your text or focal point is obscured by this, the impact of your thumbnail may be lost.

Be wary that whatever you put in your thumbnails can come back to haunt you as well. Do not use other people's artwork unless you have permission to do so. If you use it without permission, you can have a copyright claim filed against you. The argument that it is free exposure for the artist is simply the wrong idea. Artists do not create art just to have others take it and use it for their benefit. Crediting someone in the description of the video doesn't really do it justice either because the amount of people who see it will be minimal. Know if you take things you do not own that you may be held accountable.

This goes for photographs as well. Even if the photograph is of something the photographer doesn't own (like a photo of a city), the photo is still their artistic representation of that subject. People can come after you for that too! Keep in mind that fair use and transformative works can still give you some wiggle room for utilizing other people's materials. However, there isn't a defined rule for what is and isn't in these categories. It is always a case-by-case basis because the situation for each is always different. Definitely spend time to understand these concepts so that you can act accordingly in the future. Only a lawyer can really draw the line. Even then, it can be argued in so many different ways, but the general rule of thumb is that the original artist holds the copyright and use rights.

THE ALGORITHM AND METADATA

One thing you'll quickly learn is that a good video and thumbnail are only the fuel that drives the inner workings of YouTube. YouTube is a pretty complex machine with a lot of moving parts. If something isn't in order it could damage you as a creator or slow down your growth. If you haven't heard of the "YouTube Algorithm" by now that's totally okay. This section will clarify things.

However, before diving into the actual topic at hand, just know that a great deal of what is being described in this chapter is hypothetical. Honestly, the mystery around YouTube's algorithms is also a safety measure so people don't monopolize the system. It is always changing. So just know this is based off my experiences and the best practices that have worked for me as a creator, and not an official guide by YouTube itself.

The algorithm is essentially an automated, ever-adapting formula that YouTube uses to rank, serve, and recommend content. Prior to YouTube, Google used a similar system for a long time. When you search for something on Google there are plenty of things that determine the websites that show up in the search results. Things like how relative the page is to what you're searching for, how clean the code is, the structure of the website, how much inbound traffic is coming to the website, and so much more. All of this is shrouded in a grey area as well. However, this makes it so the most relevant content is delivered to you. You wouldn't want to search for something and repeatedly be disappointed. You'd want to go with the option that has stood the test of time and is a positive experience.

The YouTube algorithm is the same thing, except instead of websites, we are working with videos. There are a few layers of complexity to the YouTube algorithm that makes it different. Once again this is based on my own analysis and opinions vs breaking down code if one had actual access to the algorithm. You have the search algorithm which serves up content based on what you search for, the recommendation algorithm which automatically suggests content, and the notification component to the algorithm that tracks what you're interested in.

Sound daunting? I promise I'll break it down to make it easy to understand! Let's start with searching first. It is focused around metadata, which contains words or phrases that determine how well you rank in search.

Searching and Metadata

When you search for something on YouTube you want to see the most relevant things first. You want an answer to your question and you're seeking an immediate response.

Knowing how someone uses YouTube search can be incredibly powerful to a content creator. Building videos around common questions or inquiries is a good way to ensure someone may find your video since people are actively searching for it. This is why the name of your video, the description, and your video tags are very critical. In addition, your video title and description may also influence someone to click on your video. Your video title and thumbnail are the most powerful tools you have at your disposal and they must work seamlessly.

Video titles are tricky because you want the title to be engaging enough to spark interest in people, but you also want it to have enough keywords in it so that people can find it when they search for it. The order of the words in your title also affect the power they hold in search. Starting your video with the word "cat" can pull more weight in search for that word instead of having "cat" at the end of your title. Be aware that your titles may be cropped when you're viewing them on a mobile device. Always consider that your entire title may not be visible if it has a lot of words in it. Someone may not have enough information presented to them on the search page if the first few words of your title don't establish what the video is about. They simply may skip your video.

When I'm writing my titles, description, and video tags I am always paying attention to what people are searching for. When you start to type something into the search bar it usually auto-populates with popular searches. I'll get into this a bit more once we talk about tagging. Since I'm a gamer I often utilize the name of the game because it has the most important role in search. If it isn't centered around the name of the game, I include the video game character or topic I'm covering first. I usually present my title in a compelling way.

Sometimes I ask a question. Just know that a decked-out search-engine-slammer of a title can also make people not want to click on the video. You can have a video title that is super great in search, but if it is cropped funny on a mobile device they may not even know what the video is about. The fact always remains that if it isn't interesting, they won't click on it. The same goes for if the title is boring. Check out some larger creators you look up to and see how they do their titles. See which videos get a lot of views and which didn't.

After titles you'll want to work on your descriptions. What you write in your description plays a role in the search power a video has. Often times you will see a combination of social profiles, links to other videos, and a description of what the video is about. The order these are laid out definitely influences the search results and how people interact with them.

When you work with sponsors you may hear the phrase "put this above the fold" often. This is referring to the text that appears above the "See More" button. YouTube automatically hides majority of the video description so that people don't have to scroll through the whole thing to get to the video's comment section. If they didn't, it'd be pretty tedious. Putting something "above the fold" means to place it at the top of the description so it is visible even when the description is minimized. People will see it regardless of expanding the description. This is where people often put links because it allows viewers to click on them without having to dive deeper into the description. It's where a sponsor wants their ad or shoutout placed. One last thing to note is that your video description's first lines may show up on computers in search results, but may not on mobile devices. Even if they don't visibly appear, they still influence search results.

People tend to next write a small blurb for what the video is about. It's believed that the text closest to the top of the description has influence in search results until a certain point. This is why you want to include a descriptive blurb that has some key words and topics integrated. It may be wise to repeat keywords from your video title or focus them again in some way. Try to work it into a sentence. Three to four shorter sentences will probably work best. I'll break all of this down a bit more with an example soon.

Let's swing over to video tags. Video tags are keywords and phrases associated with someone discovering your video. Basically, you want to boil the concept of your video down to bite-sized chunks that would represent it if someone were trying to search for it. If you were showcasing a fitness routine in your video, you'd want tags that identify that. You'd also want to take it a step further and make these tags even more niche. Some appropriate tags would be: fitness routine, best fitness program, best workout, best workout for "x", getting in shape, getting in shape for beginners, getting ripped, getting ripped at home, etc. Some of these may sound redundant, but that's because you're trying to cover all your bases. There may be multiple ways to say the same thing. See what people are searching for by going to YouTube's search bar and starting to type something in. The words at the top of the results are the most searched. I advise doing this in a private browser though since your previous search results can influence what you're seeing. A clean slate is always best. You can look into Google Trends and other third-party keyword apps to see how much traffic certain phrases are getting. There are a lot available and the more you study, the better off you will be.

Title / Description / Tag Examples

Below you'll find three examples of video uploads to YouTube. Notice how the title, description, and tags are all relevant to one another. They are designed around search terms so they can be discovered easily. That's why they include keywords and phrases. For the gaming section, I've built it around a fictitious game and made the video about speculation surrounding the game's story.

Try not to include too many external links in your description when you're setting it up. An external link is any sort of URL that takes someone off of YouTube. Using URL shorteners to link to other YouTube videos is okay, but having too many external links in your description may reduce your video's visibility. YouTube doesn't mention anything about this officially, but I imagine they would like to keep people on their website. Keep in mind the examples below that list URL's first are because these links appear "above the fold" like I mentioned earlier.

Please note that the brackets ([ ]) around the tags below are just to show where the tags are separated. Normally when you type a comma it will separate them.

Pet Channel Example

Title:

Why Are Cats Afraid of Pickles and Cucumbers?

Description:
Become a Cat Mom/Dad! ▶ https://goo.gl (Subscribe link)
Funny Cat Montage! ▶ https://goo.gl (Video link)

We've all seen the funny cat videos where a cat becomes terrified after seeing a pickle or cucumber. But, why are cats afraid of pickles exactly? What about them triggers this? Join us as we explain this phenomenon!

Twitter ▶ @whateveryourhandleis
Instagram ▶ @whateveryourhandleis

Tags:

[why are cats afraid of cucumbers] [why are cats afraid of pickles] [cat cucumber] [cat cucumber scare] [cat cucumber reaction] [cats and cucumbers] [cats and cucumbers try not to laugh] [funny cat videos] [funny cat fails] [funny kittens] [funny kitten video] [pet videos] [cat meowing] [cats] [kitten] [cute] [cats] [funny cats] [*name of channel*]

Gaming Channel Example

Title:

Why Super Zarkon 7's Story Tricked Us All! | *Name of Channel*

Description:

Subscribe for more videos! ▶ https://goo.gl (Subscribe link)
This isn't the REAL Jacob? ▶ https://goo.gl (Video link)
How OLD is Zarkon? ▶ https://goo.gl (Video link)

Super Zarkon 7 introduces a big problem to the Zarkon universe. After seeing the ancient city's population, we are left wondering . . . Is Zarkon actually a human? Have we all been tricked? In this Super Zarkon theory, we'll take a crack at this complicated problem!

Follow me on Twitter! ▶ @whateveryourhandleis

More Gaming Videos:

How Super Trylord 2 Defined Speedrunning ▶ https://goo. gl (Video link)
What Powers the Monster Sphere? ▶ https://goo.gl (Video link)
Picazzo's MYSTERIOUS Paintbrush! ▶ https://goo.gl (Video link)

Tags:

[super zarkon 7] [super zarkon 7 trailer] [super zarkon] [*name of game developer*] [*name of game system*] [*name of channel*] [is zarkon a human] [super zarkon 7 theory] [super zarkon] [game theory] [zarkon] [zarkon game theory] [super zarkon 6] [zarkon gameplay] [super zarkon 7 gameplay] [zarkon review]

Cooking Channel Example

Title:

The Filet Mignon: How to Cook the Ultimate Steak!

Description:

Ever wanted to know how to cook a filet mignon? We've assembled the ultimate steak recipe. Whether you're a beginning or a seasoned vet, we'll walk you through the process to get the best cooked steak ever!

Subscribe for more recipes! ▶ https://goo.gl (Subscribe link)

More videos you may like:

Fish Fry or Die! ▶ https://goo.gl (Video link)
The Ultimate Rainbow Slushie! ▶ https://goo.gl (Video link)
Twelve Layer Birthday Cake! ▶ https://goo.gl (Video link)

Tags:

[filet mignon] [filet mignon steak] [how to cook a filet mignon] [filet mignon recipe] [filet mignon skillet] [how to] [steak recipe] [steak marinade] [how to cook a steak] [how to make] [preparing a filet mignon] [how to cook] [*name of channel*] [cooking videos] [cooking book] [cooking channel] [cooking lessons] [cooking for beginners]

Watch Time and Retention Rates

The best package for a video is having a video title, description, and tags that all complement each other. I often feel this part is like building your own car from scratch. Now that everything is in working order, we of course need to give your car fuel. This is where the second part of the algorithm comes into play. Being optimized for video discovery via search only does you so much good. Your vehicle will never move if no one is watching your videos and providing fuel for your car. Your car will mostly benefit from two things: Watch time and retention rates.

Consider watch time to be your absolute fuel for getting your car somewhere, whereas retention rates earn you bonus points and make things more lucrative for you. Watch time is how long viewers have collectively watched your video for. A viewer may attribute one view to your video, but they may add several minutes to the total amount of time anyone has watched that video. The number of minutes they watch is far more important than the view they provide. This is why you can't really succeed in the long run on YouTube if you simply trick people into watching a video. If you have a ten-minute video and majority of people leave after only 30 seconds, your video will not do well regardless of the views it may receive. You'd need twenty views that are 30 seconds long to equal someone simply watching all ten minutes.

Now I'm not saying view count isn't important because it certainly is. When people see a high view count they innately trust the video more. As a society we are trained to look for higher numbers. People may be more willing to watch a video that has established itself with viewers across the platform. However, in order to succeed, the number of minutes watched has to be increased. The more organic watch time you have, the more places your car can go to before running out of gas. I personally believe that YouTube has what I dubbed a "watch time threshold" that your video needs to break through to grow. After a certain amount of watch time, your video will begin to be recommended to people as a suggested video.

A "suggested video" is a video that appears on the right side of the page. They are recommended to the viewer based on what they watched and one of them may automatically be queued up next on autoplay. In order to find your video here, you need to have recognizable metadata and enough watch time accrued so that YouTube thinks your video is worth recommending.

YouTube is always looking to make as much money as it can to sustain itself. If a video is performing well and people are watching a lot of it, they will recommend it so that they can make money off the ads. A win for YouTube is also a win for you. If YouTube sees that people are enjoying your funny cat video, they will probably start recommending your cat video to others once it has accumulated enough watch time. Again though, this watch time threshold I'm talking about is something I believe exists but YouTube only knows how it truly works. Take it with a grain of salt!

The icing on the cake for all of this is retention rates. Watch time is great because it constantly increases with each and every view. Your retention rate is the average percentage of when someone stops watching your video. Did the average amount of your viewers leave after 30% of the video? Perhaps 45%? How long did you retain them as a viewer?

Not only does a high retention rate mean you've also accrued a lot of watch time with every view, but there are more benefits than that. Your video can be further recommended by YouTube because they know it is a smash hit. Super high retention rates make YouTube want to shovel viewers in your direction. If people are really invested in your video, that probably means they will be more willing to pay attention to an advertisement too.

This is something I have personally experienced and may not be 100% fact, but every video I've created that's had high retention rates has earned more than what an average video has. Now I'm not saying that because they got more views. The amount I earned per view in advertisement earnings is what was increased. My theory is that YouTube analyzed the retention rates of my viewers and was able to determine how much people enjoyed the video. They then put a higher paying ad on the video after it gained traction because they knew people were invested in it.

Advertisers are able to run tons of different ads— some that are cheap and others that are expensive. If they are paying a lot for advertisements, YouTube tries the best it can to make those ads successful. Putting them in front of an engaged audience is one of those ways. Placing an expensive ad before a video that no one really cares for would be doing a disservice to the business that is trying to market themselves. If their advertisement campaign is a bust, they may not return to YouTube for future business. This is why retention is so important for content creators. Look at your analytics and see where people drop off on average in your videos. Try to change something up and rekindle their interest in the video when things may become less exciting. By experimenting you can increase your retention levels over time by identifying what works and what doesn't.

Notifications and Alerts

The final component to the YouTube algorithm, in my opinion, has to do with people who have already subscribed to you. You would think that if someone subscribes to you that they would know every time you upload something. However, this isn't the case at all. This is because there appears to be another automated system governing this area of YouTube and it reacts to what people like and dislike. It's often the most frustrating part for established creators because it is the most difficult to fix. The ball isn't in your court for this one. It's up to your followers to set the precedent for you.

If your viewers become subscribers and skip a few videos, they may not be notified when future videos come out. The reason for skipping these videos could simply be that they were busy in life and didn't have the time. But the reason doesn't matter, because YouTube still takes note. If this happens on a grand scale it can become extremely problematic for your channel. You can also dig yourself into a hole by uploading content that people aren't interested in. If they subscribed for a certain type of video and you no longer upload videos like that, you'll alienate them as a viewer. YouTube will eventually stop notifying them about your latest uploads because it assumes they aren't interested in your content anymore.

This really sucks because even if they wanted to watch your next video, they simply don't know it was uploaded. If your video does get a decent amount of traction from your subscriber base, then they may notify people it previously deemed uninterested on the home page or other areas on the site after the matter. However, it still won't do it across the board.

It's all a tough subject based around hypothesis. While the whole algorithm in general falls into this category, the notification component is the biggest unknown. We can't see a viewer's email inbox or notification tab to get a clearer idea why they missed out on something. We have backend analytics which help, but ultimately the whole ordeal is guesswork based on feedback. It is alarming when people tell you they love your videos but forgot about you because YouTube stopped notifying them.

Did YouTube actually stop notifying them or was it simply user error? It's hard to tell.

This has affected channels of all sizes and similar comments have appeared all over the platform. Some people even claim that YouTube unsubscribes them from channels if they forget to watch videos over a long period of time. All of this is of course uncertain, but it is still something to be aware of. With any automated process there will be hiccups I suppose.

So how do you set up your channel for success in this category? Personality first and foremost, but the notification bell as a close second.

Your personality will ultimately be the driving force behind why people come to see you. Make your personality the thing that draws people in whereas the topic of the video is second. Personality will bleed over to other social channels which serve as notifiers in their own way. Swing over to the personality chapter in this book later on to get a greater understanding of its importance.

The second line of defense we have is the notification bell. At the time of writing this book, the notification bell is essentially something a user can click after they subscribe to a channel. In the eyes of a YouTube creator it is like the second level subscribe button. It does what we wish the actual subscribe button did. If someone opts into this by clicking the bell icon they will receive email updates and alerts whenever you do something critical on the platform. There are a few different things they can choose to be notified of. Any time you upload a video, live stream, and so on. This doesn't include things like commenting or liking. It is honestly the best thing people can do so they can stay up to date with all your latest videos. It is definitely worth letting people know it exists too, because even your most diehard fans may not know it is there.

DEMONETIZATION

Monetization on YouTube is what allows you to earn money from your videos. Advertisements can appear on your videos when you are partnered with YouTube and enable monetization. However, demonetization is what occurs when advertisements are removed from your videos. This word probably strikes a lot of fear into creators. Very recently YouTube started becoming stricter on its rules about what qualifies as advertiser-friendly content. If your content is deemed to not be advertiser-friendly, you'll find that your video will be marked with a yellow dollar sign next to it. This means YouTube found things in your video that were questionable. So to play it safe, YouTube is going to limit what kinds of advertisements appear on it or may even strip all advertisements from it. Sound horrible? That's because it is for a creator.

The Perspective of a Business

Before diving into the specifics of this process we need to understand advertisements in general. People quickly jump the gun and say that demonetization is a form of censorship for content creators. This is because controversial content triggers demonetization on the platform. In turn people will more than likely produce less controversial content since they want to have monetization enabled. The thing we need to realize is that the reason we can make any money on YouTube at all is because someone is paying YouTube to show their ads on our content. The money they put towards those ads are divided between the creator and YouTube.

Let's say you were someone trying to advertise and your ads were showing up on questionable videos. The audience of those videos probably won't pay attention to your ads due to the nature of the YouTube video they're watching. You'd essentially be wasting your money. You may not want your brand associated with certain topics as well. This started to become a more mainstream issue when advertisers noticed their ads showing up on videos that promoted cyber harassing, tragedy, and other negativities. The kinds of people who were tuning in to watch these sorts of things couldn't care less about advertisements. They had zero interest in anything other than the video. This continued to spiral out of control until YouTube ended up reworking their entire advertisement system. The goal was to give as much control to the advertisers as possible so they could achieve better results and become a recurring customer for YouTube.

The issue with this is that the system put into place started alienating creators of all kinds. For example, positive videos focused around negative subjects like depression would be demonetized across the board. A lot of creator's livelihoods were in shambles due to these new changes. Even though YouTube had written guidelines for what was considered advertiser-friendly, there was really no way to tell. The other issue was that controversial subjects could really be anything. If two people have powerful contrasting viewpoints, even if one of those people is truthfully wrong, it is still controversial.

I know earlier in this book I said it was important to branch out as a creator and not focus on ad revenue for your livelihood. Those who have done that may not see demonetization as a huge issue because they earn their income elsewhere. However, losing advertisement revenue on your videos is only the beginning of the problems that demonetization brings. The worst part of all is actually what isn't readily explained.

The Real Reason Demonetization Hurts

The things I'll be talking about next are simply based off of my own personal experiences and analysis. I don't know what exactly takes place, but I can certainly see the results. So, don't take this as the almighty guidelines to how YouTube operates. That's still a mystery!

Much like the YouTube algorithm, demonetization appears to have its own algorithm as well. When your video gets flagged for demonetization you are able to submit an appeal, but if that appeal is denied, that video is essentially dead content. When a video is marked as not being advertiser-friendly, YouTube stops promoting that video in its entirety. This means people can only discover the video by searching for it or by going to your channel specifically. This is an issue because most traffic for YouTube videos comes from recommended content.

When you're done watching a video you typically look to your side bar for what is coming next. YouTube even queues up a video automatically for viewers based on what it seems they're interested in. This allows a viewer to watch several videos in a row that are related to their interests. Often times this takes viewers from channel to channel and they discover new ones. This is usually the highest traffic source for viewership that any YouTuber will experience. This is why demonetization is such a huge problem for creators. If you've been demonetized that video will no longer be recommended or suggested to viewers. Without this traffic your channel will grow much slower than it would have otherwise. To top things off, you never know what will trigger the demonetization of your video. That's a problem in itself.

Not too long ago I had one of my videos demonetized. This was shortly after I launched this video so it was still actively being promoted as new content on YouTube. About a day after it was uploaded the video became demonetized and went from receiving 3000 views an hour to 10 views an hour just as it had started picking up traction. I was worried about this video in particular because it had a few buzz words in it that I suspected may trigger demonetization. Even mentioning the word "drug" and other words in the context of games didn't matter. YouTube automatically assumed the video was about questionable things without considering context. The video was demonetized and after a manual review 24 hours later it had monetization reenabled.

Now the problem with this situation is that I lost out on about 25,000 – 30,000 views during this time period. When monetization was activated again, I had already lost out on the hype of it being a new video. It wasn't like a switch was flipped and the viewership started coming back. It felt like the video started on a clean slate and I had to earn back my place so the video would get suggested to viewers again. For the first eight or so hours after the video was remonetized it brought in about 100 – 300 suggested views an hour. It eventually got back up to a thousand or so over time though.

All of this occurred because of a bad call on YouTube's end though. The system it had in place at the time was faulty and by going through this ordeal my earnings from the video were what took the fall. YouTube lost out on their share too, but ultimately it is the creator who suffers most.

One thing I have heard from other creators is that if you are a repeat offender of getting flagged, YouTube may watch your channel more closely than others. This is all speculation of course, but they believed that their videos were getting preemptively flagged because of their past videos that were flagged. Because YouTube deemed their videos non-advertiser friendly in the past, they would mark their newest videos the same way as soon as the videos went live. This is awful as it meant they couldn't gain any residual traffic at all from other videos recommending them. They essentially had to upload the video a few days early, mark it as unlisted, and see if it would get flagged.

I can see this being super problematic for news-related channels that need to get their content out as soon as possible. What makes it worse is there is no way to tell what causes the issue. However, from YouTube's perspective, I can understand why they set the system up this way. If it didn't work this way then bad videos would still get majority of their advertisement earnings before YouTube realized the video was not suitable. It's the lesser of two evils, I suppose, and the process is something they are continually trying to improve on.

How Demonetization May Occur

At this point you're probably thinking about how all of this happens. How does YouTube know whether a video is good or bad? Once again everything in this section is going to be hypothesis-based. We don't have any other information other than their official advertiser-friendly guidelines, but we do know it has to be detected somehow. The believed answer is that YouTube can only determine what is in a video by the information surrounding the video. Your title, tags, description, thumbnail, and auto-generated captions all probably play a role in this.

Text can be analyzed and images can be reviewed by an algorithm. It is believed that YouTube has a program that can scan your thumbnail images to look for specific things. It's kind of like that creepy feature when you upload an image online and it recognizes one of your friend's faces in it. However, not much information is known about this or if it truly even exists. Text in your thumbnail can be read to some extent. Anyone who has ever used a program to identify fonts inside of images knows that this technology exists.

The biggest issue in my eyes is the automated captions that are created. When you upload a video to YouTube it tries to transcribe what you say in the video so that it can create automatic subtitles. While it isn't confirmed, I highly suspect that this is where they gather the most information about the video. While YouTube can't watch and understand a video fully like a human can, it can analyze a block of text that was derived from the video. They could then search this text for offensive language, controversial topics, and other things it may deem as not safe for advertisements. Using this in conjunction with your title, tags, description, and potentially how people are reacting in your comment section could determine whether they flag your video. On the flip side, if you fail to fill in enough information about your videos you may find yourself flagged as well since YouTube doesn't know what your video is.

One final thing I want to touch on before wrapping up this section is that advertisers are able to avoid content with swearing. If someone is creating a video ad campaign they have the option to exclude videos that have swearing in them. The interesting thing is that they can take that a step further. They have the ability to exclude censored swearing. So even if you uploaded a video that had bleeped out swearing, there's a chance your video can be still excluded from advertisers it normally may have attracted. I'm not sure if this means they have audio Content ID in place for certain censorship tones to detect this, but it is certainly worth being aware of.

In conclusion, all of this doesn't mean you should change the direction of your content if it is affecting who you really want to be. Just know that with YouTube becoming more critical with choosing ad-friendly videos, things may become more difficult for you if you choose to ignore their guidelines. Ideally YouTube will adapt over time so that videos that are unfairly caught in the crossfire won't be punished. But if your videos are flagged for demonetization, just know that your growth will stagnate. Consider this as the system will be working against you.

Please note that everything in this chapter is based on experience and may not be 100% accurate. This is based off my experiences and is no way directly from YouTube itself. YouTube evolves daily, so they may come up with a solution for this in the future. However, based on how everything works right now, this is the most accurate representation of the demonetization process that I currently know. Hopefully it was insightful!

FAIR USE AND CITATION

If you've been around on YouTube in the past few years you've probably heard some furious debates over something called fair use. This essentially allows someone to use copyrighted materials without actually getting permission from the creator. The work itself has to be transformative and fall under specific categories like commentary and criticism. A lot of YouTube videos operate in the realm of fair use as they often contain assets that were created by other people. These original creators hold the rights to their work, but under fair use creators can sample these creations for transformative works. I'm speaking about fair use under the American system of law, that is.

However, there isn't a golden rule book that outlines fair use. Only a lawyer can tell you that and even then, it is usually a matter of arguing your case. So just know that everything presented in this section is subjective and if you have more questions about it, I highly recommend seeking out a lawyer to help you. I'm not a lawyer, so if you're creating videos that invoke fair use, certainly be mindful of what you are using. This is merely to outline the topic at hand and is not legal advice. Let's go through a few different things you may encounter.

Music is always a hot topic with fair use. Using someone else's music for an extended period of time generally isn't fair use at all. If you're deliberately using someone else's creation in its entirety you definitely are not safe. Even if you sample music for a few seconds in your video and it falls under fair use you can still be hit by a copyright claim. While fair use is a grey area, so is the Content ID system on YouTube. It is constantly searching for copyrighted songs in its library and when it finds a match it sends out a notice regardless.

Even if you're technically safe you can still find yourself dealing with a claim. On top of this, if a certain part of your videos always uses the same song, even if it is only for a few sections, you may find yourself in another unique problem. Hypothetically let's say for some reason you were using the same copyrighted song for all your video closings. Even if it is only for a few seconds, you're using it in all your videos. Someone may come knocking at your door about this and it has happened to creators in the past. Be extremely careful when using music made by others. Try to seek out royalty-free music tracks that have the appropriate licenses for videos. Just because music is free to use doesn't mean it is free to make money off of. There are rules and stipulations with every piece of music so make sure you seek out the proper information for it.

Video footage is another area to be mindful of. You're free to sample video clips from things within reason, but just know that the copyright holder may be the one who ultimately decides what is overstepping the boundaries. If you are using bite-sized chunks of a video to support your message you will probably be okay. However, don't use too much of the video. If you're sampling a two-minute animation and you showcase all two minutes of the animation in your 12-minute-long commentary, it probably won't be fair use. Their entire video is included within yours. Someone may not watch the original video because they already did so through yours, and it holds true even if you split it up into four to five second chunks and talk critically about the things in it. Your work has to be transformative enough to be considered acceptable.

A situation like this is honestly dabbling on the dangerous side of things because it would have to be decided by lawyers. On top of this, just like audio, YouTube has a Content ID system for video. Even if you use footage fairly in your video you can still be hit with a copyright claim by YouTube's automated system. It is simply just checking for the footage. It can't really tell if something is fair use or stepping over boundaries.

Keep in mind that multiple rights holders may be involved for video footage and music. This is especially likely if you are showing a clip from a movie that also has part of the soundtrack playing. These rights holders differ from country to country, which means you could be getting hit on the same clip from different people. It can get pretty detailed and complicated. One may simply track your clip, another may monetize it for themselves, while others may choose to block it.

Even the use of images can be considered not fair use. Certain images can be used that are in the public domain, but images are different than video or music. An image's lifespan is someone looking at it. It's consumed much faster than other media. While you may not find yourself being auto-flagged by using someone else's images, it doesn't mean you can't be punished for it. If you plan on using someone's image, reach out to them or at least provide a link to the source content. Even this won't protect you fully though. Images are actually one of the biggest grey areas because some can be used without any issues while others cannot. It's not like footage where you can use a limited amount and still be safe. It's not very likely that someone will come after you for using images, but if it is an independent artist or a giant image conglomerate, they may do so.

Photographers, illustrators, and graphics designers need their work protected from people who steal it too. Think about how many people online steal images and pass them off as their own. We have fake Instagram accounts, portfolio sites, sketches, and that's just the start of it. Sometimes merchandise is produced with stolen materials as well. Artists need to be defensive about their work because so many people cut out watermarks. Do not grab artwork and use it in your videos without the creator's permission because they can submit a copyright claim against you. If you use their artwork in your thumbnail there is an even higher chance of that happening. Your thumbnail is essentially promotional material for your video. It is the thing that convinces someone to click on it. Artists and photographers certainly don't work for free and their art shouldn't be used for free either.

Technically, if someone spends several hours on artwork and it is stolen and used to promote a video, wouldn't that be equivalent to someone stealing your video in its entirety and uploading it elsewhere? I'm sure that probably wouldn't make you too happy, especially if someone was profiting or gaining tons of exposure from it. You may put in just as many hours for a video as an artist does for one image. Be very mindful of other creative professions when you are operating under fair use.

One common occurrence you may find happening is your own videos being used in other people's videos. Remember, it's your video so you have the rights to it. If it is being used fairly then so be it. However, if it isn't, I recommend filing a copyright claim against the video. Many people will advise you to reach out to the infringing creator to talk about it first. However, to be blunt, I've been burned many times before by doing this. Often times you may be ignored, especially if the person is trying to get away with the act. It's incredibly frustrating when you're a small creator without a voice too. A larger entity may just ignore you.

Perhaps I've just become jaded with the whole process because it happened to me too many times. I've had people cut up my entire videos and recreate the same video with a different voiceover. All my animation and supplemental footage being used for something I didn't make. The forty hours I spent making it was used by someone to make a video in less than an hour. I don't have the patience for people like that so I let YouTube handle it. Filling out the copyright claim is lengthy enough. Even if you don't share the same viewpoint as me now, you may find yourself changing in the future. Repeated stolen content will do that to you, unfortunately. If you produce heavily animated or edited videos, Content ID may be a blessing for you.

One thing I always try to do is cite the sources for things I use in videos. I typically have a white box that pops up that states the name of the work, the creator, and a web address to the source material. I honestly do this with any other creator's footage that I can too. I'm not perfect at this but I think it's incredibly important to do so. I always imagine it from the viewpoint of discovering artwork but not knowing who the artist is. We need to give credit where credit is due. Just like when we used to write school papers and cite our sources, it's important to do this online as well. Lots of people have stopped doing this over the years and truthfully, I could get better at it myself.

The reason why some people stopped doing it is because sometimes they have the hardest time trying to find the source of something. They discovered it through a particular outlet which got it from a different website and that chain goes on and on. If it is an image try to do a reverse image search on Google and see if you can identify the creator. For footage, see if there are any details in the footage that hint at where it is derived from. Same thing with music. I know this is a little preachy, but we're all artists so we should coexist in the best way possible. If someone helps you out in some way take the time to thank them. We take so many things for granted.

MULTI-CHANNEL NETWORKS (MCN'S)

If you don't know what a multi-channel network is now, you certainly will once you start finding some success on YouTube. Multi-channel networks (MCN's) are companies that partner with several channels to assist them with many different things. This could be in the realm of cross-promotion, convention / conference involvement, integrated brand deals, free products, channel optimization, legal assistance, Content ID, and a whole lot more. The network typically takes a percentage of your earnings on YouTube for exchange of their services. Typically, you'll be assigned a partner manager who you can reach out to when you have issues. This person will then try to help resolve your problem and get you heading in the right direction. It can be extremely helpful when you find yourself stuck.

MCN's can be mentioned in both a positive and negative light. Depending on what creator you talk to will change the answer you get. Some consider them to be leeches who suck away your revenue while providing lackluster services, while others will claim they have been monumental in their success. Let's start by talking about good MCN's and great behaviors.

A great MCN will do everything in their power to help you. The value they provide to you will be clear. I've had amazing opportunities granted to me through good MCN's and their affiliates. I've received free access to expensive conventions, been flown out for speaking opportunities, and been given some pretty cool free products. I also met some creators at events my MCN threw that I may have never met otherwise.

By far the greatest value I got out of my network was protection though. Not only did my MCN act as a shield for me, they also have helped me out when I was in rough spots. I've been protected from bogus Content ID claims for things that were certainly fair use and I've also had help getting my videos into Content ID. My videos often got stolen due to their higher quality. People would see my animation work or my cinematic shots and want to take it for their own videos without crediting me. They'd even crop out my watermarks.

My MCN helped me register my animations in the Content ID system so that any time someone stole my work YouTube would defend me. It really sucks working 40+ hours on something and having someone steal it to make money for themselves. Content ID makes sure the earnings for those videos go to the original creator. Unfortunately, Content ID isn't available to average creators without a MCN that is capable of doing so. A channel opting into the service on their own needs to have a pretty reputable following and thousands of videos according to what YouTube prompts you with when you try to apply. Content ID has been helpful for me because the amount I earn from claims also offsets the cost I pay for the MCN. Of course, this won't apply to all creators, but if you do something mind-blowing in your videos they are most likely going to be stolen.

The way you know you're dealing with a bad MCN is pretty straightforward. You signed up for something and aren't getting what you signed up for. Often times these red flags are visible from the first email they send you. If you feel like the person reaching out to you hasn't even watched the videos you make, chances are the multi-channel network is garbage. They are merely trying to partner with as many people as they can and they don't care about what you do. Their contracts will be horrible as well, and you'll be stuck with them for several years if you sign one. Avoid these MCN's at all costs. They will focus on how much more money you will make and how much you'll grow as a creator, but I promise you the real value of a MCN doesn't come from anything like that.

A common occurrence of a lackluster MCN is that your channel partner will never respond to you. You will feel like you're shouting into a void. If you do get a response, any questions you ask will be deflected elsewhere. It leaves you feeling taken advantage of and trapped. Which is exactly what you are. They will continue to take a percentage of earnings from your channel and you can't opt out of their service until the contract is up. If you are a small creator, you will find yourself in a bad spot because your channel may not be earning them enough money to warrant them paying attention to you. Be very careful when you sign up for any service and read through the contract carefully. Ask them tons of questions too. If they don't respond right away or give you clear answers, walk away. Take it as a warning sign. If the potential MCN is ignoring you while they are supposed to be winning you over, that is a sign of things to come once they have your business. Remember, you are valuable to them as well!

There are a couple tidbits of information that are worth noting about MCN's as a whole though. For starters, check to see if your MCN also gets royalties from your stream donations. This isn't something that a lot of MCN's do, but it is important to still ask. If you're live streaming on YouTube and someone donates ten dollars through Super Chat or some other feature, that ten dollars will still be divided up between YouTube and you. If you don't ask about this, the MCN you sign up for could possibly dip into that as well. This only applies if the donation is given through YouTube's system though. Always ask about everything the MCN gets a percent from before signing. Be wary of long term contracts as well. Nothing is worse than being misled into signing something you don't actually benefit from, only to find out you can't cancel it for two or more years.

Sometimes a MCN offers "royalty free" music that you can use in your videos. This music won't be claimed by Content ID and can really add some life to your work. However, be careful when utilizing this music. Read into the use cases for the music and what happens if you ever leave the MCN. A while back a MCN actually pulled a shady move where they essentially Content ID claimed all the videos that used their music if those people had left their network. Always read the fine print. If your video gets claimed that means you no longer receive any money from it. Make sure your videos are safe even after you leave a network. Ask about the terms of the music before using any of it. You just might save yourself a ton of hassle in the long run.

Overall, multi-channel networks can be both good and bad. They aren't a requirement for all creators, but they can also be the saving grace of some. Definitely consider your options before signing up for one. Don't underestimate the value of them either solely based on the percentage they take from your earnings. Some of the legal advice and help I've received certainly would have cost me a lot more if I had to actually seek out the resource on my own. On the flip side, if you feel like you won't utilize all the services a MCN offers, then it makes sense not to partner with one. There are positive and negative reasons on both sides of the argument and ultimately only you will know what is right to do. Do not feel pressured into signing up for one. You can be just as successful without one, so be sure to always remember that!

TAXES

After a certain point our YouTube channel grows into a small business. For some of us, it may be viewed that way from the moment we start. If you are pursuing YouTube with the intention of it being your job in the future, make sure you keep track of everything that you do and purchase.

Despite naysayers, being a YouTuber is a real job. It requires a lot of work to be successful at it, and if someone claims otherwise, it is simply because they are misinformed. Just like any career endeavor, it is extremely important to pay attention to the not-so-fun stuff too. Taxes in particular. Now, for this section I'll be explaining things from the perspective of living in the United States since that is where I'm from. These things can differ per region, so I would highly recommend looking into your own country's system. Consult with an attorney versed in tax law or an accountant depending on the situation (even if you live in the United States this is still advisable).

If you are purchasing something for the betterment of your channel or your YouTube career, keep track of it. These could very well qualify for business expenses and be deducted at the end of the year. It's important to create an itemized list of every expense that is tied to your channel. Camera equipment, computers, software, printed materials for conventions, travel to industry events, hotel lodging at conventions, meals purchased while attending events or while talking to people about YouTube, your measured office space within your home, a percentage of your electricity/phone/internet bills, and other related expenses. All of these things should be considered and can save you money when it comes to filing your taxes. Keep track of everything. Take photos of your receipts and throw them into a folder. Save all your invoices and do the same. If you don't do this you'll be taxed on money you already spent that should have rightfully not been taxed.

At the end of the day everything I mentioned above is merely to spark the idea to educate yourself about taxes. I'm no tax specialist and certainly only know the basics, so seek out someone who knows this way better than I do. Everything you collected over the year should be brought to them and they'll help you sort it. The reason I included this in the book is because of the amount of people I've encountered who don't do this. Research the topic and get in contact with someone who specializes in taxes. You'll lose out in the end otherwise. Keeping track of everything can be tedious for sure, but the amount it can save you is its own reward.

DON'T WAIT

People often daydream about the things they want to do and the success they may find afterwards. I know I was always daydreaming whenever I had the opportunity to do so, but daydreams fade as fast as they come about. The grand ideas we have often stay locked away in our brain because we feel actually acting on them is impossible. We think we aren't good enough or that whatever we are dreaming of simply will never be reached. We pretty much cut ourselves down. It sucks.

Regardless of how we look at it our uncertainties talk us out of it. We fear change or even the thought of having to give something up in order to move in a different direction. A lot of these factors are why humans in general stay at jobs or in relationships that may not be the best fit for them. Change is too great of an obstacle for them and it is simply easier to settle.

If you only take away one piece of advice from this book, let it be this: throw away that feeling. Don't wait for what you want to do. You have to go after it. Today.

The reason I feel so strongly about this is because something happened to me that I'll never forget. I was so happy with how things were going on YouTube that I didn't even think something bad could happen to me. I know that sounds extremely silly, but once you strike a stride with creating you're constantly thinking ahead and about what comes next. You become so focused on what you're accomplishing that you may even forget about the present. I'll touch on this concept in a different note a little later on, but this played a role in what occurred with me.

I was a guest at my first convention ever and I was so excited about the weekend that was ahead of me. I attended conventions and gave speeches before, but I had never officially been booked as a guest. This was new territory for me and I was being paid to come to a convention and talk about video games. Not a bad gig, eh? As you can imagine that's precisely why I was ecstatic. However, later that night an incident occurred that reversed my thoughts on everything.

I was out at dinner with my significant other enjoying the night before the convention started and all seemed right with the world. I was thinking about my panels tomorrow and my first time signing things as an official guest. However, right before leaving the table at the restaurant I felt a pop in my chest and my whole world turned upside down. And I don't mean that as an idiom. My perspective of the restaurant before me grew bizarre and skewed as a pain raced across my body. I tried to tell my significant other that I couldn't talk but I could barely get the words out before everything went black around me. I felt like I was in a dream. I saw fields of flowers before me and then suddenly I was in the back of a car on a road trip out west. It was as if someone pulled random footage from my brain and cut it all together into a montage. They say your life flashes before your eyes before you die and I totally understand why they say that now.

When I woke up I was in a daze and couldn't really talk to anyone. Paramedics surrounded the table as they tried to figure out what was wrong with me. The world around me was still blurry after I woke up and I felt like I was looking at everything through a rain-covered window. I was absolutely terrified. After all the commotion stopped and I recovered from what happened, my outlook on life had changed. They weren't able to identify what happened but it seemed like I was okay from what they could tell. I'm honestly surprised they didn't take me to the hospital since they weren't able to diagnose the issue, but from that point forward I was in a funk. I remember lying down at the hotel that night thinking about how fragile human beings are in general. Even though I hoped I would live a long and healthy life, there was never a guarantee.

If I had died in that moment would I have been happy with the life I lived?

That's a question I still can't answer truthfully. YouTube had finally started to pay off for me but there was so much I still wanted to do. I wanted to write books, make video games, and travel the world. I've had an idea for a killer fantasy series in my head for years now and if I died no one would ever know about it. It's quite a grim thing to think about.

How many amazing stories are left untold simply due to time constraints we have in life? How many people never took the first step to sharing them? That's why you don't wait. You don't wait because you really have no idea how long you will be here. You don't wait because you don't know if your life will completely change in an instant. It doesn't even have to be something health-related either. Your life could simply become busier and your free time may eventually be replaced with responsibilities you have to address. The more you wait to do what you want to do, the more you will regret not starting it sooner.

Waiting may even be the defining factor that prevents you from starting. I mean, when you see people who are farther along then you in something you may simply talk your way out of it.

"I'm starting too late. I'll never catch up."

Defeating thoughts like this are real and it's weird because that particular instance doesn't even have anything to do with your ability as a creator. It just has to do with the fact that you waited too long to do something and you feel you missed your window of opportunity. That feeling will only get worse and it doesn't go away. That's why starting today is so important. You may not feel completely ready, but the truth is you never will be. Your first video will feel like garbage and it honestly may be garbage, but that's okay. Everyone started out that way. What's important is that you give it a try, because you may surprise yourself in the long run.

I know if I wouldn't have tried I would have regretted it for the rest of my life.

THE IMPOSTOR WITHIN

Our journey as creatives is filled with a multitude of feelings. Sometimes you'll be super empowered and filled with joy as you create, and other times you'll be depressed and barely scraping by. Creating is truly an emotional rollercoaster, but a big part of it is that our perspective is constantly changing as we continue to grow. Our successes sometimes feel like they are never enough, but our failures always crush us.

The community shares a large role in our outlook as well. Unfortunately, humans will naturally compare themselves to others. In the online world this gets very extreme too. The reason I say that is because we are judging from afar and in isolation. Nothing is worse than feeling frustrated or insignificant while sitting by yourself in front of a computer screen. We have no one else to bounce those feelings off of besides a chat window or some other outlet. It makes us feel more alone than ever.

A big hurdle I had to overcome while creating on YouTube was the feeling that I didn't belong. I would look at other creators having conversations on Twitter and wish I was a part of that conversation. I wished I had more friends than I did. I think more than anything I wanted to be recognized for my work because I thought I made really good videos. When I didn't get the recognition I expected, I became jaded and sad.

Was my work really not that good? Why didn't people like me? Why didn't I fit in? This was extremely demotivating because for the longest time nothing ever changed. I wanted to be a part of a community that I thought was open to everyone. In reality it was, I just didn't give it the time it needed. Because of this, I felt like an impostor even though I had some success on YouTube. Little did I know this was something almost everyone feels at some point, and even though I felt like I was the only one, I surely wasn't.

My problem was that I was overlooking everything about these online interactions that made them human. For as openminded as I felt I was, I was missing so many things that were really obvious when I stopped to think about it. Circles of friends form naturally online, but they take time to do so. A lot of the people who I saw were friends honestly had shared years of time together on the platform. They had met each other while attending conventions and over time this slowly led to the great friendships they had today. My expectations were simply betraying me because Twitter seemed so accessible. I may have felt like I knew the people I followed, but truthfully, I knew nothing about who they really were. It was a one-sided friendship that I had formed simply based on what they decided to share online. So, when I would reach out and not get a response, I had to take a step back and consider the possibilities that may have happened.

Was my message ignored? Possibly. Did they not know how to respond? Possibly. Do they get tons of messages in a day and it's impossible to hold one-on-one conversations with everyone? Very likely.

Beyond this, people often have to be careful online as well. When you let someone into your life there is a certain amount of vulnerability that comes with it. If the intentions of the person you are letting in are simply self-serving, they may leverage you to reach success faster. Fake people are truly the worst, but the reason why so many creators online have their walls up is because they have been burned in the past. They let someone in and that person hurt them. After a while that creator will only talk with their friends because time and time again outsiders have brought them stress. They do it in order to protect themselves.

These are things I wish I had realized right off the bat while creating. My expectations led to my downfall and I truly felt like I didn't deserve anything because others didn't recognize my efforts like they did their friends. To some degree I even became cynical about it because I was jealous. However, the worst part of all of this was all the time I spent worrying about these things. It actually harmed me as a creator. I would lose motivation to create because I felt like I was creating in a vacuum and no one would truly care if I stopped.

To make matters worse, when someone would criticize my videos or leave a mean comment online, it would slowly cement the idea. One by one these occurrences would make me believe that I truly was an impostor in my craft. Little did I know that wasn't the case at all. The problem is that this behavior repeats itself for a long time because without an inciting incident to make you think otherwise, you simply operate on a cycle believing it. The reality is that these things honestly don't matter at all.

I essentially created my own problems because I was constantly comparing myself to others and hoping to have what others had. I failed to recognize the entire journey that these people took to get to where they are. I was only seeing where they were now and I didn't account for anything else.

Ironically, even people we deem successful still share the same feelings we do. You can be successful and still have impostor syndrome. You can feel like you don't deserve the success you have, and when someone pays you a compliment you simply disregard it.

Friendships in general take time to develop and you have to be comfortable with waiting. When the time is right you may run into these people at conventions or a conversation may spark up. If a friendship sparks because of it, great. If not, then it simply wasn't meant to be. When you're creating on your journey be aware of the signs of impostor syndrome and truly try to take a step back from everything. It's very easy to dig yourself into a hole that's much harder to climb out.

AN INTERNET FULL OF HATE

"This video was a waste of time."

"Your voice sucks! You slur all your words."

"You look like a potato."

The internet is quite the vile place sometimes. For every good thing that is on it, there are often just as many negative things as well. Regardless of what you do you will always receive negative feedback. Sometimes people leave the most damaging comments to make other people laugh at your expense. As the content creator, you are typically at the butt of the jokes. You better bring your best armor before you wander out into the comment section. It's a battlefield!

I have decently thick skin as a person so the comments I would encounter on YouTube didn't affect me too much. However, I'm also a straight white male. I never had to deal with anything extremely racist, bigoted, or sexist at all. I was on easy mode, where as other people would encounter things viler than I could ever imagine. It's sad that this is the way the world is. But hopefully we can all work to change that. Please do not let this discourage you from your dreams though. For every toxic person knocking at your door, there are a handful of people who will want to stand by your side.

My drive to make YouTube work often overshadowed the idea of letting individual haters slow me down, but that doesn't mean they didn't sting once in a while. More than anything I wanted to know why people felt like they needed to be super vile. What made someone so agitated that they had to insult people? Especially about things that have nothing to do with the video itself? I was determined to figure out why and started to ask questions. Sometimes you wouldn't get a response in return and sometimes they would simply hit you harder than they did the first time. By enduring the hateful atmosphere and forcing myself into conversations with these people, I learned something invaluable as a creator. From that point forward my perspective was changed forever.

There is one story in particular that really shaped the way I handle all hate comments now. At this point in my YouTube career I simply cannot respond to every comment, but it doesn't mean I don't read them. After one of my first successful videos began to gain traction and I had broken 1,000 subscribers, comments began to pour in all over the place. There were people who really loved the video, people who wanted to offer their own thoughts on the topic, and people who came to hate. One hater in particular dropped the spiciest hate comment I had ever read before. He hit everything on the hate list in a grand fashion: From telling me to drink bleach and kill myself, to saying that everything presented in the video made absolutely no sense. He went on and on belittling me and took pride in doing so.

This was a comment that stung, but it made me scratch my head. How could someone get this worked up about a video that is speculating about the story within a game? A video built on the premise that everything within the video is just a hypothesis served as an introduction to the topic? Regardless of what type of videos you create on YouTube, I'm sure you may run into a similar situation.

So, what did I do? I decided to take the bait and respond. Of course, my response was only met with more hate even though I tried my best to address the situation. At this point I realized that there would probably be no way to reason with this person, but I was still curious about his purpose behind it all. Lots of other viewers began to chime in as well and this only added fuel to the fire. The comment chain itself probably got around 300 comments before something happened that I would have never expected. During the entire ordeal this person continued to spit vile towards anyone who opposed him, but in the end, they ultimately broke down and apologized to everyone. It was the grand finale that no one would have even thought was possible given that internet trolls will often argue to simply argue. But the act of apologizing was really only the beginning. His reasoning for why he acted this way changed my outlook on a lot of things.

This person was a content creator. His hatred stemmed from seeing others succeed while his channel remained stagnant. Now that reason alone seems very childish of course. However, while that may have been what ignited the backlash comment, it certainly wasn't the only contributing factor. This user went on to talk about how they had a bad life at home and things weren't going very well for them in school. They were depressed. I got the sense that they were still pretty young, too. All of this started to make me think about people in general and how they can be influenced by others.

Take for example a kid who is bullied at school. If a kid is bullied at school you would think they wouldn't reciprocate this behavior themselves because of how bad it makes them feel. However, if they feel invisible in school and the only time they are noticed is when they are getting teased, it can emotionally scar them. This same person may go online when they get home and digitally bully others to make themselves feel better. They can stand up to anyone through the internet and for the most part, there are no repercussions. They have a voice when they normally don't have one, and that pent-up anger is released to the world through the web. If you're usually ignored you can become desperate for any kind of validation. You want to be acknowledged by people. Feeling invisible is horrible. However, it does not justify behaving terribly online.

Now, this isn't the outlook for every troll you encounter online, but it does boil it down to one thing: We should never judge people. Often times we do not know their full story or why they are acting a certain way. They may simply be angry at you because they are angry at themselves and the internet is the only outlet they have to make their voice heard. That hateful comment is only the tip of an emotional iceberg that is peaking through the surface of the water.

At the end of the day this creator wanted to be a good person. They truly did and on their own channel it was apparent. These factors were corrupting them and making him do these things out of anger and jealously. This made me realize that I should never take comments at face value. I always take the time now to consider the possibility of where this viewer may be coming from. Do they really hate you or is that hate coming from somewhere else? Everyone has their own story and not everyone's life is the same. You should really consider this before deciding to respond or regretfully attack back.

I didn't want to be known as the person who argues constantly online. I would take a step back from the situation and try to consider all the possibilities. I strongly believe this helped me grow as a content creator because vile comments don't affect me as much now. This of course does not excuse someone for being vile though. Toxic comments are still toxic regardless of why they are said. The important thing is that I won't let this stop me from creating. If you build it, the haters will certainly come. Do not let them distract you from what you are trying to achieve.

Remember why you started creating in the first place.

THE IMPORTANCE
OF PERSONALITY

When I first started creating content for YouTube over a decade ago, the world of online video was still a foreign land to all. Later on, when I landed a job making videos for companies, things were still backwards. For the longest time "killer content" was all the craze, and people would swear by the power of it. While these people weren't wrong, I felt like they weren't seeing the whole picture.

How do I know this? Well, I used to be one of those people.

For quite a while I simply focused on the quality and message behind my videos. I felt I excelled at presenting interesting topics that were delivered through high quality editing. After some time it paid off because people flocked to my channel to see my latest videos. However, what I failed to realize was that while my videos were great, I simply wasn't memorable. Anyone could have been narrating these videos and they would have turned out the same. On top of that, my voiceover work in the videos wasn't really good at all. It was a hindrance to the video while the editing was a blessing. The problem with this approach is that it doesn't work forever. Eventually you'll dig yourself into a hole because the topic of your video is more important than the person making it. That really sucks to realize, but it happened to me. I wasn't showing the world enough of me to make them understand who I was. I was the man behind the curtain that the world couldn't relate to. This is what made me realize just how important personality truly is.

Personality has the power to bring people to videos for topics they might not even be interested in. They may not even consider watching the video without it. As a YouTuber, your number one goal should be to connect with your audience in a way that makes them feel like you're a friend. You want your audience to be emotionally invested in what you're doing. The reason why so many vlogging YouTubers have success is because they end up feeling like a best friend to you. Personality is their defining feature and the video topic comes second. It is very clear as well, because people who are on camera in their rawest form crush it on all social platforms outside of YouTube. Facebook, Twitter, Instagram—you name it, they have high activity on it. Super passionate fans seek you out on other platforms and it is usually a decent way to measure one's reach as a creator. But don't let that completely discourage you. It isn't the case for everyone!

This is why live streaming is also very helpful. You may not get the biggest turnout for your live streams, but it offers you the chance to connect with your audience in real time. For a moment you're not just a person in a video. You're a real human being they can converse with. During that moment you have the power to strengthen your relationship with everyone watching because they feel like they're a part of an exclusive club. It feels intimate. Live streaming certainly pays off in the long run too. The more invested people become in you, and the more they enjoy you as a person, the more opportunities that will eventually come your way. Not only that, but these people who now have a pure taste of your personality will seek you out specifically in your videos that they may have not felt connected with before. It keeps you in their thoughts. They may even live through you vicariously and use that to try new things.

Your number one goal should be to present your topic in a way that puts your personality first. You want them to come back because they want to hear your personal take on something. It takes a while to figure it out, but after releasing video after video your personality will eventually shine through if you give it the time to. If you write scripts for your videos like I do, consider ad-libbing part of your scripts. Just start recording and talk. Don't be afraid that people won't like the unstructured you. It's always rough before things get better. My voice used to be why people stopped watching my videos and now it is the reason they come to watch. By listening to feedback from my audience and injecting more and more of myself into each of my videos, my audience started to become more familiar with me. They were also willing to come out and see me at conventions because they enjoyed me as a person. I was scared to be myself for the longest time and my audience could see that before I let myself be free. I didn't need to shape who I was or act like I was someone else. I just had to be me.

Anytime you start a video, consider how you can maximize your personal touch in it. Plan to have sections that allow your personality to shine. Personality is the single most important thing for a YouTuber to have. No amount of tagging, optimized titles, or killer video concepts will ever rival what human interaction can. When the YouTube algorithm is working against you, personality is the one trait that can save you. People will come to watch your videos regardless of any notifications that are sent out. They will seek out your channel on their own just to see if you've uploaded. You mean something to them and that is the best spot to be in as a creator. Continue to deliver your value fueled by personality and you'll definitely find growth!

THE NEGATIVE INFLUENCE OF NUMBERS

In today's society we get swept up in numbers. How many likes did I get? How many followers do I have? I wish I had more "x". We are being divided into social influencers and followers and we lose our humanity in the process.

I have gone to many conventions in my YouTube career. One time I even did almost twenty in the span of a year. However, each and every time I go to a convention or conference I learn something new. After my first trip to a Maryland convention I left feeling more sad than happy. The convention itself was amazing and I met a lot of awesome creators, fans, and game enthusiasts in general. But some of the interactions left me feeling depressed and it was something I couldn't get out of my mind on the eight-hour drive home.

The problem with conventions is that everyone is on uneven playing fields. There is a social hierarchy that is artificially created for everyone attending. Instead of people wandering through a convention center, we become numbers. At this convention in particular it hit me a little harder than it usually did. Often times when you are talking with people at a convention they may ask you what you do if they don't already know. I would tell people that I was a YouTuber and that I made gaming-related videos on my channel, SwankyBox. Now this is when the conversation would completely change for a multitude of reasons. What I started to realize was that people often didn't recognize me since I didn't show my face much in videos at the time. However, they remembered the name. This either made them excited or it made them distant. When I would ask what they do in return, I would sometimes get the response, "Oh me? I'm a nobody."

I can't tell you how heartbreaking this feels to hear. It's common to think this as just a reactionary phrase, but the body language does all the talking. They don't look you in the eyes from that point forward. When I think of the response "I'm a nobody," that means someone or something had to make them feel that way, whether they feel like an impostor themselves or because an earlier conversation made them feel inadequate.

The truth is these people are not nobodies at all and I hate that we as society started to define ourselves by numbers. People feel that a number next to a name directly reflects someone's worth and it is a horrible precedent. It really pains me to know that these people feel like they can't talk to me because they think they aren't worth my time. I'm pretty much one of the most easygoing and welcoming guys ever! Please come say hello if you see me! I hate having to toot my own horn like that, but I just feel everyone should be accepted. At the end of the day we are all people and no number should define or separate us. When a person approaches me and someone has already instilled in them that there is a hierarchy, it really makes me sad.

Placing people we look up to on pedestals is a horrible thing to do. It dehumanizes people. Creators who act like they are on a pedestal only amplify this horrible behavior. Those at the top who claim others are "irrelevant" are awful people. With creative success also needs to come humility. When I was at this convention I heard three people tell me they were "nobodies." But how many more people in the crowd also thought that same thing? There were plenty of people I wasn't able to talk to. Anytime someone would mention this to me I would immediately stop them and tell them it doesn't matter. I wanted to talk to them for who they are and not for what number they stand for. By not taking the time to say this I feel like it only continues to damage their confidence. It slowly divides us more and more over time. We should be empowering each other and not reinforcing social barriers.

On the flip side of this you have the people who seek out people with numbers tied to their name. Any creator can tell you that this is extremely bothersome because the reason they are approaching you doesn't actually have anything to do with the creator themselves. It's because they want something out of you and that is why they are trying to force themselves into association with you. There have been times at conventions when people found out I did YouTube and their approach to me completely changed. They suddenly got overly friendly, wanted to take photos, and tried to plug their own creative endeavors as much as they could.

There is nothing wrong with wanting to share your creative passion with people, but just make sure your reasons are honest for doing so. If you flock to people who have a larger following just because they have a larger following, you aren't doing YouTube for the right reasons. Most of these people don't even see the person or understand their story. They see a large number and they see an opportunity.

I've been introduced as a number before too and it is extremely uncomfortable. I know some of you may be reading this thinking that's a great problem to have, but you have to take a step back and look at it for what it really is. You're being introduced as a number because the person introducing you is showing off. This isn't the case always, but in private conversations it certainly is. You can become a bargaining chip when you are included in conversations because you provide instant clout. You are being leveraged for what you've accomplished. I totally understand why some people do this even though I still find it annoying. In a business sense it's essentially like cutting to the chase. But in a circle of strangers who may not necessarily care, it's bothersome.

When we are first starting off we become extremely focused on subscribers, but over time as a creator this begins to wear off. The number doesn't matter as much as the value and entertainment you provide to your audience. More people following can certainly help, but it becomes less important as you grow. You can be an extremely successful channel with only a few thousand subscribers compared to a moderately successful channel with a few million. Numbers only define you if you let them. If you strip all these numbers away, we are the people we always were.

If you develop an ego as a creator and lose your humanity in the process, just know you will be directly

influencing the behavior of those around you in a negative light. You will be the one who creates the idea that
these people are nobodies. So please, always make sure
your status doesn't change who you are at your core.
I've even had people with large followings interrupt
one on one conversations as if they had the authority
to do so. It really is a sad state of affairs sometimes, and
every time it happens it reminds me to never become
like that. You can even be standing with a group of
people talking and the people in the circle will ignore
you on purpose and only talk to their peers. I get that
a great deal of us may be introverts, but the behavior is
absolutely baffling. For someone who has been out of
high school for a while now, it's almost comical to see
people who may be in their late twenties still portraying
this high school behavior.

On the flip side, recognize when people are busy
and try not to interrupt them. Intruding on people
isn't cool either. Be welcoming and accepting of those
around you. We are all equal and it doesn't matter who
you are, what you do, or where you're from. No number
should ever change that. Talk to someone as a human
being and not as an expectation.

THE DANGERS OF INFLATED NUMBERS

"If you subscribe to my channel, I'll subscribe to yours."

The dreaded sub 4 sub mentality. If for some reason you haven't witnessed this yet, you will once you start poking your head into YouTuber communities online. You want to grow as fast as you can when you are starting off. You are so focused on the number next to your name that you will do almost anything to make it larger. While you shouldn't be focused on the number, it's hard not to be. Often times we are attracted to bigger numbers and give them the benefit of the doubt. A channel that has hundreds of thousands of followers and millions of views makes us innately trust their content enough to check it out. Whereas when a creator has seven subscribers and only forty views on their video, people may judge the video before giving it a chance. It absolutely sucks to be in this situation. Unfortunately, it's just societal behavior at this point. However, you cannot let this drive you to artificially inflate your numbers. Following others to get follow backs is a horrible concept. Please don't ever buy illegitimate followers or views either. The number may make you happy for a moment, but it will wreck your foundation as a creator.

We've all seen the Twitter account that has thousands of followers but zero interactions. Anyone can see through that right away and it's only doing your future fans a huge disservice. Certain platforms factor in your number of followers into the equation. It measures how interested they are in you as a person based on how they've interacted with you.

In YouTube's case, if you have a huge subscriber base but they're all illegitimate subscribers, your channel is doomed. Those people didn't subscribe to you because they wanted to watch your content. They couldn't care less about what videos you're uploading. They only subscribed to you so you would subscribe to them. They might even be bots. There is no connection between the viewer and creator, thus the relationship is meaningless. The worst part is once you get fake followers, you can't really get rid of them. They have to unsubscribe themselves or you have to hope that YouTube somehow unsubscribes them for you. These subscribers are essentially dead weight to your channel and it will make things more difficult for you.

YouTube will send out notifications to subscribers to alert them about new content. If your audience doesn't seek out the videos though, YouTube assumes you aren't putting out videos your audience wants. No one showed up to watch the video after all. Because of this, YouTube starts to notify people less and less. These people who don't show up still affect your ratio of people who do show up. While it isn't set in stone if this principle is an exact factor in why viewership can decrease, it is a theory that is sort of established. It is like multiplying fractions because each video you release ends up bringing less and less people. This in turn means that the potential audience for each video decreases with every upload. Hypothetically, even if all your true fans showed up you would still have the dead weight of inactive subscribers harming your reach as a creator. This is why fake numbers can be extremely dangerous.

If you find success after dabbling with fake numbers it can still be something that harms your channel for a very long time. Obviously it can be overshadowed with time if you truly discover an audience that resonates with you, but it is still extremely dangerous. It is something than can come back to haunt you in the long run. Make sure the people who follow you are actual people who are interested in you. If you beg for a subscription, the person may just do so out of the kindness of their heart and not because they want to see your future content. There is always this rush to grow as fast as we can but every number next to our name is a person. A relationship takes a lot of time to build and if you rush that you will only lose in the end. The best fans are the ones who thought you were worth following and supporting themselves.

If you run giveaways and other promotional events make sure you don't force yourself into a fake fanbase too. Doing giveaways is totally fine if you do it sparingly, but if it is a frequent tactic then you are really betraying yourself as a creator. People will show up for the giveaway and not for you. If you ever stop doing giveaways your channel will immediately take a huge hit in viewership.

It's also important to know that doing giveaways with other content creators your audience is unfamiliar with can be dangerous as well. Hypothetically, let's say you had five separate channels doing a giveaway that all had entry requirements of subscribing on YouTube. A typical viewer will subscribe to all five channels simply to get more ballets into the drawing for the prize. You may gain a few thousand subscribers through the amount of exposure the giveaway brings, but these people will not stick around. You just dug yourself into a hole you may have not even been aware of. They are fans of the channel that brought them to the giveaway and probably won't care too much about the other channels. There is no human connection present.

They will surely be factored into the reach your channel has if they are subscribed though. I've seen a few creators actually wreck their viewership by holding a few giveaways with other channels that produced different kinds of content. The process is irreversible and the damage remains. Please be careful with any kind of tactic that artificially inflates the numbers of your channel. Organic growth is slow, but it's the best kind. Trying to game the system may bring you temporary gains, but sooner or later it will all come crashing down.

BURNED BRIDGES

I feel like I'm navigating a land of burned bridges fairly often in the YouTube space. What do I mean by that exactly? A burned bridge is a severed or damaged relationship. You can't use that bridge to cross the water anymore metaphorically. What you were able to do before can no longer be done. However, the bridges I'm referring to were not burned by me. The environment around me has been damaged by others and once that bridge has been burned, there's no going back. Trying to rebuild a relationship from the ground up is a ton of work. Even so, it's the only way to move forward.

This concept certainly isn't unique to YouTube. However, I find it more difficult with YouTube. Not every YouTuber acts professionally in situations where they should probably do so. Those on the receiving end of this behavior will always remember it.

There have been so many instances where a bridge has been burned before I even had a chance to start crossing it. It's incredibly frustrating. I spend majority of my time re-educating people since others before me have ruined their viewpoint towards content creators. For all of us who take YouTube seriously, there are an equal amount of people that don't realize the damage they cause when they misbehave. When they do something bad it reflects on all of us.

People can of course act how they want. That is their choice. The problem is a lot of times people may have such a large following that it doesn't matter at all what the repercussions are. But a leak at the top will trickle down and harm those working their way up. With great power comes great responsibility. Listen to Uncle Ben! The bigger your following the bigger your impact. If you're having public fights on Twitter and are known as a YouTuber, you are slowly damaging YouTubers in the eyes of others. Every public action you take shapes how content creators may be viewed.

The actions of others can affect you as a creator in many ways. For example, let's talk about conventions and conferences. As a YouTuber you are going to have to branch out and establish other ways to make a living. Uploading videos is only the start and conventions are a perfect way to do so. This is where you might have difficulties though. Other YouTubers may have actually ruined your chances to get involved with certain conventions.

This became apparent to me as I began to branch out. I would be judged before people even got to know me. My chances would be pretty slim if that staff member was jaded from a horrible experience with a past YouTuber. Perhaps they paid this YouTuber to come out and do panels or host certain events. If this YouTuber got drunk and was unruly, or if they simply didn't show up to their scheduled events, that is a wasted investment for the convention. The convention has to make ends meet too. When someone else comes along, they may not even consider it an option simply based on their past experiences. You start buried six feet under. You have to build the relationship up before even approaching the starting line because they are afraid to make that investment again. Some conventions may even fear taking legal action against YouTubers with large followings because the fan backlash could ruin the image of the convention. I know that sounds super silly and that's because it is. Don't be that kind of YouTuber.

A lack of professional experience on the YouTuber's side can lead to these incidents. Interacting with others professionally and keeping your word are both incredibly important. All of these fuel the fire for my next point: Understating your value.

A big problem in the gaming space is that YouTubers and streamers in general will opt to do things for free when they rightfully should be paid for doing so. You see this happen a lot at big gaming conventions. For example, for the past few years now opportunities have been canceled for people because others have opted to do it for free. You can do a live performance at a booth during a conference and companies are absolutely willing and able to pay for your time.

That is until someone else says they will do it for exposure. The company then immediately cancels the opportunity with the initial person and books the person who will do it for free. It is smart for the company because they get similar value for spending nothing, but it is horrible for YouTubers and streamers because it sets the precedent that what we do has no value. Anytime they work with a creator in the future they will operate on the assumption that they can probably get someone to work for free. And yes, what we do is often "fun" and does not feel like work, but we offer skills, personality, and audience reach. All of that has real-world value. Often times there may be clauses in contracts so that companies can opt out if other circumstances arise. Because these loopholes exist, they can adjust accordingly on the fly without repercussions. A YouTuber may not even know what they can do legally in a situation like that either. Only a lawyer would know what is best.

Every time this occurs, the price of our talents gets lower and lower. Of course, there will always be competition and people will argue that undercutting others is just the nature of the game. However, just know every time this is done you are damaging not only your own worth but the worth of all the creators around you. Playing games for people live has value because people tune in for the person playing them. There is a personal experience and that individual has the power to direct attention to things that people may have not looked at otherwise. That is your entertainment value.

This same situation can also occur with any type of public appearance for a YouTuber. They don't necessarily have to be a gamer. I imagine musicians and even artists may run into similar experiences. Regardless of what you do on YouTube, you may one day be confronted with a live stream convention opportunity because of what you have built. Keep this in mind because the same type of situation can occur!

Sponsorships and brand deals fall into this same category. If you need a refresher, feel free to drop back to the "Adapting to the Wild" chapter.

KEEPING YOUR WORD / COLLABORATIONS

If there is one thing that bothers me about the online world, it's reliability. I think it's unfortunately just a trait of the society we live in. It is much easier to agree to something and then become a ghost when the person you said yes to follows up. We are afraid to tell people no and the value of someone's word has become nothing. When someone tells us they will do something, we get antsy because we know there is a strong possibility they won't. It is quite the ugly trait.

When you start to collaborate with people this may become apparent right away. There will be a moment where everything is great because both parties will be working on something neat together, but then it falls through. I think this is what I always hated about group activities in school. They were supposed to make you familiar with working on a team, but that was never the case. One or two people always did all the work. If they didn't, they would fail the assignment. The other people in their group would make promises they couldn't keep and it would make it twice as stressful for the people who had to pick up the slack.

Online content creation is no different when it comes to collaborations. If you're going to work with someone you should definitely pull your weight. Many creators have been burned by such poor collaborations that they end up closing their doors to the possibility of new ones. Always make sure you are giving 50% out of the 100% needed for the project. Keep people updated as you work as well. Nothing is worse than scheduling your weekly video to go out and then finding out the person you're collaborating with dropped the ball and didn't finish their video. You never want to be that person because it will almost immediately burn your bridge with your collaborator. They will put up with your behavior until the project is over, but they will never want to work with you again. Reliability is so important and so few people understand this.

There are a few different types of collaborations and each requires a different amount of work. There are single-video collaborations, dual-video collaborations, and long-term or multi-person collaborations.

Single-video collaborations are when one creator creates a video on their channel and invites someone to take part in it. The owner of the channel runs the show to some degree. If you are the collaborator in this scenario, make sure you are accountable because the channel owner can't make the video until they get all of your assets. This could be you recording yourself on camera, giving them voiceover audio, or some other sort of footage. The longer you make them wait, the more stress you put on them. Having your collaborator deliver assets late is incredibly frustrating. The deadline for the owner of the channel may not be flexible. Since you got your files to them late, they now have to work nonstop to get it done on time. Beyond this, always make sure what you are delivering is what is expected. If you dump a bunch of unedited audio on someone who was expecting to just plug your edited voiceover in, now you've doubled their workload. It also makes it look like you really didn't care about the collaboration to begin with. Communication is the most important thing and if you fail to do so properly, your relationship with this creator may fizzle out.

Dual-video collaborations are essentially when there are two videos in total and each creator has a part in the other's video. One video goes on each channel and they link to each other's video at the end. In order to do these you need to settle on a deadline that both creators can meet. If something changes and you can't make your deadline, you need to immediately notify the other party. Don't be the person who magically forgets. The person you're working with will grow to dislike you. Personally, I always operate on a schedule and if someone fails to upload their video at the same time that means I have to delay mine to compensate. That could cause me to not upload during that week because someone else didn't take things seriously. It is incredible frustrating to say the least!

Multi-person and long-term collaborations are the last of the bunch. Multi-person obviously has multiple people involved. Sometimes this means that someone failing to meet their deadline isn't the end of the world. You might just scrap them from the video. These types of collaborations typically have multiple people contributing their thoughts on a topic and the flow of the video doesn't necessarily rely on any key player. It's a montage of thoughts. If someone fails to deliver, they simply don't make the cut. It isn't as dire because the video can still happen without them.

Long-term collaborations are more or less a series with someone that will include multiple episodes. Chances are you already have a great relationship established with this other creator and you trust them. It wouldn't make sense to embark on a long series if someone was going to flake out on the third episode. Creating a series takes a lot of planning. Make sure you outline the terms of the collaboration if this is a path you are going down. The series has to be uploaded to only one channel, so before doing so make sure everyone involved is okay with this happening. Also work out how compensation will be dealt with. People's opinions may change if you start a long-term series and it becomes super successful. It can be messy if you don't outline everything beforehand. Treat this seriously or it might come back to haunt you in the future if things turn sour!

YOU COPIED THEM!

After creating for a while you are going to run into some people in the comment section claiming that you've copied someone. The response can come in many forms, but in the gaming community it typically comes in the form of "so-and-so already did this." Whether you were covering a specific topic or playing a certain game, these comments will appear below your video. This will even happen if you are doing things besides gaming. People will accuse you of things you may not even be aware of and it is going to feel weird when it happens. It's important to take a step back and understand why this happens though.

For starters, the core problem is that this particular viewer is trying to stand up for another creator and say what you're doing is wrong. If you're doing the same thing as someone else, surely you stole from them! The issue with this is that stealing does take place on YouTube all the time and it is a huge problem. Not every case is stealing though. If you want to make a video on a topic someone has already covered, you are absolutely able to do so. However, you need to absolutely credit people if you used someone else's research or leveraged another video to make yours. There's a difference between plagiarism and referencing. Be mindful of others' work and make sure you stay within the lines of fair use.

Making something that someone else has made before isn't stealing. That's actually very hard for me to say because I've dealt with real stealing many times, which is often difficult to prove. Someone creating a video, however, doesn't mean they have the absolute authority to claim stake on that topic forever. You have the power to create whatever you want. Why not give it a whirl if you can put a different spin on the topic? On the sillier side of things, some gamers even get criticized for playing the same games as larger creators. That mentality is absolutely absurd, yet people still vouch their concern about it. Just know that if you're going to make a video that is similar to someone else's, credit them if you use information from that person's video. It's really that simple. You don't have to if you arrive at the same conclusion by yourself though.

This is why there is a grey area with thieving. A lot of intellectual thefts can be argued that someone thought of it on their own. It makes this whole process incredibly frustrating because the thieves will usually prevail. What can make matters worse is when it is a larger entity that does so. If someone plucks your idea off of Reddit, Twitter, or from your video itself and creates it without crediting you it is very hard to fight back. There are some creators who deliberately do this. They wait for smaller channels to come up with good ideas and they simply take the idea. They even use the same tags and title. The larger channel's video will outperform the smaller channel and if the smaller channel tries to complain a few things may happen: They will either get muted in the comment section or the fan base of the thief may attack the smaller channel.

If this situation sounds absurd that's because it absolutely is. Hardcore fans unfortunately tend to attack first and then ask questions later. They won't even bother to check the upload date of the videos either. I've been criticized for copying videos that were uploaded a year after mine. I've also been called an idiot by people who tell me to go watch another person's video who clearly copied mine. Welcome to the silly world of YouTube. When the time comes and this happens to you—because it will—hopefully you'll recall this and the experience won't be as mentally taxing!

Unless you're stolen from. Then it will be awful! The Traveler's Note section on "Dealing with Content Thieves" will be your next destination then.

JUMPING TO CONCLUSIONS

One of my biggest flaws as a creator was that I jumped to conclusions all the time. I assumed people should know what I know, that people willfully ignored me when I reached out, or that people stole ideas from me. I was a very guarded individual and I overthought things way too much.

To be blunt: I was foolish.

Often times my mind would create scenarios that simply did not exist. However, perhaps part of this was because once you are burned by someone those wounds may never heal. That may lead you to believe that everyone has bad intentions or is ignoring you. This isn't the case at all and I realized this as time went on.

Something I needed to realize when reaching out to other people was that they have their own lives. I was tied to my computer for the first part of my YouTube journey and that painted the illusion that everyone else was as well. Of course, this isn't the case at all. People are out and about during the day. They work jobs or disconnect and go outside. While we are all bound together by the internet it is important to know this balance. Sometimes I would get heavily discouraged if I reached out to people and saw them posting online at the same time. In my mind I would determine that they had to have seen whatever I said, and I would grow anxious because of it. I was worrying about things that were out of my control. I wasn't thinking about it from their perspective.

We've all gotten emails and messages we don't respond to right away. Some we never even do. We could just be busy doing something when the email comes through. We may forget that email exists even though we glanced at it in that moment. Since it was marked as read it gets buried further in our inbox and we don't think to check back on it. Meanwhile someone like me was sitting at home growing anxious that the person thought I wasn't worth responding to.

Perhaps I wasn't. Or perhaps it was a million other things that prevented them from doing so. Maybe there were a hundred other emails just like mine and they simply could not respond to every single one. You always feel like your message is super important when you send it out, but in the scope of everyone else, it's just as important as theirs. Growing comfortable with this feeling is something we all need to do. You won't grow into a stress ball if you just accept that state of mind.

This same thing occurred to me when I thought people stole ideas from my videos. Is it possible they stole the idea from me? Of course. But it's just as possible that they came up with the same concept too. Since I typically made videos centered around the stories behind new games, anyone who was trying to do the same thing could potentially connect the same dots. Just because I uploaded it first didn't mean that everyone after me was a copycat. Even when I was certain people stole from me I could never prove it. It's funny because I would paint pictures in my heads of these people and deem them as thieves. In reality, majority of them were blissfully unaware. When I would finally meet them in person I could tell they were genuine people. My defenses were simply getting the best of me.

Although being stolen from sucks, holding yourself back because you felt you've been stolen from is no better. It still stops you from creating and you're probably overthinking things as well. The more you dwell on it the worse it gets. This doesn't mean that thieves aren't out there. They are and they're abundant. However, just be cautious so you don't jump to a conclusion that may come back to haunt you. Nothing would be worse than burning a bridge that should have never been burned. Whatever you say on the internet stays forever. Be mindful of this.

DEALING WITH CONTENT THIEVES

Probably the most soul crushing, lowest points of my career as a YouTuber came from dealing with content thieves. A content thief is someone who steals your video and uses it for their own benefit. This practice comes in many forms and by far the most notorious is freebooting.

First and foremost, "freebooting" is a phrase that people use online when someone steals a video in its entirety from YouTube or another social platform and uploads it elsewhere on the internet. It's kind of like committing a crime and fleeing the country to avoid punishment for something. I was so afraid of this when I first started that it almost stopped me from creating content in the first place. The issue is that most people don't even recognize this is a problem. If you write a book and someone takes the story and presents it as their own, that's plagiarism. The same goes if you're a painter or a photographer and someone duplicates your work and sells it for themselves. That's stealing.

Freebooting is that same concept, but it affects content creators of all kinds. It is the act of downloading a form of media that someone else made and uploading it as their own. For me, I worry about the video aspect of it. But for others, it could include artwork or photos that other people steal to use for their own benefit. I see radio stations, news sites, and other random social media accounts stealing media and using it to promote themselves all the time—Facebook being the most prominent.

Viewers are exposed to this so often and they probably don't even realize it is a stolen video. And honestly, they might not even care. However, I always ask them to think about their own job or career for a second and try to imagine the following scenario: You spend forty or more hours at your job because you need to earn money to make a living. You use that money to purchase goods, pay bills, or even support a family. Pay day rolls around and you're really looking forward to picking up your check. Once you have it in your hands though, you begin to panic. The amount you earned this month was far less than you expected because someone didn't have to watch your channel's content to support you. They found it pirated elsewhere.

That may seem like a drastic comparison, but every stolen view damages a creator's ability to support themselves through their work. Advertisement money is a creator's immediate form of payment when it comes to making videos. While it isn't great to rely on that completely, most creators start off with that in mind. The problem is that the smaller you are, the more difficult it is to fight against content thieves. Often times you have to jump through several hoops in order to even attempt to get the content removed. By then the damage is already done.

Shady Facebook and Twitter accounts prey on up-and-coming creators because they can. They know nothing will happen to them in return because most of the time the people they stole from don't have a voice to defend themselves. The second you try to confront them about it you get blocked. Or your call out is simply swept up in a wave of comments. Think about one comment trying to stand out in thousands of incoming messages on a popular Facebook video. It seems super grim. And the appeal process for these websites is often horrendous because they take forever.

When you finally are successful in getting the content removed, it has already gained hundreds of thousands of views if not millions. The thief has already won because even if that video is removed they still gained tons of followers from it. They took your hard work, cropped out your branding, and leveraged it for their own social gain. Eventually that social gain could be used to promote anything they want when it comes to converting that following into money.

It's a common case of the rich taking from the poor. How can you even stand up to someone with a million people blindly following them unaware that what they are enjoying is actually your hard work?

The short answer is you can't. It really hurts me to say that.

I've spent so much time fighting theft battles that it left me jaded about creating in the first place. I've even had huge companies take my videos, cut them up, and re-upload them to their Facebook pages netting in millions of views. Now one may suggest taking legal action at this point, but not every creator has tons of money to pursue costly and long legal battles. There's also the chance it could just be ruled fair use in the end. I only know this because I contacted lawyers about this and they felt it would be a lost cause.

I realized something though after all of this turmoil and repeatedly going through this process. I was beating myself up over something I could do nothing about. Not having a voice is like being packed into a room with thousands of people. No one can hear you whisper when everyone else is capable of shouting. And because most websites cater to those who have more followers, people may not even see your notification. It's unfortunate, but is something we have to deal with until policies are changed on external social websites. This is why I started watermarking my videos and including branding that simply couldn't be cut out. It didn't stop it from happening, but it would make it an annoying process to do so.

Utilizing Content ID

It isn't entirely a lost cause on the YouTube side of things, however. Since the content I produced was animation heavy and contained unique visuals, I was able to put some of my videos in Content ID. Content ID is basically a system that checks to see if your video exists elsewhere on the platform. It is why you can't have copyrighted music in your videos because it will trigger a match. Think of it as your video or audio file having its own unique fingerprint. Anytime that fingerprint is detected elsewhere on YouTube, the system takes actions.

A big problem I was having with my videos was that people in other countries were downloading my videos and translating them into other languages. From an accessibility standpoint that sounds great. People I could never speak to could watch my videos and understand my messages. The issue is more complex than it seems though. Someone who only translates other people's work only has to put in a fraction of the time that the creator did. Yet they make just as much money off it. They never have to think of new ideas and can build a huge following by leveraging others. It's sort of like skipping to the finish line. Animators get hit the hardest by this because a great animation can take a month or longer to make. Yet a translation of that animation by a bilingual individual may only take a few hours.

Locating translated versions of your videos is almost impossible to do because often times you don't know what to search for to even find it. The keywords it is tied to are in a different language. How would you even take the first step to locating a video titled in Russian or Japanese characters? This is where Content ID helps a ton. It would locate these things for you and claim the work as your own. This means anyone who uploaded it won't receive ad revenue from the video. You will instead.

Now some people who translate videos aren't necessarily thieves. Some people honestly do it from the goodness of their hearts and it does reach new audiences. But at the end of the day it is someone using your work without your permission in a way that doesn't classify as fair use. You wouldn't let someone take a paper you wrote, translate it, and make money off your thoughts, would you? You might even consider them a plagiarist. It's important to protect what we can of our work. On YouTube we have a fighting chance at least. Not everyone will have ill intentions, but in order to protect ourselves the best that we can we have to be stern about people using our work properly.

The unfortunate part is Content ID isn't something that is available to every channel though. It is typically a function only granted by certain multi-channel networks. This means unless you are contractually bound to a multi-channel network, you more than likely won't be able to utilize Content ID if you don't have thousands of videos. YouTube has strange requirements like that. Being part of a multi-channel network has some perks and drawbacks as well, and you can read up on that in an earlier chapter. Some MCN's may allow you to put videos in Content ID through them without officially partnering. They will still take a certain percentage of the earnings though and it will differ with each case.

Copyright Claims

You can always file a copyright claim on a particular YouTube video if you happen to stumble upon someone taking your work. Be very careful about this though, because if it ends up being a false claim, you will be the one that suffers consequences. This is pretty much like opening a legal case against the person you're reporting. If things are found in your favor the content will be removed and they may receive a copyright strike. Do not take this lightly because abusing this feature will get you in serious trouble. If someone samples your work in a way that classifies as fair use and you submit a claim, you may be the one who faces punishment. Please be aware of what is considered fair use. A lawyer or a MCN can always shed some clarity on this as well.

Don't feel bad about issuing a content claim if it is deserving. I know that sounds a bit heartless on my end, but I became cutthroat about the process after having dealt with it so many times. If someone accidentally commits a crime, it is still a crime. A lot of people mention reaching out to the person before issuing the claim because they may not know otherwise. You can certainly try this and you may get some results, but I found out that most of the time I never got a response back. They will ignore you on purpose because they will think you can't do anything about it. Especially if you're a smaller channel.

I started hitting people with copyright claims right off the bat because they willingly would crop out my watermark on the video and strip out all branding that was associated with me. They'd just use my footage to suit their own needs. They'd just reuse or recreate the message of my video with my own actual video. That's not okay at all. When confronted they'd try to play innocent and act like they didn't know, but you have to be stern. It isn't fun being stern, but protecting yourself is so important. Don't let others walk all over you. Fight back when you can, but on the flip side, draw the line somewhere. Being frustrated about thieves 24/7 will only drain you as a creator. It's impossible to fight them all.

Someone once told me that you can't build a following defensively because you will spend all your time defending yourself and not actually creating. I was bitter about thieves at first, but ultimately had to swallow my pride and focus on my creativity. I fought battles occasionally but I couldn't let other people be the reason I stopped creating. It took me forever to realize this and it certainly isn't the type of solution I'm fully on board with, but it's very true. It's a delicate balancing act and you can't let it control you. Know when to let it slide when the outcome won't benefit you in the long run. Your heart will be telling you otherwise, but in order to grow you absolutely have to.

THE NOTIFICATION / DEMOTIVATION SQUAD!

New things will occur for you once you establish a notably sized fan base. One of the most interesting things is the sense that people will be eagerly awaiting your next video. When you first start off this isn't something you would expect to occur. However, when it does occur, it is a really neat feeling. Someone raced to the video because they were so excited to see the notification come through. That's pretty darn cool. I always picture it as a grand opening. Once you cut that ribbon in front of the building, everyone comes rushing in to see what this new venue has to offer. That's exactly what this is—in video form.

This group of people will eventually come to be known as the notification squad. Every established channel has it in some form or another. People rush in because they want to be the first to comment or crack a silly joke. Sometimes it is simply because they want you to see their comment before it gets buried beneath everyone else's.

This is a perfect time for you to interact with them. Try to be online any time you upload a video. The first thirty minutes or so after a video is uploaded is when your super fans show up. Whatever they were doing wasn't as important as watching your video, so be sure to see what they have to say! You'll make their day if you take the time to have a short exchange with them. Highlighting their comment with the heart icon is another great way to let them know you saw what they wrote. Doing this repeatedly will make your fans want to show up to your videos early. Your notification squad will grow and grow. The first hours after your video is uploaded is really important as YouTube uses this time to determine if your audience truly enjoyed your content. If it brought a lot of people to the video immediately, it lets YouTube know you did something right. By interacting with fans in the comments, your notification squad will also super charge your video launch. Building up a lot of viewership when a video goes out is pretty important and this is one way to help out.

However, with every good thing there is always a bad thing as well. Alongside your positive notification squad will be a group of people who are showing up for not the greatest of reasons. This is what I like to refer to as the demotivation squad. These are the people who show up as soon as a video is uploaded to simply dislike your video and complain in the comments. After uploading a video, you may notice you will already have dislikes before anyone could have honestly watched your video. That's because they didn't even watch it.

This can occur for many reasons, but the hateful comments and dislikes can certainly sting. Sometimes they disliked your video because they have a grudge against you. Sometimes they do it because they are jealous of your success. It's important to keep an open mind about things though. Their reasons can be perfectly invalid, but that doesn't mean that every time they are. If you left out a crucial detail in your last video, or if they feel you are milking a topic for views, this is their way of calling you out. Hate can be unwarranted, but it's always worth considering that it could be derived from a misunderstanding. Perceiving yourself through your audience's eyes may help clear this up, so always make sure to indulge in what they are saying in the comments. Communication is the ultimate remedy to confusion.

LIVE IN THE MOMENT

When I first started creating I paced myself the best that I could. There wasn't much to look forward to because no one was watching my videos anyways. I took the time to develop good video concepts and tweak them to my heart's content before releasing them to the world. Once I started getting traction though, things changed. I understand why these changes came about, but sometimes I wish I wouldn't have been so blindsided during the process. Looking back, I felt like I had missed out on a part of my life while also experiencing one of the most unique moments in it. If that sounds confusing, that's because it absolutely is. Let me explain.

Adrenaline kicks in when you start achieving success on YouTube. More so when you have your first break-through. It's an overbearing feeling of excitement and it truly feels magical. You want to keep the feeling going as long as you can and you suddenly become way more serious about your journey altogether. Once this occurs you sort of end up in a vacuum. You love the success you have and it empowers you to pursue it harder than you ever have before. This happened to me soon after breaking one thousand subscribers. My channel was performing very well and in only two months it was at thirty thousand subscribers. The following year was a complete blur for me as I broke one hundred thousand only twelve months after I had broken one thousand. But during this process I realized something quite grim. While this success felt amazing, I realized I had forgotten to live. I existed in a perpetual state of running towards my next goal. I was blinded by the grind of YouTube.

Time is a funny thing. You can be present and absent in the same moment. For the past year I was always living in the future and reflecting on the past. I forgot what it was like to live in the present moment and to enjoy the small things in life. I took a leap of faith and chased after a crazy passion of mine, and while it has been rewarding to the core of my soul, it severely damaged the old me.

During the holiday season soon after I broke 100,000 subscribers I revisited my parents' house for the first time in a long time. This wasn't like any other visit though. I actually left all my worries, expectations, and general life busyness at my own home. This trip was extremely hard on me because I realized my life had been nothing but a goal-driven vortex for the past year. I remember arguing with my mother that the family pets looked different and I was so certain that something had changed about them since my last visit several months ago. In my mind I wasn't wrong, but it wasn't until I left that I realized I was. It wasn't the pets, my parents, or their house that had changed. It was me.

My pets had merely aged and I couldn't believe that this physical change had occurred. I was so driven that I stopped paying attention to the small things in life and in the end, it broke me down. Accepting that I was the one who had changed was very hard to do because even though everyone was happy for my accomplishments, I lost the old me along the way. Somewhere along this winding path in life I took a separate road and left my old self behind. For someone who was often praised for their memory, I realized by living in a constant state of goal-driven flux, I had lost my memory and perception of the current day. I lived in the future and the past, but I forgot to cherish the present. And really, that's what the holidays are all about. Taking the time to celebrate with those you hold dear, as the memories will last you a life time if you keep them close.

YouTube pulled me away from all of that. I missed an entire year of my life because the only thing I paid attention to was my channel. The adventure was certainly life-changing, but in ways that weren't positive as well. I was too aggressive and too driven for my own good. I'd end up being the person who pushed so hard for success that they drove everyone else away in the process. When I finally made it I would be alone because of what I neglected along the way.

That's precisely why I changed my approach to YouTube. Living in the present moment and appreciating life was far too important to give up. You may not realize these things when you are stuck in the funnel of creating, but the second you step out of it life comes back and punches you in the face. It's quite the wallop too! The pain it leaves lingers for several days as you slowly have an existential meltdown.

So just know that while you may want to sprint the

entire time during your YouTube journey, it is incredibly important to slow down and live life. YouTube isn't a race and the path we take as creatives isn't meant to be powered through. It is a life journey and if you force it, you'll more than likely have regrets in the end.

RECHARGING YOUR CREATIVITY

After you've been creating for a while it is easy to become completely burned out. You may become so process-driven that you find yourself operating on zero creativity. If this energy was gasoline, you'd be running on fumes. When this happens, the quality of your work will take a hit and it will not feel as genuine. You won't be creating because you want to. You'll be creating just to get something done and your audience will be able to tell.

So how does one prevent this from happening? The answer is pretty simple. You turn everything off. You turn off your email notifications. You shut off Twitter. You power down your smart phone.

Told you it was pretty simple! But honestly that's only the first step. The funny thing is it took me forever to realize how to properly recharge my creativity because I wanted to always work on the next thing. I didn't always understand the value in disconnecting from everything because I forgot what it felt like. The best thing you can do is leave all your work behind and go and do something fun. Go hang out with your friends or go take a walk in the park at sunset. It will honestly do you wonders. I strongly believe that creativity is a renewable resource. We just need to give it time to recharge. Think of yourself as a walking solar panel that only recharges once you disconnect from everything. Sounds silly right? It totally is. It's also totally true.

I often get my best ideas when I'm not staring at a computer screen. When I'm out and about on a walk my mind is truly free. I often feel like it's meditation in motion. Because my body is moving, the gears in my head just turn naturally. My mind can simply wander once I remove the complexity of my to-do list. When you're in this state of wander you may find yourself coming up with the best ideas. Almost all my greatest videos came to life this way. Heck, even majority of the chapters in this book were birthed through this process. You plant the seed in your mind while you're walking and it grows into something amazing by the time you're done. The idea is free to grow without interruption since you have no other thoughts conflicting with it.

I find walks in nature to be the most rewarding. However, you can recharge your creativity in a ton of different ways. The beauty of it is that the process is different for everyone. The way you recharge may not be the way I do it. If you don't know how to recharge your creativity—experiment! You'll know right away if it is working because you'll find yourself at peace. You won't be thinking about the things you have to do when you get back. You'll get lost in the moment and enjoy what is happening in the present. You will be supercharged when you go to work on your next video after achieving this.

HOW YOUTUBE CHANGES YOUR LIFE

One of the questions I get asked all the time is what it is like to be a YouTuber for a living. My first response is that I absolutely love it. It has changed my life in so many positive ways that I am truly grateful for. Soon after though, I follow up and say that there are a lot of other ways it affects your life. The thing is, you can't really anticipate these changes when starting out because you haven't experienced it yet. Having gone through the journey myself, let's talk about a few!

First and foremost, public recognition is a big one. If you show your face in your videos you may find yourself running into a fan out in the world who recognizes you. These experiences are honestly awesome because you get to connect with a person you may have not talked to otherwise. If they didn't recognize you, you'd just walk on by and would have never met them in your life. I love talking to fans, but at the same time, you can never predict when this will happen. I've been out and about in cities foreign to me and ran into people when I was in a hurry before. I always feel bad when this happens because I have to quickly say hello and scurry on. Most people understand this. However, sometimes when you're not in a hurry you still don't want to talk to people.

If you're shopping for clothes in a store and someone recognizes you from afar, you can't really stay isolated. And if they start a conversation, it is hard to decline chatting. Even though you're there to just relax and shop, you may be pulled into a conversation you may not be feeling. It isn't fully the fans fault because they simply saw a creator whose videos they like. Sometimes when this happens back to back or in places you don't want to, it can get draining.

Also, we've all had those moments when we say bye to people and we leave in the same direction. Imagine saying bye to one of your favorite creators and then continuing to shop alongside them. You'd still be paying attention to them because it was so random that you ran into them. However, from their perspective, they may be self-conscious now. Even though you aren't talking to them, you're still in their bubble and they aren't a face in the crowd anymore. It is a one-sided conversation where they don't fully know you but you know them. Sometimes it is nice to just exist in your own world while you're out doing things. Conversation isn't always welcome but the creator will probably still chat. Just know that this may happen to you one day.

In the most extreme cases, super fans may not know the boundaries between fan and stalker. They usually have the best intentions, but if they are trying to figure out where you live to come and say hello, that's crossing the line. Even though creators care for their fans and appreciate them, they still have their own lives. No one really likes strangers knocking on their doors. Especially when they know everything about them. It's a little creepy.

Never feel bad about having to skip out on a conversation either. While you love your fans, you don't owe them a conversation if you can't have one at that moment. Just because someone stops you to talk doesn't mean you have to. As you grow as a creator this will happen more often than you know. I usually don't flat-out ignore people but I understand why some people have to. I try my best to explain that I'm in a hurry after waving and saying hello.

Often times small- to mid-level creators may struggle with this because they honestly don't earn a ton of money. However, they still have the attention that a celebrity may have. Sometimes this can leave you feeling unsafe because you never know who is out there watching. If your address becomes public knowledge and you have a divided fanbase, you may not know who will show up. You may not have the time or resources to move either.

Be extremely careful where you share your information as a YouTuber. Set up a Google Voice for your phone number so that you can always adapt if things turn sour. Most of these things probably won't happen but I highly recommend taking the precautions regardless. Set up a P.O. Box to use as your address for things that absolutely don't need it. Beyond that, make sure all your accounts are super secure. You wouldn't want an account being compromised that has access to your information. Although it is honestly impossible to truly mask your location and contact info, it doesn't mean you can't take the best precautions you can to minimize the risk. Treat this stuff seriously.

The last thing I want to mention is how your life can become divided further by being a YouTuber. You have your private life and your online life. To make things more complicated, if you play a character on your channel, now you have a further divide. When someone talks to you in person, what category do they fall in? Is this someone you know privately? Do you need to speak to this person professionally out of character yet still as a YouTuber? Or is this a fan who only knows you in-character? In that scenario you have a triple life you are living.

If you're known as a character but are out of character when people meet you, some fans may not make the connection right away. I know it sounds silly, but it is something to think about. If you ever stop being that character people may have trouble growing accustomed to the real you too. It will probably be a drastic change in the eyes of some people. Your true fans will understand, but it may take a while for the public to adjust. This is why balancing your life as a YouTuber can sometimes be difficult.

YOUTUBER
STORIES

YOUTUBER STORIES INTRODUCTION

It's always beneficial to get knowledge from as many different sources as possible. That's why I felt it was important to share the stories of ten other YouTubers. My story may not be the same as yours, but these other creators may be more in line with what you want to pursue. These are creators I absolutely love and I think their stories have a lot of valuable insight in them. They all chose different passions on YouTube and each one found success in their own way.

In this section you'll encounter interviews with all the creators listed below. I asked them a multitude of questions about their own journeys on the platform. I hope their stories further inspire you to continue your YouTube journey!

MAQAROON /
CUTE LIFE HACKS

youtube.com/Maqaroon
youtube.com/CuteLifeHacks

Joanna's channel Maqaroon was one I became familiar with early on in my YouTube career. When I first
started to gain traction I remember seeing some of
her comments on my videos. It honestly made my day,
because when you're still small on YouTube it's really
heartwarming when a larger channel stops by to share
their thoughts and drop a compliment. You are filled
with hope and it empowers you to keep creating. I knew
right away I had to reach out to her about the book I
was writing because of this. She runs a few motivational
crafting channels, so for those interested in pursuing a
similar path, this interview may be right up your alley!

• • •

SwankyBox:
Thanks for joining me Joanna! You currently run a few channels on YouTube and I was hoping you could tell us about them. What types of content do you create and what is the inspiration behind each channel? How long have you been creating for?

Joanna:
I'm really happy you chose to include me in this book! Back in 2013, I ran my own jewelry label called Maqaroon. It was a fun, one-person business and I did all the typical things such as selling on Etsy, at craft fairs, attending trade shows etc. I didn't have any money for promoting, so I decided to create a YouTube channel where I'd craft things on camera while wearing my own bracelets. I started out by demonstrating Japanese needle-felting kits, air-dry clay tutorials, and how to make stuffed animals using socks.

The first two years of YouTube was more of a hobby as it didn't generate enough money to live on, but it did help sales in my online shop so I was happy about that. In summer 2015, I decided to start a more trend-driven YouTube channel called Cute Life Hacks featuring mainstream content (slime, lip balms, edible DIY's, etc). By a massive stroke of luck, the first video I uploaded to Cute Life Hacks (Nutella EOS Lip Balm) went viral so it basically kick-started that channel from day one. By summer 2016, I decided to close my online shop because it was becoming far too much work for one person and I became a full-time YouTuber. In 2017, I teamed up with another blogger from Austria (Lisa) to launch a German channel for Cute Life Hacks.

SwankyBox:
In your past videos on your channel you talk about how

you used to be a manga illustrator. That sounds so cool! I imagine it was probably very time-intensive as well. What made you decide to start pursuing your own creative endeavors? Was there a moment when you knew this was something you absolutely had to give a whirl?

Joanna:
Yes! I loved manga illustration and worked for many years as a manga artist for magazines and various clients. My biggest dream was to write and draw a graphic novel and I sent out countless pitches to publishers in the USA, UK, and Germany. Sadly, I was rejected for all of them. I slowly realized that my underlying goal was to simply create things and then share them with people. All of that is obviously possible through YouTube and that encouraged me to get started. Shortly after uploading my first few videos, I discovered that YouTube essentially connects you directly with people who love the same things you do. This was a lot more fulfilling than working through editors, publishers or other traditional "gatekeepers" in the media. I knew from that point on YouTube would be my perfect job!

SwankyBox:
Is there any reason you decided to become a crafting channel instead of focusing on your other interests? I know you have a background as both a graphic designer and an illustrator. You seem to be interested in gaming as well. What made you settle on crafting and "do it yourself" projects?

Joanna:
I decided to go for crafting because it's the most accessible to a wider audience. My goal was to make tutorials

that people can actually follow. This might sound obvious, but the majority of YouTube DIY videos actually fall under entertainment. They showcase projects that are too complex or extravagant to replicate. I feel the most important thing is to make a physical impact in the life of a viewer. For instance, there's a huge difference between someone watching a video of me speed-painting versus someone spending hours making a gift based on my tutorial and giving that to a loved one. I absolutely love gaming, but that's one area which I promised myself to keep "off limits" from my work so I can forever enjoy it as a hobby!

SwankyBox:
Who are some of your favorite YouTubers? Were there any creators who inspired you to start creating in the first place? What about them made you decide to start carving your own life path?

Joanna:
I was inspired by the Japanese channels Mosogourmet and RRCherryPie when starting my channel. I loved the first-person ASMR-style of filming which made their videos very calming and immersive to watch. I know this sounds very strange, but my favorite YouTube channels actually have nothing to do with DIY. Crafting and lifestyle videos now remind me too much of work and I find it difficult to wind down when watching them. My genuine favorite channels include This Is Dan Bell (extremely talented filmmaker who does vaporwave, urbex, and creepy videos), Steve1989MREInfo (taste tests extremely expired military meals) and How To Cook That (crazy desserts and cakes).

SwankyBox:
Were there any hardships with your channel? I know
for myself I had lots of times where I second guessed
myself if everything would work out. I kept myself
focused, but my mind still tended to wander. What
kind of difficulties did you have with your channel?
Any particular moments you can recall?

Joanna:
One thing I struggled with was having my DIY ideas
stolen by other channels. I have no problems with
people re-filming my tutorials as long as they just
leave a link to my video somewhere in the description
box—which is completely free and requires virtually
no effort. However, you'd be surprised by how many
"creators" feel the need to pretend that a particular
tutorial is their own, or believe that if they re-film
another YouTuber's video step-by-step then this actually makes it their own rightful creation. This bothers
me less now because both of my channels are large
enough so I don't lose out on significant ad-revenue
even if my ideas get copied. I've learned that the best
strategy on YouTube is to keep moving forward and
focus on coming up with new ideas. There's no point
getting angry at plagiarists or trying to chase down
credit, because all of that doesn't help your community
or your channel growth.

SwankyBox:
This honestly happens to me all the time as well. I'm
a strong advocate of giving credit where credit is due,
and thieves really make my blood boil. Your response
resonates with me because I was one of those people
who spent all of my time hunting thieves. I lost out on

so much productivity because of that. It was an unhealthy place to be since I was stressed constantly.

• • •

SwankyBox:
How has Maqaroon and Cute Life Hacks evolved over time? Where do you see them going in the future?

Joanna:
Cute Life Hacks recently crossed 1 million subscribers which is something I'm so proud of. Maqaroon is close behind. However, based on my experience with two channels, I realized that the "sweet spot" of being a YouTuber is between 100K - 500K subscribers—so you must enjoy it! This is the phase where your channel is growing steadily and you gain new, supportive fans with each upload. All the comments tend to be positive and the quantity is manageable for you to read and respond to people individually.

Sadly, once a channel starts reaching 1M, it becomes increasingly difficult to make content that pleases such a huge number of people. This results in a vocal minority of viewers who will constantly leave snarky comments on your videos about how you've changed, sold out, or how they miss the "old" you. Instead of supporting the person behind a channel, many viewers turn against creators once they realize this person is becoming too successful. You may also notice that each new upload triggers a sudden drop in subscribers, which is quite demoralizing no matter how big your channel is. I suspect this is actually caused by YouTube's algorithm rather than active unsubscribes, because it's a phenomenon that suddenly popped up in early 2017. I would love to grow both channels even larger over the next few years, but I have to develop a thicker skin to criticism and try not to please everyone.

SwankyBox:
If someone wanted to start a DIY crafting channel, what kind of advice would you give them? What would you tell your past self based on what you know today?

Joanna:
The best advice I have is to treat your channel like a business—together with a business plan, market research and view/subscriber targets. Lots of people hear stories about the first generation of successful YouTubers who simply filmed vlogs for their family, and believe that passion and luck is all you need to succeed. That may have been true 10 years ago, but YouTube is very different and an incredibly competitive environment right now.

One of the easiest things to do is to research your competitors. Which of their videos are most popular (length, title, thumbnail) and how can you put your own twist on the same theme? Track those channels religiously on analytic websites so you know exactly when they're growing and when they're stagnant. Use that knowledge to your advantage by optimizing your own content so you're always aligned with the most popular people in your niche. Go crazy with SEO keywords without actually being deceitful or creating clickbait. I know this sounds clinical but I found that gathering and analyzing huge amounts of data is the only way you can possibly tackle YouTube's algorithm. I really loved your SwankyBox video on this topic! I think lots of creators go into YouTube being quite naive about how the company and how the world in general works. Every creator is disposable if they don't serve Google's purpose of generating advertiser-friendly views and communities. Just like in a real job, you need to work with the company values in order to advance and every creator should be aware of that.

SwankyBox:
What I love most about your channel is the mission behind it. The idea to inspire girls to live creatively and pursue their ambitions is amazing. I think being content creators really puts us in interesting positions because it grants us the ability to use our creativity to help people. I know with my own channel I try to instill life advice and teach concepts through my videos. I want viewers to walk away having learned something and in some ways I always wanted to be a source of inspiration for the next generation of creators. For my last question, I was hoping you could share your thoughts on the driving force behind why you chose this angle for your channel. It's definitely a very important issue to address in society and I think future content creators could really benefit from hearing your thoughts. Perhaps it may empower them to align their channels to important causes as well.

Joanna:
Thank you so much! There's that famous quote by Simon Sinek which is "People don't buy what you do, they buy why you do it." My YouTube journey started from there. I was personally tired of seeing so much content aimed at females that was solely dedicated to make-up, beauty, weight, and fashion. Social media peddles the notion that a woman's self-worth is almost wholly derived from her physical beauty and her ability to spend money on tasteful things or experiences. There's a thinly veiled connotation in there that physical attractiveness will help you find a man to provide the rest, since there's

also zero emphasis on how women can earn the money required for such a lifestyle themselves.

I think this makes young people unhappy on many levels. Girls are obsessed by the Instagram / YouTube lifestyle and seek out partners who can fulfill this. This also leads to a lot of unhappiness and self-doubt in young men, who are constantly rejected for superficial reasons that may not have existed prior to social-media.

Growing up, I was very nerdy and loved manga, video games, fan art, and anime conventions. Like all teenage girls, I wasn't confident in my own skin but I found comfort in drawing. I realized that the ability to create art or crafts made me happy in a very different way than being asked on a date (which was none anyway) or being invited to a popular party. This is the experience that I want to give my viewers. I wanted to create a place for girls where they are free from the pressures of having to look a certain way or having to buy certain things in order to feel accepted. My content is whimsical, fun, and the vast majority of DIYs are affordable (under $20). Originally, I never wanted to show my face at all (again inspired by Mosogourmet / RRCherrypie), thus reinforcing the idea that it's about what you create and not how you look. However, I realized that this isn't realistic because after a certain size on YouTube your loyal fans do have a right to know who is behind the channel.

Another thing that many viewers may not realize is that I'm actually quite a bit older than they think. I'll be turning 34 in November, so I can work on my message and goals for my channel with the responsibility of an adult. I feel that being given this platform is the biggest privilege of my life and I don't want to let it go to waste. I still have a childish imagination so that's why I genuinely love coming up with all the content and DIYs. But I do feel that being older gives me more distance to see what YouTube can truly offer, rather than just using it to boost my own ego and bank account. Even ad revenue is increasingly unimportant. On our German channel we recently donated €5000 to UNICEF in response to backlash about "wasting food" in our videos. I enjoy SwankyBox because I also feel you're invested in using YouTube for spreading worthwhile messages so I love connecting with the few creators who hold the same values.

SwankyBox:
I think it is truly a blessing. There are honestly so many issues with society in general. One day I hope I'll be able to do more than I am now. I came from a non profit where our mission was helping people keep their promises, and I feel part of that still calls to me. I know that is where my future may end up taking me as well.

● ● ●

I highly recommend checking out Joanna's channels for some awesome crafting videos. They are full of awesome content and perhaps may inspire you to consider a crafting-focused channel as well!

SHESEZ

youtube.com/Shesez

I discovered Shesez's channel through the same blog that originally shared my work. It was amazing to see a breakthrough happen for someone the same way it happened for me, and I knew he was destined for greatness. Shesez is one of the most humble YouTubers around and that spoke to me right away. I was instantly attracted to his Boundary Break series because it was created in a similar fashion to how I produced my videos, but his approach to the medium really stood out. He takes the cameras in video games and shows us the video game world from perspectives we could never see before. It has truly been amazing watching his gaming channel grow and I can't wait to see what the future holds for him.

• • •

What is unique about your content on YouTube? How is it different than most gaming channels out there?

Shesez:
Starting off, I made sure that what I was doing on YouTube was different than what anyone else was doing. I pretty much thought that was the only way to get into YouTube. So having an original idea, which was essentially taking a game camera to find new secrets or perspectives in the game itself, was the way I differentiated myself from other YouTubers. As I was doing that I looked at ways that I could maintain a level of entertainment while at the same time try not to blend in with everyone else. I'm not sure if I ever effectively pulled that off, but seeing other creators helped influence this. I'd see other creators come off very informative but very monotone. They essentially checked their personality at the door. My goal was to see how much of my personality I could fit into the program without distracting the viewer from what they came for. I knew if I walked down this path there was a really good chance that I'd just become someone who just talked about cool discoveries and there wouldn't be much creative freedom for who I was as a person. That's why I always shaped the content the way I did with my personal outros.

SwankyBox:
I think that's the best perspective you can have. For the longest time my personality was secondary to my content and it eventually came back to haunt me. While people loved the topics they didn't get a sense of who I was. Instead of showing up to see me they came for the topic. This would be very clear when I would upload a video about a topic that people weren't completely thrilled with. Viewership would be extremely low because my audience wasn't coming to see me. I was

putting personality second which actually was pretty damaging to my channel.

• • •

SwankyBox:
When you first started YouTube, did things go well or did you run into issues? Were there things that didn't work out?

Shesez:
As for issues along the way, the "adpocalypse" was probably the biggest. That started immediately as the channel started pushing itself over the hill. I had one month of what seemed to be a normal and immediately after that things started going south for the channel financially.

As for creating things and not having it work out correctly, of course. You always want to fight against the machine. You see all these other YouTubers only sticking to one type of video and you want to do all these different types of videos yourself. Unfortunately it doesn't really work that great. If you were solely a personality-based YouTuber you might be able to get away with it, but at that point, you also wouldn't have to think too creatively. You'd just be a viewing glass for the viewer and whatever you decide to do they will follow along with. Whereas on my end, even if you're creative and come up with new ideas they often times won't stick. Or at least in my case, I haven't come up with the right approach to it. I put out a top ten video one time and I knew it would do okay because it was so relevant to what I'm already doing. That's a good example of coming up with an idea that is a compromise between what I'm currently doing and what can be done differently.

SwankyBox:

What moments from your journey as a YouTuber do your remember most fondly? Is there anything that sticks out in your memory when you think back to what you've accomplished?

Shesez:

There's a lot of great highlight moments, but I think the number one thing that made it closest to a heart attack was when I was at my office job. I was typing away at my computer and I just happened to check my Twitter real quick and I saw a whole bunch of people posting links. People were rushing to notify me that my video had been picked up by a pretty popular blog. Sure enough, when I clicked the link there it was. It was the first time they had written about my show. Now I was very familiar with this site and had gone to it for years and years. I would have never imagined in my life that anything I ever produced would be featured on that website. But seeing it there was such an amazingly surreal experience and it made my mind go foggy. It was like my body couldn't handle that level of excitement. So lots of things have gotten me incredibly excited and happy, but never to the point that I felt I had to come down from the excitement because I was worried I'd have to go to the hospital otherwise. That was definitely my number one moment.

SwankyBox:

I know that feeling as well. One of my posts hit the front page of Reddit and it was one of the most crazy things I had ever experienced. You know you typically post something on Reddit and it gets an upvote or two, but coming back to your computer and seeing ten thousand upvotes on your post with it still rising definitely made my heart shoot out of my chest. It's a crazy adrenaline rush.

● ● ●

SwankyBox:
When did you know you wanted to give YouTube a whirl? Were there any creators you had watched over the years that had inspired you?

Shesez:
My number one inspiration without a doubt is the Angry Video Game Nerd. His show was the very first one to ever enlighten me to the idea that video entertainment for video games could even exist. For a long time I just wanted to be a reviewer, not necessarily a mimic of the Angry Video Game Nerd, but I always had strong-minded opinions of video games and I could always break down what I thought logically. I believed that was a good ability to have for reviewing video games. So for a while I wanted to do that on YouTube, and even in general before YouTube I knew I wanted to entertain people. I made stuff on Newgrounds and other websites like that. But James Rolfe was definitely my biggest inspiration. I owe a lot to his videos for inspiring me.

SwankyBox:
How has your series Boundary Break evolved since you started? Where do you see it going in the future?

Shesez:

It's been a pretty fun journey. I had an idea from the very start that I wanted to be more personality-based compared to the more informative YouTubers I've seen in the past. That started in the most purest form in the first few episodes of the show where I 100% did not edit my audio, use a script, and I used one-take clips. Over time everyone was incredibly kind to me in the comment section as I was trying to figure out what people were wanting to see. Constructive criticism was always given out to me and I was told I should work on certain areas of my videos. The more often I saw the feedback the higher chance I actually adopted it into the show. If you watch the first episode on Super Smash Bros Brawl and then my latest video, all the big changes you've probably seen over time were influenced by viewer comments.

The funniest thing that I could probably bookend this question with is that I used to always say "room", but my audience let me know I was saying it odd. The way I said it felt natural to me and those in my immediate area. The internet actually let me know that I was pronouncing it incorrectly, as I wasn't annunciating enough. I very quickly adjusted how I said it because as a viewer, when I'd be watching something on YouTube I would also get irritated when someone would mispronounce something. This is why I try to maintain the mindset of the viewer. If enough people are making a complaint or have a suggestion it's probably a good one. That's how the show has been steered.

SwankyBox:

I had this same thing occur with me since I've always struggled with slurring words and phrases. I'll say "I 'member" instead of "I remember" very often. I'd say the start of "remember" so fast that it would come across as just the word "member." My biggest hurdle as a creator has been around correcting my diction and it has been something I've honestly worked towards my whole life. I was in speech classes when I was younger but I still have a slurring problem to some degree. The feedback in my audience has been very helpful for me.

My most famous mispronunciation comes from one of my most popular videos. It currently has around 1.5 million views. I mispronounced the word amalgamates. I was writing about a topic in a game and when I came across it in my script I just tried to wing it. So I pronounced it as if I was breaking down a Spanish word phonetically. "Ah-mal-ga-mott-tes."

That was the final nail in the coffin. People still tease me about it to this day.

• • •

SwankyBox:
If you could give one piece of advice to an aspiring content creator who is starting today, what would it be?

Shesez:
I've heard this question asked by lots of other people. When I read the answers to it, I often disagree with it entirely. Some of them are just like, "Keep doing it. No matter, just keep doing it." Or they'll be like: "Audio is key. If you don't have good audio, you're not gonna make it." That's all bull crap.

The number one thing that will get you noticed on YouTube is either A: Having an idea that no one's ever done before—but everyone would want to watch. Remember to encapsulate that advice all in one sentence, not take just part of it and assume that it will work because it's a different idea. It's either that or B: Do anything you want, but have the most distinct personality that attracts people. It has to be one or the other. I've never seen a boring person with an unoriginal idea rise through YouTube. If you can do both, then you're gonna rise really fast. One or the other ought to get you somewhere on YouTube, I think.

SwankyBox:
Strong advice. People often asked me why I didn't create my videos with the same energy I often had in my vlogs. I think my problem was that I was a writer first and foremost. I always wanted to write my thoughts down first instead of speaking them. Sometimes I'd lose my personality in the script because it shaped who I was. What I'd end up with was an interesting video that lacked soul. Personality is so important. If you're forgettable people will surely forget you. On the flip side, if you try to act like another creator who already exists—why would someone watch you? They'd just watch the person you're aspiring to be instead. You have to let you personality shine and truly define yourself.

• • •

SwankyBox:
What is something you learned through your audience's reception that you never considered until you started to gain traction as a creator?

Shesez:
One thing in particular was that I was saying "um" and pausing a lot in my commentary. When enough people had said that, I was like, "Well, that's something I can work out. I can go into the audio recording and just clip

it out." A lot of what you hear on my show is actually intense audio editing. You get my personality essentially, but without any of the hiccups. So, like any dead air, any time I hang there for a minute to think—that's all gone in post. It just becomes a fast paced, energetic commentary. I just kept retooling how my commentary worked until people stopped complaining. But, even though they were complaining, it really did put things into perspective. The changes were certainly for the better and I have my audience to thank.

SwankyBox:
When did you know you had to leave your job? It certainly isn't an easy thing to do and YouTube can feel like a gamble. What made you take the leap?

Shesez:
So, I was fiddling with YouTube here and there for a while, but I also had a full-time job. In my mind, that was where my future was. I mean, at the time. I was trying so hard to move up on the ladder, and there was lots of people stifling my success. I'd put in the same amount of work there as I do now as a YouTuber. I always pushed myself a little harder than I should and I took my job very seriously. I think the part of me that took it seriously didn't mesh well with the laid-back nature that you kind of need to have to get along with everybody.

Funny enough, when the YouTube thing started going well, to a small degree I was like, "I gotta basically take care of this baby. I need to be very attentive to YouTube, 'cause it might be my shot of finally getting out of an office job some day." My thoughts did go that far back, admittingly, but if you watch my old Real Talk episodes, I admit that I had no intention of making money off of YouTube. And it's true to an extent. I was comfortable with the idea of never making money off of YouTube and the expectation was never really there. I was willing to make these videos for free, essentially. But when things really started to pick up, that's when things started getting exciting. I was like, "This might actually be a thing that could happen someday."

On the same side, with the office job, things were finally starting to go well too. I basically skipped over a whole bunch of people on the ladder and got the attention of the CEO of the company. The CEO was starting to get pretty impressed with me, and he was inviting me to do more things. This lead to the proposition of actually getting a promotion. He wanted to, basically, give me any kind of job that I wanted. I knew what I wanted to do, but at the same time, my YouTube channel was starting to gain traction. I was beginning to think, "Maybe it's time to take a loss here. Make less money for now with the idea that I could probably turn this YouTube thing into something special. Something career-worthy." Unfortunately what stifled me for a couple of months was this idea of a really well-paying office job with a lot of security to it.

I was at such odds. I didn't know whether or not it was the right decision to stick with the office job, or if it would be the right decision to abandon all of that and start doing YouTube. I stuck out for as long as I could just to test the waters and see what exactly was going to happen to me if I chose to stick around in the office. Although there was a lot of hardships, and a lot of times where it just felt like a natural choice to walk away—I stuck it out. I ended up getting promoted to a job that promised a lot of money. But at the same time, this is when Boundary Break was making 90,000 views a week. Sometimes 110,000 if the game was popular enough. These views equaled a fair amount of income. There was even a month where I made the same exact amount of money doing YouTube as I did with my office job before the promotion and stuff like that.

So, again, the feeling of being at odds only grew more and more. But then it finally started to pull me in the right direction. The YouTube direction of course. When I was test driving this new job for a while, my CEO was just the most . . . I don't know how to put it. He was the most aggressive human-being I've ever had to work with in my life? I don't think that he was a monster. I think it was just the way he plays the game. You either sink or swim. You have to be tough on everyone to get the best out of everyone. I knew that, but at the same time it's like, "Do I have to put up with this, or can I spend a week doing something I love? I could be playing video games, making discoveries, and editing fun videos. Not only that, but my end product would then be cherished by thousands of people."

To summarize, it's A: deal with a person who's yelling down your throat. Or B: have the respect and appreciation from thousands of people. When it got to that point the answer was clear to me. I had to quit this job. I know it's gonna upset some people in my family in close proximity, but I have to do this for me.

So, one day my CEO threatened—well, not threatened—he pretty much said "You are fired." It was a fear tactic he was using against me. I went back to my desk, and I said, "You know what? I'm gonna send an e-mail and say I'm coming right back into your office to talk about something." I went back into that office, and I told him, "Listen, this isn't working out. I need to leave." It was at that point I went into my car, and it was a little shaky and a little scary, 'cause that world was ending. But very quickly my heart rose right back up knowing that I could spend 40 plus hours a week dedicated to YouTube. I have to say it wasn't the worst decision and things are going pretty well now.

If there is one takeaway from this story, it's that I didn't see an immediate opportunity with YouTube and suddenly quit my job. I toughed out both options for as long as I could. I choose the one that stood the test of time for me and offered the most control. So, although there was a lot of anxiety and stress—holding out and letting the two paths show themselves in a much clearer way was probably the smartest thing that I could've done in that situation.

SwankyBox:
The moment I felt like I was no longer in control was when I threw in the towel myself. I was creatively burned out and I felt that my role was expendable. I think sticking it out was a smart choice because jumping into YouTube with no plan or stability is quite the daunting task. I hope your story helps people who may be stuck in a similar situation!

• • •

If you want to watch some of the most innovative and educational gaming content out there, swing over to Shesez's channel and watch Boundary Break. You'll certainly discover some new secrets and perspectives to your favorite games!

SEFD SCIENCE (JABRILS)

youtube.com/SEFDScience

I met Jabril from SEFD Science not too long after I had my breakthrough on YouTube. Fair use was a hot topic on YouTube at the time, and he had produced a few videos on the subject. I recently was dealing with a lot of stolen content on my end, so I ended up sharing my thoughts with him. We synced up over a call and overall it was a great experience. Since that time I've followed him online and have watched his YouTube career evolve. I always love tuning in to see what he's cooking up next!

• • •

SwankyBox:
Now I know your channel changed directions in the middle of 2017, but I as hoping you could tell us a little bit about your channel in general and the new direction

it will be heading in for those who may be unfamiliar with your work.

Jabril:
Absolutely. So I run a little channel called SEFD Science on YouTube, although I might be changing it to simply my name "Jabril" soon. [laughs] In its original inception, I was going to focus on presenting science research in a documentary-style kind of way. I'd then exemplify that research with some sort of in-public demonstration at the end of each episode. But I quickly learned after producing a few episodes that the production turnarounds for such a show on YouTube would make it near impossible for me to compete—especially while being on the wrong side of a million subscribers. So I removed the in-public demos and stuck to just presenting science research in the most fun and coherent way possible. This helped improve my production turnarounds, but they still take a long time due to being on average 20 minutes per episode.

But as you've alluded to, in the middle of 2017 I changed the direction of my channel yet again to focus heavily on computer science. Although this might be considered a huge change, it's still my goal to keep most of what my audience expected and loved from my old show despite the focus change.

SwankyBox:
I originally discovered your channel when you had switched over from doing pranks a while back. What made you decide to change directions and start a new channel focused on science? Choosing to start over when you already had a decently large following surely is a difficult move. But not only that, you chose to move into an entirely new genre. What lead to this decision?

Jabril:
Believe it or not deciding to start a new channel focusing on a completely new category was probably the easiest part about that entire process.

Back in 2015 I had celebrated my four year anniversary with producing my prank channel. When reflecting on those four years it all just felt incredibly empty and almost useless. The original team of three that I started with was reduced to just myself and our relationships were in questionable states due to creative differences. I had collaborated with a decent number of people within the prank space, but could only get a reply from maybe two or three tops. I'd worked with huge companies like Nickelodeon for example and even had the honor to premiere a few exclusive videos on live television. I had a few projects that went viral and I even became an internet meme for a bit (search "little pot gif" if you're interested). I experienced a lot of really cool stuff that sounds great on paper. But after it was all said and done, my Nickelodeon contacts wanted nothing to do with me. Again, I couldn't ask any of the people I've worked with for anything. The top people within the prank space didn't really care to empower those below them.

The prank space had drastically changed and the only stuff that was getting views and attention were things I did not morally agree with. I felt the general prank audience was actually pretty abusive and didn't have a great appreciation for the content and its creators. Not to mention the biggest issue above all, I started thinking about how my projects weren't helping to make the world a better place. That mentality is what inspired who I am today.

In 2015 the main thing on my mind was obviously that this prank operation had ran out of value in relation to my goals. So what was next? It was this that lead me to launching an educational show. Out of all of this mental chaos I went through, the true beauty was that I essentially got a great opportunity to update what I spent the most time on in my life: YouTube. I could reflect on the person I became over the past four years. I could only imagine how miserable I would be if I were still trying to produce competitive prank videos today—oh geez.

When I started SEFD Pranks in 2011, I was pretty much fresh out of high school and super interested in hijinks, social experiments, and what not—but during those four years my interests evolved into discussing more complex ideas, watching a crazy number of documentaries, and overall just learning. So it only made sense to not only try to contribute to the science community with my own unique spin on it, but also update the focus of what I spend the most time on—which was YouTube. This in turn resulted in spending a lot time researching and learning about new fascinating things.

SwankyBox:
Do you have any advice for creators who are still trying to figure out what they want to do? Going from entertainment, to science, to eventually branching out into computer science specifically for your own research is quite the journey. I know often times people get frustrated because sometimes they don't know what they're supposed to be doing. I was hoping you could shed some light about that experience.

Jabril:
I think the best advice I can give is to stop worrying about what you think you're "supposed to be doing" and simply "do what you want to do." I think whomever is constantly searching for what they're "supposed to be

doing" in regards to YouTube will always be behind the curve. When they think they find the answer, they are simply unknowingly copying someone else's success. They will become PewDiePie Clone #31,765 or Casey Neistat Clone #234,234.

My advice is simply do what you want and most importantly do what makes you happy. Even if that sounds completely backwards. If something as obscure as collecting cereal boxes makes you happy, don't ever underestimate the value you could bring to the world by sharing that passion. The best part is, it will never feel like work because you already do it for free!

Furthermore, I think a really important thing that a lot of people interested in growing a large audience on YouTube should internalize is that growing a channel is statistically about personal journey. It's all about expression. Large audiences on YouTube generally explode because of their videos, but in large part due to personality, relatability, and novelty. Think about it this way: There are only 24 hours in a day. Do you really want to watch YouTuber A and three people trying too hard to be YouTuber A? Or would you rather watch YouTuber A, B, C, and D who all bring something unique to the table even if it's the same topic? I think the answer there is obvious unless you're doing a research paper on YouTuber A or something. My final piece of advice is to fully embrace who you are as a unique individual and use that to drive your content. This is the beauty that most people still don't understand about the internet. It's a place where anything is possible, even something as scary as, dare I say, fully expressing your weird and natural self. Dun dun dunnnnn!

SwankyBox:
I definitely hid who I was for the longest time online. I was a shell of a person because I feared what the world

might think of me. Breaking out of that feeling truly made me feel free. It was a weird mental prison I was keeping myself in. I think a lot of creators suffer from similar issues.

• • •

SwankyBox:
When you first started creating on YouTube did you have any issues? What was the hardest thing to overcome?

Jabril:
I think the hardest thing for me when I first started creating YouTube videos was coming to terms with imperfection. As anyone who creates anything would know, when you have an idea, it is utterly sharp and shiny in your mind. As it rightfully should be. But when you bring that idea to life, there's a low probability that it will be an accurate representation of how you envisioned it in your head. This is most likely for many different reasons. The most difficult thing for me was just coming to terms with the fact that I had to show people something that wasn't the best work I was capable of. My perfectionist tendencies hated this!

But I think this was a really important part of my journey as this process yielded a very valuable lesson. Perfection only exists in one's mind. Perfection is subjective and merely a construct. No one knows intent vs mistakes except the artist. Just keep your mouth shut and move on to bigger and better things. [laughs]

If you ever watch the director commentaries of your favorite films or TV shows, you'll find this apparent. Things that you really enjoy as a consumer might actually be a frustrating or disgraceful mistake on behalf of the production team. If you struggle with this as I used to, watch a lot of DVD / Blu-ray commentaries on some of your favorite stuff. You'll learn that even the things that you use as inspiration are riddled with mistakes and errors outside of director's intent. [laughs] Your thoughts are completely normal.

Ultimately, I learned that especially with YouTube, perfecting projects isn't the important part. Learning how to complete something and becoming more efficient at finishing projects holds the real value.

SwankyBox:
Absolutely. [laughs] Perfectionism is a creator's worst "best" trait. I can't echo your thoughts enough. I take pride in my work, but I would spend all my time on one video making it the best it could possibly be. However, all that time I spent over-polishing it could have gotten me through my next video. It can also stop you from creating in the first place.

• • •

SwankyBox:
Who are some of your favorite YouTubers? Were there any creators who inspired you to start creating in the first place? What about them made you decide to start carving your own life path?

Jabril:
Aww man, don't get me started! [laughs] Mega64 was my first ever favorite YouTube channel and they still are champions till this day for me. In fact, their channel was a huge inspiration for us launching our prank channel back in 2011. They were just doing incredibly cool and hilarious things. It was super inspiring. But I think the biggest draw was that they were completely

self-funded. I was going to film school at the time and they were teaching us all the traditional routes in film, but Mega64 were shining beacons that completely went against that convention. It corrupted my little brain and made me start a YouTube prank channel. Little did I know this easy barrier-to-entry would later completely ruin the prank space. [laughs]

Vsauce is still an all time favorite. He was the first educational channel that I gravitated towards as I am sure he is for most people. But he really showed me that educational content can also be highly interesting and entertaining. After realizing this, it lead me to start my own education-based channel.

I am enamored with the channel Lemmino. I think the draw of Lemmino for me is that his accented voice is super calming and inviting. Sorry to get ultra poetic about a dude's voice, [laughs] but his voice mixed with his choice of scoring for his projects just takes me to a place. Mentally like a warm cozy cabin with a fireplace burning in the winter time, [laughs] I digress. He spends a lot of time polishing his projects—arguably too much time. He has a great eye for finding facts and tidbits that I almost have *never* heard of but are extraordinarily interesting. His content always takes me to a great place.

Allen Pan's Sufficiently Advanced channel is also one of my favorites. I am honored to be able to call Allen a friend now, but the draw to Allen's channel for me was that he was an engineer that just built a bunch of cool things just to see if he could. Probably the coolest thing is that he has a book filled from front to back with million dollar video ideas that everyone wants to see but hasn't yet. I am always anxiously awaiting to see what ideas he decides to bring to life with every upload.

There are countless others but I am going to lump both That One Video Gamer & SwankyBox as my last pick. The draw to these channels for me is that I would wager most kids born from the 80s+ played many video games in their childhood. The aesthetic of these channels bring me back to when I was a kid with almost endless free time to play video games. There are a good amount of number of channels like these out there, but I think these two are near the top for me because their aesthetic is rather consistent and I really enjoy that. I love playing these channels before I go to sleep to give my dreams a little encouragement. [laughs] Don't tell anyone my secret, alright?

SwankyBox:
I'm flattered that you included me! When I was younger I realized I used to love watching Mega64's videos despite not ever realizing it was their channel. I remember the video where they dressed up as the merchant character from Resident Evil 4. It was honestly amazing. Hard to believe it has already been 10+ years though!

• • •

SwankyBox:
How do you balance all of your passions at once? YouTube itself can be considered a full time endeavor. Being someone who juggles many interests, I still find myself having difficulties doing so. Any words of wisdom in this area for new content creators who may have multiple interests?

Jabril:
It definitely isn't easy but after being forced to confront this for mental health precautions, I think I have something very valuable to share here: Stay completely mindful of your thoughts and enable them to the best

of your ability. The best way I know to explain this is just to share my own personal story.

In 2016 I was one year into producing my educational channel and absolutely loving the content. I was loving my audience, the growth, and the things it enabled me to do. Interviewing experts and visiting various locations for video ideas felt amazing, but I also had this super burning desire to write games and software again. I couldn't fight the desire of wanting to solve interesting problems, imagine new game ideas, and produce products. So I tried to do both. I'd produce videos for my educational channel and write games and software on the side. The result of that solution was that I ended up producing both mediocrely. None of it felt meaningful. My YouTube growth stagnated because I was spending half of my days coding something up. I wasn't making any great game / software progress because I was afraid. Afraid to start projects that would keep me away from thinking about my upload schedule. I was stuck in complete limbo and it was a mess.

So eventually I hit a fork in the road. Most of my friends and family advised to choose either my educational channel or developing games / software. I thought for sure this would have helped me finally escape limbo. However, being mindful of my thoughts at the time and enabling them the best of my ability is what lead to the realization that obviously these both occupied my mind in a relatively even manner. Eliminating one or the other might of caused even more stress or non-satisfaction in my life. So why not instead just figure out some cool way to merge the two? Which is exactly what I eventually did and is the reason why my channel is based on computer science today. I kept my best interest in mind, and because of it, I am able to do all the things that I love completely stress free.

Thankfully, I have the absolute best audience. They overall trust that I will deliver them content that they know they'll enjoy regardless. They understand that people evolve with time. They've been very accepting of my channel change to computer science, and it's honestly the best feeling ever.

SwankyBox:
What is the most difficult part of creating on YouTube? Anything come to mind right away?

Jabril:
I think the most difficult part of YouTube is that competing on YouTube over the years has gotten layered with dimensions.

When it first started off, you were just competing with other YouTuber for subscribers and views. Then the dimension of ad revenue came in and now you're also competing for ad dollars. Then these huge production companies came in with big budgets and now you have to take that into consideration. After that celebrities came in. Now your competing against other YouTubers, production companies with big budgets, and celebrities which all require their own optimization techniques. Then came this crazy thing called the algorithm that gained a lot of power over content. You're competing to optimize that while also having to produce videos around automated systems. Fair use consideration and demonetization principles are then added. [laughs] It has just became so layered, so many things you have to think about consciously or subconsciously when producing content. That's the first thing that comes to mind.

SwankyBox:
What does the future look like for your channel? Any exciting things you're working on that you want to share?

Jabril:
Man the future for my channel is looking incredibly magnificent and I am able to quantify this because finally my collaboration pitches are garnishing interest! Since the beginning of my YouTube adventure I think I've been sending out the same rate of collaboration pitches. Finally with this computer science passion, people are interested in what I am pitching and I can't help to take that as I've finally got something good brewing. It's all thanks to enabling my thoughts!

As for exciting things I'm working on, I've got a lot of really drool-inducing collaboration pitches out but most aren't confirmed so I wont speak about them in detail. Mainly because I believe being boastful about unconfirmed stuff is the fastest way to ensure it doesn't happen. [laughs] But there is one coming up very soon and it may be out by the time this book is out. I might be collaborating with Physics Girl to create a hologram video game. I can not *wait* to do this one. Fingers crossed! Another I am hoping to do is an unseen Dragon Ball Z hardware/software collaboration idea which I think will be a lot of fun. Lots of machine learning AI stuff is coming up as well.

To say I am excited for the future is a *huge* understatement!

• • •

Looking for some quirky computer science videos? Hop on over to SEFD Science and give it a gander. Great topics and brain food all around!

LIGHTSEN

youtube.com/lightsen

Lightsen is a creator that popped up in my comment section not long after I started finding success on YouTube. She's an incredible animator and we bonded over the love we had for the same games. She was definitely an inspiration for me as I started to get a footing on my grand adventure as a YouTuber, and I certainly cannot recommend her humorous animations enough!

• • •

SwankyBox:
Thanks for agreeing to do this! I was hoping you could start off by telling those who may be reading what do you do on YouTube as a creator?

Lightsen:
Hey! I'm Lightsen, a 26 year old geordie from the UK. I like to spend way too much of my time animating

slapstick cartoons for YouTube. When I'm not animating, I'm playing games, messing around on the piano, and recently learning the trombone for purely comical sound effect reasons.

SwankyBox:
One of the things I really like about your channel is that it has simply stood the test of time. A lot of people abandon the channels they started when YouTube first came out and start new ones. However, you have videos all the way back to 2006! I think that's pretty cool! Over the years you never lost your passion for drawing and it has certainly evolved. Did you know you always wanted to be an animator on YouTube? Why did you choose animation and YouTube specifically?

Lightsen:
Thank you! I always feel ancient every time the odd comment comes in along the lines of: "This was uploaded before I was born!" but on the other hand it's a huge privilege to be told that your videos are a part of someone's childhood, no matter how small.

I think it's a huge shame when people abandon their channels so easily. No matter how bad my first videos were, it's really nice to look back at how far I've come in skill and quality now. And hopefully new artists can look at my early stuff and say "I can already pass this point with my art skills now, so there's nothing stopping me from working hard and improving over the years too". It can also be an encouragement for those who's YouTube growth is very slow. It took me 6 years to pass 3k subs. You never know what may happen if you just stick to it!

You mentioned an important point though—not losing your passion for art. The best way to do that is to draw and create what you enjoy of course! I think people can tell if you have a real interest and enthusiasm in what you do, and it makes everything better. If you have the enjoyment and passion to go that extra mile when creating, the viewers notice, and it's an everyone-wins situation!

Looking back to before I joined YouTube, I didn't even know the term for animation. Here I was in school, making basically a slideshow of MSPaint drawings with a mouse, and mistakenly naming them "movies." After making a few, I realized that the site I was using to post drawings didn't support video uploads. Later, thanks to a recommendation by a friend, I finally joined YouTube in 2006 with the sole intention of having a place to host my videos. What I wasn't expecting was for a few comments to trickle in and encourage me to post more. At the same time I was influenced a lot by Newgrounds, and wanted to make my own cartoons pretty early on. One day, my school got a bunch of new programs on our computers, Flash8 being one of them, and so I ended up spending every single lunch and break time working on my first animations. Some of them got found by the teachers and got deleted! Probably for the best though. I pressed on, and since then animation has always been by biggest hobby.

Looking back now, although what I have made in the past is definitely amateur—and that's being generous—the support I got from a few random viewers back then is what led to me sticking with YouTube for the longest of long terms. The site has changed a ton over 11 years, and the community is thousands of times bigger. But there have always been fantastic, supportive, and constructive people out there, and they know just how to make your day when you post. I'm so happy to have been a part of this fun community for so long.

SwankyBox:
Animation is one of the most time-intensive forms of content creation out there. Even though my animations are relatively simple on my channel, they certainly take a lot of time. How long does it typically take you to make an animation from scratch? If it is a long time, is that amount of time daunting or do you enjoy the process?

Lightsen:
Your animation work was always my favorite part of your videos. It made them really stand out! For my own projects, it has been around 4-8 months to finish an animation depending on complexity. It definitely can be daunting if you don't thoroughly enjoy the process. Sometimes I remake or change completed scenes, making days worth of work a waste. Nevertheless, animating has so many different parts to it. You don't have to get yourself stuck doing the same thing for too long. There is script writing, storyboarding, lip synching, sound effects, scene transitions, backgrounds, effects, etc. Personally I really enjoy the process, especially if it's good old-fashioned slapstick!

SwankyBox:
I'm glad you enjoyed it! Honestly, I put the animation work in because I saw no one else was doing it. I saw it as an opportunity to differentiate myself. Although, my animations are a tad easier since I'm working with developed assets already. Creating everything from scratch would surely take a long time!

• • •

SwankyBox:
I noticed you have two types of content on your channel. You do fan animations of some of your favorite games,

but you also have your own original series called Lizard Cops. How did Lizard Cops come about? How is it balancing between the two types as well?

Lightsen:
Lizard cops was actually a project I did in animation class. We could pick what we wanted to do for our 3rd year. Since I wanted to work on my YouTube channel, and I happened to love reptiles, I thought, "finally, this is my chance to make a cartoon series!" It's been a dream of mine since I was little, so I'm overjoyed to see it reach a small audience.

However, it's also a lot harder than I realized. Balancing between the parodies and originals is a tough call. People are a lot more critical on an original series because it has other animated originals to compare to. There are some absolutely fantastic original cartoons and pilot episodes on YouTube! Since I found Lizard Cops to be a much bigger project than I expected, I didn't feel skilled enough to really showcase how I wanted it to be from my imagination, and put it to the side after the second episode. I've decided to return to it only once I felt skilled enough to bring it to life properly. It does make a nice break from the parodies though. It's really rewarding to make something 100% original. I'm just about ready to bring it back though—bigger and better I hope!

SwankyBox:
For those who want to start animation on YouTube, but may feel too intimidated or simply don't know where to start, what advice could you give to anyone aspiring to follow in your footsteps?

Lightsen:

Don't feel intimidated by the YouTube system, or by other YouTubers, and do your own thing. Do it for fun and don't focus on the numbers. It took me many years to improve, and I focused completely on my content. Rather than focusing on tags, algorithms, self-promotion and trends—you can more wisely invest that time into improving your content first. All those other points are important to consider, but don't wrap yourself up in them so much that you ignore the actual videos. Just go ahead and create, don't worry about how bad your first animations will be. Every post is a stepping stone and you will probably learn something new each video. The more mistakes you make and fix, the more you improve!

With regards of getting a foothold in YouTube with animation, I would recommend asking creators you really like. Smaller channels will be easier to contact of course. Ask if you can have their permission to animate a short scene you enjoy from their videos, or perhaps an intro for them. Gamers and vloggers are always very happy to have animations made for them, and you'll likely have the mutual benefit of them shouting you out. Some channels like GameGrumps actually pay animators for their hard work if they apply through them. The final video is posted on their channel though. This is a great place to start since your audio/music is provided for you with the clip, and it's likely some of the channel's fans will be excited to see their favorite moments animated.

And lastly, please don't hesitate to reach out to other animators! The animation community on YouTube is very welcoming. Having friends to work alongside with will make YouTube even more enjoyable for you. Reach out to them on Twitter and art sites.

SwankyBox:
What has been the greatest obstacle you've had to over-come as an animator on YouTube?

Lightsen:
Probably coming up with an idea your super excited about, and having to wait half a year before it ever sees the light of day! The struggle to remain patient is very real.

From a technical standpoint, the hardest thing for me to get right is joke timing and sound/volume levels. But thanks to comments pointing out the flaws, I've learned what it is I need to improve on. Getting fresh eyes to look at my work and giving me feedback is great, but taking on board criticism has been absolutely vital to my art improving over the years. I can't thank them enough!

SwankyBox:
What software do you use to animate with? I feel like a lot of times there are so many options out there and people don't know what to use. Do you have a specific process for your animations?

Lightsen:
This is probably the most common question I get online. I like to use Flash CS4, though the work I do with it can be performed with any version of Flash new and old. Probably like most other animation software out there. Other very useful tools I use are Audacity and MPEGStreamclip. Audacity is a free sound recording and editing program. MPEGStreamclip is another free program that can convert a huge 10GB .mov file into a manageable 20MB .mp4 without any loss in quality.

The animating process is pretty simple. Write a basic script, then storyboard it out in Flash as an animatic. That's basically an animated comic. Usually I add the sound in next, but lately I've been leaving the vocals until later so I have more time to change my mind on lines. Next, I split the animation up with an estimate of the timing, and chop it into separate files for each minute's worth of animation. This helps keep you free from lag! Once everything is fully animated, I export all the files as a .mov and import them into After Effects. There I just clip them together and re-export it as one file. However, there will be easier ways to do this I'm sure!.

SwankyBox:
What are your hopes for the future? Are there any cool projects coming down the pipeline you'd like to talk about?

Lightsen:
I hope to be able to continue with animation on YouTube for as long as possible. It has been a huge privilege to have so many supporters and it drives me to make each upload better than the last. For the future, I have plenty planned with animations ranging from a new Pokémon mini series, a Spyro the Dragon 3-part series, continuing with Twitch Plays Pokémon Animated, and also bringing back Lizard Cops bigger and better. Now If only I had more hours in the day to get this all done!

• • •

I highly recommend checking out Lightsen's channel on YouTube. If you're looking for some comedic animations, you'll certainly enjoy her work!

COLE AND MARMALADE

youtube.com/chrispoole20

A few years ago I was obsessed with internet cats. Who am I kidding? I still am. During this phase is when I stumbled upon the channel Cole and Marmalade. Having moved out of my parents house and not having any fur babies of my own, I lived vicariously through several pet channels. Up until this point I didn't know the full story behind it though. Chris, who runs the channel, was still a bit of a mystery for me. He seemed like the perfect person to reach out to about running a pet-focused channel and it was great chatting with him.

• • •

SwankyBox:
How would you describe your channel to someone who hasn't watched your content before?

Chris:
The channel actually includes a lot of different things.
We have videos focused around the efforts of big cat res-
cues and also educational and awareness-raising videos
with Cole and Marmalade. We do stuff to promote black
cats—showing people how great they really are. We
touch on pet adoption and spaying and neutering too.
There is feral cat stuff with TNR (Trap-Neuter-Return)
and of course funny videos as well. We try to keep a
good balance!

It's a family-friendly channel. I'm pretty aware
there's lots of kids watching our videos so we keep it
all family-friendly. When there's a more serious educational video we do a warning before. That way people
are aware in case the video covers anything gross or
maybe surgery or something like that.

It's a good mix of fun stuff and educational content.
We're just trying to make a difference. That was my
main goal when I started the channel. When we rescued
Cole, we wanted to show people how cool black cats
are. To raise awareness about their low adoption rates
and try and make a difference through video and social
media basically.

SwankyBox:
I think that dovetails into my second question, which
is what made you decide to start creating on YouTube?
Out of all your passions, why did you choose to focus
on cats?

Chris:
I'm not sure if you knew this, but I used to work at a
big cat rescue in Florida. That's where I started making
videos ten years ago. I was the social media video guy at
a big cat sanctuary. We used to shoot news about tigers

and lions being rescued, and people keeping those pets in America—believe it or not. They're rescued from police raids or they're ex-circus cats. That was my day job and I used to live on the property. I used to have tigers, lions, and leopards as neighbors.

Then, we adopted Cole in 2012. We found out about black cats being the first to be euthanized and last to be adopted in animal shelters. So, me and the wife decided to make a video called "10 reasons to adopt a lucky black cat."

It kind of became my hobby on the weekends to film Cole and put together funny, silly videos. We wanted to try to show people that black cats were cool. They've always been my favorite kind of cat. I used to have a black cat when I was growing up as a kid. When I found out that they had low adoption rates, that became my hobby. Making big cat videos during the week at work, and then making small cat videos on the weekend. That's how I started five years ago, now it has grown into this giant thing, but it's cool.

SwankyBox:
I always found the whole black cat thing interesting. Is it a result of people thinking they bring bad luck? Or is it a different thing altogether that causes the low adoption rates?

Chris:
It's the bad luck and stigma surrounding them from hundreds of years ago. Still exists today. It's different depending on the country. I think in Japan they're good luck. In England, if you give a black cat to the bride on the wedding day, it's a sign of prosperity and good luck in the future. There is a thing surrounding the bad luck, but then it's also because people always want

to choose the more colorful cats. The cats with pretty patterns—they photograph better. So, people always tend to choose them over black cats. They can't win, really. With all the shelters out there, there's always just more black cats than other cats.

SwankyBox:
I have a lot of friends who have two black cats. All of my friends have always had them in pairs, which is kind of interesting now that I think about it. Going back to the reason why you started pursuing this, that's also what I loved about your channel. I did not actually know about your past, but I knew about what you were doing. When I emailed you, you said you were going to a big cat sanctuary in Africa. You were gone for an entire month volunteering and that's really cool. I was hoping you can tell me a little about that experience. And beyond that, what advice do you have for upcoming content creators for aligning their channels to things that they are truly passionate about, or causes that need champions?

Chris:
Africa was really cool and I went to two sanctuaries while I was there. One was called Emoya. I spent two-and-a-half weeks there and then I went to Panthera for a few days. After that I then spent a few days in Cape Town visiting some local shelters.

It is believed that there are 10 to 20 thousand privately owned big cats in America. It's legal in many states and it differs from state to state. But then in states where it's illegal to sell big cats, people tend to own them anyway and get away with it because there's just not enough money or manpower to go around checking all these properties and enforcing the laws. As for how it's enforced, it's normally just a slap on the wrist—a small fine—and they get to keep doing what their doing. It's a massive problem from an animal welfare standpoint. Tigers being kept in garages and small backyard cages. From a public safety standpoint, there's people out there who don't even know their neighbors have a pet tiger. Hundreds of big cats have escaped in the past. People get attacked and killed. It's a giant problem people aren't aware of. That was why I was involved in a big cat rescue in Florida.

As for advice to future content creators, make your passion shine through the content you produce. If you're passionate about something, do your best to educate people and raise awareness. I always do it in a fun way too. Sometimes you can get too preachy and start making videos that are too serious all the time. You have to try and keep people's attention. The bottom line is, your passion needs to show through, and if you're truly passionate about a subject or cause, that's normally evident in the videos you make. Just be yourself and do your best to communicate the information in a fun way. Think outside the box. That's what I always try and do.

SwankyBox:
I think that's good advice, even for myself to hear. Sometimes I would try to instill life-concepts or ways I would want society to be. People have said it comes off too preachy. I think what you said is a good point. You have to find a middle ground for that. We would love to just be able to talk about it, but unfortunately, in order to get people to listen who may not be on the same page, we have to take extra steps.

• • •

SwankyBox:
How do you constantly keep things interesting on your channel? Often times whatever passion you choose to create around can feel like work if you don't approach it the right way. You wouldn't want to put any additional stress on your pets either. If you have a pet-focused channel, you have to be mindful that you're not stressing your pet out or forcing them things they don't normally do. If someone wanted to start a pet channel today, what advice would you give them so they approach it correctly?

Chris:
Working with cats can be difficult at times. You want them to go left and they go right. You have to learn how to fully earn their trust. Since we built this relationship with Cole and Marmalade we have it pretty easy now. We involve them in everything and keep them excited. We try our best to give them a good life. We never force them to do anything if they don't want to do it. That kind of goes without saying for me, but other people might be so focused on trying to get video views and they forget that.

SwankyBox:
Obviously my focus is gaming, but when we started our pet channel on the side, we wanted to make sure that everything we were doing involved our cats having fun naturally. Even though I liked all the internet cats, I think a big problem with them was people were taking these cats to conventions and social gatherings. The cat would stress out and I would feel super bad for them.

Chris:
Yeah, that's another good point. I feel bad for all our fans because they see me with Cole and Marmalade all the time. I just recently went to Cat-Con in LA. It was literally 12,000 cat people, 2 days in LA, and they all wanted to meet Cole and Marmalade. They're all saying "Why didn't you bring them so we can meet them?" That would stress my cats out, stress me out, and it's not worth it in my eyes to do that to them.

In regards to creating content in the home, I've got a list of different subjects and video types. I'm always jotting ideas down and have a video camera within arms reach. If the cats start doing something funny and crazy, I can just grab it and start filming. I then organize all the footage for future videos.

Going back to what you mentioned before, there's a lot of people out there that go to animal shelters and adopt a weird looking cat or dog. Or they go buy from a breeder. They look for a specific breeds and a certain look. They do this in hopes of trying to make their cats and dogs famous. You have to be responsible about it.

SwankyBox:
I agree wholeheartedly. Remember why you started creating or why you want to do it. Don't make it a fame thing. I think that's the biggest issue. If you go into a YouTube channel with the idea that you want to become famous, you're doing it for the wrong reason. Whereas, if you want to create something cool with your pet, then you're still enjoying that moment. You can of course branch out, but make sure your actions aren't being guided by the wrong reasons.

• • •

SwankyBox:
Obviously you had success on your first channel Cole and Marmalade. What made you decide to start a second channel? I'm not sure if you started that second channel before or after. How has this new endeavor been? What made you decide to make a second channel where it's more focused on you as a person?

Chris:
That was pretty recent—like a year ago. I wanted to start vlogging while going to cat shelters and events. More day-to-day unedited stuff. Clips from whenever I shot the clips. More personal. With Cole and Marmalade videos, they're all like edited to music. I wanted this second channel to be more natural like a video diary. To do more big cat content and be more on the preachy side of things. I wanted a different channel that was more education-based. Still going to have fun on it, but I wanted it to have less to do with Cole and Marmalade.

SwankyBox:
I think it's a really cool outlet. Your mission is to entertain and to educate people through your main channel. However, I think your super-fans have also navigated to your second channel. They know you a little bit better, and they don't mind the preachy content because they can see the direct results in action. The videos of you taking in rescue kitten may inspire them to go and volunteer at a shelter. Perhaps adopt themselves. All of these things have more impact because it's not a glorified video—it's literally how it is and what is happening in that moment. It's raw.

• • •

SwankyBox:
When you first started on YouTube, did you run into any hurdles or did you start to gain traction quickly? How did you gain traction before you established yourself?

Chris:
I had it pretty easy because I was used to making cat videos from doing the big cat rescue videos. I think it was like four or five years before I started making Cole and Marmalade videos. I had my style pinned down and knew what worked and what didn't work. People seem to share a lot of our videos, like the first one we made "10 reasons to adopt a lucky black cat." That went viral. I had it pretty easy compared to others. Different sites picked up on the concept and shared it and then we started getting a pretty good following easily. Then Marmalade came along and that's when things apparently started to get crazy. He's got that pretty unique looking face. I had it decently easy, honestly, compared to other people.

SwankyBox:
I had a very similar situation happen to me except it was a little later on. A few websites definitely helped me get some of my first viewers when they shared my videos. I had even sent them over myself. Something like that can definitely jumpstart a channel.

● ● ●

SwankyBox:
So I guess for my last question, what does the future look like for your channels? Are there any exciting things that you're working on?

Chris:
Mainly I just want to keep up the production rate that I've had so far. That's the danger for some creators—myself included. You get to that point where you've got a good following and then you start slacking off somewhat. You start creating less or put less effort into videos. I just want to keep making good stuff.

Now that I've got this big following I can reach and educate more people. I just want to make sure I keep up with the quality content while inspiring and educating. To make people laugh and feel better with consistent, good videos. No real major plans at the moment. There's no Cole and Marmalade Movie coming out anytime soon, let's put it that way. [laughs]

• • •

If you're looking for some good cat fun, swing over to Cole and Marmalade. There are a lot of fun and insightful videos on the channel!

ROLY

youtube.com/RolyUnGashaaHD

I recently discovered Roly during the process of writing the beginning of this book. I was randomly recommended a video one day and from that point forward I binge-watched a ton of Roly's content. Honestly, the energy and vibes of the channel are so great I felt I had to reach out for an interview. Beyond that, I find the content very informative and it's amazing how many people struggling with identity gain a sense of direction from Roly's videos. Certainly check out Roly's content when you have the chance!

● ● ●

SwankyBox:
Starting off I was hoping you could tell me a little about what you do on YouTube for those reading who may be unfamiliar with your channel.

Roly:
My channel is called Roly, which is what my name is. On my channel, I do LGBTQ+ videos, talk about coming out stories, and things that the LGBTQ+ people have to go through in our daily lives. Also, just to tell people that you can be yourself regardless of what people say. I also do piercing and body modification videos, and share my thoughts about it. Like how to do it safely, or what good or bad piercings to get. I also like to do videos on funky piercings, or a piercing lookbook for a set of styles.

SwankyBox:
I know when I first started YouTube I really didn't know what I wanted to focus my energy on. However, you seemed to have found an awesome balance between two of your passions. On top of that, both are these are extremely helpful things for your viewers. What made you decide to focus on the LGBTQ+ community and body modifications for your channel? Did you always know that would be your direction?

Roly:
I have been doing YouTube now since 2008, so I've been here a very, very long time. When I first started my channel was basically a mess. I didn't really know what I wanted to do. I did LGBT things. I did some music. I kind of did piercing things, but not too much. Very, very rarely. I did vlogs about my life, and it was just basically all over the place. And so for the first seven years, I only grew about 30,000 subscribers. That's a lot of people, but in the course of seven years, you think a lot of those people had probably disappeared by the seventh year mark.

I have a few people that did stick around, but most people did kind of die out. So my channel never really grew and I think that's what put people off subscribing to my channel. Because it was basically a mess that you didn't really know what you were subscribing for. When I moved to London in 2015, I got in with the YouTube crowd here. I went to the YouTube Space a lot and I got a partner manager there. We had a few meetings about how to grow my channel.

We talked about focusing more on specific content, and we found that doing piercing stuff was really good for my channel. The interaction, the watch time, the audience retention—all of that stuff was really good for it. So I started doing more and more piercing stuff, and literally my channel exploded. Within a year my channel had quadrupled in size. I went from 30,000 to 120,000 in that time.

I was like, "This is clearly what people want to see," so I really grafted my channel towards modification stuff. It was gradual. It wasn't like one day I was doing a video a week, and then all a sudden it was like, every single video was this. It was a slow progression. Now I've got a nice, healthy balance between LGBT stuff and modification.

I think, for me, I'm so dedicated to LGBTQ+ things that I had to do that. I'm never gonna stop doing that because it's very, very important to me. I had to make sure it was something that I definitely carried on. I found a healthy balance between the two, and now my channel grows at a nice rate. Overall I just feel very happy now. It was kind of an easy decision because I want YouTube to be a full-time job for me, so I never thought I was selling out because it's something that I really want.

SwankyBox:
What I love about your channel is that you champion a much-needed cause in such a fun way. A lot of people often have difficulties accepting who they are because they are afraid of what other people will think. This keeps the real them trapped inside and living a life that is not true to themselves. Now that you're older, how has being a champion for the LGBTQ+ community affected your life?

Roly:
Being someone in the LGBTQ+ community who now gets looked up to for inspiration is literally insane. It's completely changed my world and my life, and just my perception of who am I as a person as well. It's a lot of pressure. There's so much pressure when you're an influencer, or someone in the LGBTQ+ community who is being looked up. People sometimes ask you really in-depth things, or will ask you advice on stuff that you're not necessarily trained for.

Sometimes I get people asking about, "How do I come out of these suicidal thoughts?" or, "How do I stop self-harming?" and all this stuff, and it's like, I'm not trained in that. So in some ways, it can be very overwhelming, but also I do feel very lucky that I can be there. People look up to me in that way, and that has completely changed my life. It's weird that I'm now on the other side of it, because at one point I was looking up to people and needing this help. Now I'm doing it for other people. It's overwhelming but also rewarding, and I wouldn't change it for anything. It's just completely altered my life, and now I have an amazing family here in London. I have an amazing friendship group, and I have an amazing audience who are so interactive. It's just absolutely amazing and I wouldn't change it for the world.

SwankyBox:
I've had a lot of similar difficult situations as well. When I cover games that relate to social issues or depression, people reach out to me for help. I've had plenty of suicidal people show up in my live streams and in my chats who need someone to talk to. At the end of the day, I'm not qualified to do so though. I can lend an ear, but ultimately I feel I'm the wrong person for it since there are people who are trained for that exact situation. It is definitely an incredibly difficult place to be since we don't really have a rule book on how we're supposed to handle it. We just point them to the right places if we can.

• • •

SwankyBox:
What advice do you have for the next generation of content creators who may be struggling with identity?

Roly:
I would say just don't be so strict on yourself when it comes to labels or putting yourself in boxes. There are so many labels out there, and I think it can be very easy to do that when you're confused about who you are. You find a label, and then it's like, "That's me and that's who I am." But don't be scared about going outside of that. Don't be scared about changing your mind about who you are. I always used to consider myself just as a cis male. Over the years of exploring who I was, I now identify as non-binary rather than just male. It's something that I never thought I would be four or five years ago.

I was so intent of just being, "I'm just a gay man," and that was it. But now that I'm able to open my mind up and be more free to be who I am, I've realized that

I'm non-binary rather than just cis male. I think a lot of people growing up now will get labels and then latch themselves to it because it's like, "Finally I have some sort of identity." They then stay with it and they're too scared to explore other things. I would say just be free, be open, but don't limit yourself. Literally don't limit yourself to one specific label because you do change over time, and it's absolutely normal.

SwankyBox:
Out of curiosity, were there any people who influenced you to start creating online?

Roly:
Oh my gosh . . . First people. Obviously I'm from the early, early days of YouTube, so I was watching people like Chris Crocker, Love B. Scott, William Sledd, Michael Buckley, all these people from the glory days of old YouTube. They really, really helped me to discover who I am. There was loads of old English creators as well. I had my friend Michael James who's now transitioned to Luxeria, and I used to watch their videos all the time. They had collab channels, an androgynous channel where there was five people who were androgynous, and I'd never seen androgynous people before. It was crazy for me to look up to these people back when I was like 17, and be like, "I wanna be like that. I wanna be able to be that free, but I can't." A lot of these people were from the very old days of YouTube.

SwankyBox:
I totally remember watching Chris Crocker and Michael Buckley! Such a nostalgia bomb!

• • •

SwankyBox:
What is your process like for YouTube? You run a personality-focused channel which is a bit different than mine. How do you go about creating and planning your videos?

Roly:
I get a lot of my ideas actually from my audience. I go a lot by the news, and what I feel like over time. That's for more pop culture-like things. With LGBT things, I look for what's going on now. With piercings and modifications, it's quite easy because I always have an influx of questions. On my piercing stuff, people are so interactive. My audience is amazing for that kind of stuff, so for me I'm able to get topics and questions and everything really, really, easily. There's always content for me to make when it comes to piercing stuff, because I've always got questions.

There's also a lot of things because I'm still modifying myself. I always do videos about what's the next thing that I'm getting done. When I do get something done, what was the process of getting it done? Modification, for me, is a never-ending process. This is always something that I'm gonna be doing for my life. Sometimes I might take something out or put something new in. I've always got a list of content ready to go because this kind of stuff is like an ongoing journey. It's a never-ending journey.

When it comes to my personality, people comment quite often, "I came for your piercing videos but stayed for your personality." So, I don't know. I think creative people just go through creative blocks, and there's times where we don't come up with the best ideas. But there's always an out. There's always a light at the end of the tunnel, you could say. There's always some other idea that will come to me eventually. I just feel like creative people can just think up things relatively easy. Ideas can just pop into your head.

SwankyBox:
The world is full of tons of people who will spew hate and won't bother to try to understand you. How have you dealt with this kind of hate on your channel specifically?

Roly:
Gosh. I see it as, now that I'm older and been here for a while, it doesn't obviously affect me. I look at it as they're basically making me famous. They're making me have better interaction on my channel, which boosts my videos on search. Obviously quite minute, but them commenting and viewing my videos obviously adds to my revenue and my ad share, so it's like you're basically giving me money still. Also I think of it as these people are just crying out for attention. What actually goes on in their mind and what really is going on in their life that's made them so hateful? I find it really difficult to hate them too much, or retaliate too harshly, because it's like they're obviously going through something themselves. People aren't born horrible. People aren't born nasty. That's a learned thing from somewhere, so I don't necessarily always hate people who do that. They're giving me more content too. The more hate I get, the more videos I can make about it. Hate comment videos are definitely ones that my subscribers love as well, and they interact really well with those. I just think of it as like, well, give me more attention, because you're making my life easier.

SwankyBox:
What does the future look like for your channel? Any exciting things you're working on that you want to share?

Roly:
Because it's been relatively recent that my channel has grown quite quickly, I'm gonna just continue doing what I'm doing at the moment because it's working. Obviously within six months, I will adapt a little bit more for whatever the YouTube algorithm does then. So for me, I don't plan too much ahead because I think, well, YouTube could suddenly change and then this algorithm's different, or that you have to do this to get noticed or whatever. I do have new merchandise and music coming out though.

Hopefully I can get a manager soon, like an actual agent, because now that my channel's grown, it has a nice size. I'm starting to get more brand deals and things, so I can be a little bit more useful to agencies and stuff.

Within the next year I'll be full-time on YouTube, which is amazing. Finally, after all these years, I'm actually getting there and I'm actually getting to that place where I can do this full-time. And it's finally, well, it sounds a bit weird to say this, but it's almost like a middle finger to everyone who said to me years ago that I was wasting my time and I'd never get anywhere on it. Because I'm like, well, I have now, thanks. So, you know, dedication and hard work really pays out.

Some people do get lucky and they get big instantly. They have a viral video or whatever, but I'm one of those people who had to work for a long time at it. Lots of dedication. And I think, in some way, it's made me a very grounded person. It's made me very humbled to have what I have, and I'm very appreciative of my audience and everything that I do have because I've had to work really hard for it. Instead of just going viral overnight and then being like, "Well, I earned this because blah, blah, blah." Like, no. You just got lucky. So yeah, I think I'll just carry on doing what I'm doing at the moment.

Obviously I need to make sure that I focus on what's coming up on YouTube. Things might change and alter the way I have to make videos. Either way I'm just going to keep moving forward.

• • •

Roly has awesome content focused on body modifications and the LGBTQ+ community. The channel has amazing energy and I always find myself laughing along! Do yourself a favor and swing on over to check it out!

ROTOR RIOT

youtube.com/RotorRiot

Chad from Rotor Riot was someone a friend introduced me to. He runs a channel focused on high-performance drones. Since we were both in the YouTube space, we met up for lunch one day and from that point forward have continued to talk. Honestly, this book you're reading right now is a result of one of those lunches. It evolved from one of our conversations and I attribute him with planting the seed for the idea. I think my nerdy YouTube side was shining strong that day!

• • •

SwankyBox:
For those unfamiliar with what you do, I was hoping you could tell us a little bit more about Rotor Riot and high-performance drones.

Chad:
Rotor Riot is actually kind of three entities, but starting with a YouTube channel based around high-performance drones. A primary revenue stream comes from our retail store, where we drive traffic to the store by creating great content around these drones.

What I mean by high-performance drones is, our pilots and our hosts are racers and freestylers. A lot of people are familiar with standard camera drones, like the Phantom, and some others that you might see in traditional stores. The next most popular kind of drones are these newer selfie drones. Then, of course, there's toys. A little lesser known is in the hobby industry, or kind of DIY drones.

High-performance is two areas. Competitive and art. Competition would be racing, where speed, agility, timing, accuracy, all of that is super important. Then you have the art side, where it's very much like skateboarding, where you pick a location and you fly through that location. The key, or the definition of success, would be to create a beautiful HD video, sometimes even shot in 4K, from the drone's perspective of flying through these interesting locations. That's what we do in our content.

Rotor Riot is a lot more focused on the freestyle side of high-performance drones. While we carry products in our stores for both freestyle and racing, because a lot of the products are very similar, or the same, our content is based on the more visual aspect of this sport/hobby, which is called FPV freestyle. Or mini-quad freestyle.

SwankyBox:
Rotor Riot was not your first channel in this category, correct? What was your first channel about?

Chad:

Correct. What got me interested in even working on YouTube was back in 2010 I created another channel called Flite Test. That channel was primarily focused on electric RC flight. At that time, brushless motors, lithium polymer batteries, all the technology was getting better, stronger, cheaper, and it was kind of a re-emergence of the RC flight hobby.

I was just getting into that hobby about nine months prior to starting the channel, and I had a production company. I had been doing production at that point probably for around 12 to 14 years. What I did was I merged my hobby with my profession, and thought, "I'm going to create a show."

I had the time at that point in my life and my career, and I had the passion. I just really made a show that I wanted to watch. When I got into the hobby, it was hard to find good content that was educational and inspirational. That lack of that content was the inspiration for me to start my own channel.

Flite Test, much like Rotor Riot, got immediate traction, and found its audience very early on. Which, I would attribute that to the research phase. With Flite Test, it didn't start in October of 2010, it started about six months prior when I started working on a logo, and started thinking about, "What do I want the brand to be about? What do I want it to cover?"

A lot of thought went into the initial inception of that whole brand. Just like Rotor Riot. Very similar. The creating phases of both channels were very similar to start.

SwankyBox:

Why did you choose high-performance racing drones as your focus? I know for myself, when I started I was thinking about doing travel vlogs and other things. Ultimately, why did you decide on the drones?

Chad:
What got me interested in the hobby back in 2010 in the first place was multi-rotors. These are non-traditional RC aircraft. I was very interested in them. What had happened was, back in the Flite Test days, I had built a quadcopter and it just flew horribly. Nobody was really building well-flying multi-rotor aircraft at that time. There were a couple emerging, but it was really clunky.

That kind of got my feet wet. Then I started flying other things. I flew Warbirds, and then I started doing scratch building, where you build planes from foam, and expendable materials. Then I got into even gliders, and wings, and lots of other things. That's what got me interested in the whole RC flight hobby.

Now, once Flite Test had run its course for a little while, I kept exploring things like FPV, first person view flying. That was where my real passion was. I loved putting cameras on planes, the multi-rotors, and flying as if I'm in the aircraft. The next evolution of that was drone racing. That was very obvious to me at the time, just because of my involvement in the hobby, and I could see the momentum picking up there.

Freestyle wasn't even really a term. People were doing it, but they weren't calling it freestyle, they were just calling it flying mini-quads. When I saw this, and I saw that people were starting to get very interested, there were some people talking about starting leagues. Because I enjoyed it, and had kind of a revived passion through this, I thought, "I want to follow this, and I want to see what it becomes."

That was the inception of Rotor Riot.

SwankyBox:
Were there any people who inspired you to start creating on YouTube? Do you remember if you were watching anyone at the time?

Chad:
Oh, boy. Yeah. There were. I'm trying to think if they're around anymore. It's also hard to remember which channels I was watching before Flite Test and after, because once starting Flite Test, I actually started watching more and more.

One of them was RCSparks. He did DJMedic's. He covers all kinds of RC products. But he primarily covered RC vehicles, like cars. There's this whole sub-genre of construction equipment, and trucks, and things like that that are all radio controlled. So, he's definitely one of them.

Then there's DaveSuperPowers. He was scratch building aircraft and then making videos. A lot of these people that I've mentioned are probably not huge, but they were very influential in that space. There's NightFlyer. There's RCModelReviews. He's out of New Zealand. Let me think of who else.

Most of my inspiration at that time was other small YouTube channels. A lot of these guys only had maybe 10,000 subscribers, or maybe not even that many. It's hard to remember.

SwankyBox:
While you were creating on YouTube, were there any hurdles you ran into, or things that may have stifled your growth or made you second-guess creating a series?

Chad:

Yeah. I would say it was always difficult to work with sponsors, and trying to figure out the model of what the best way to work with a sponsor would be. I do have the say the first six months was a whirlwind. It was amazing. It actually came too easy, because we were having fun, we were gaining subscribers faster than we thought we would, and we got sponsorship within like a month of starting the channel.

The sponsorship was fairly substantial. I think it was a total year, probably somewhere between . . . I don't know, somewhere around $15,000 a month in sponsorships. Then, of course, you get the YouTube ad revenue. But that was always fairly small.

I sold Flite Test in 2014. So, after that I wasn't as involved in it, but I think the most I ever got for a month through YouTube was a fourth or half of what was gained through sponsorships. Which is good, but when you're getting $15,000 to $30,000 in sponsorship money, the YouTube ad revenue becomes secondary.

SwankyBox:

I definitely agree. I think for a lot of creators, YouTube ad money is . . . it's interesting, because a lot of people go into it focusing on that. If they have no prior business experience, or don't really know what they're doing, the ad revenue becomes super important. However, it's not a good idea to focus on it. Especially if you plan on growing your business out. Actually, this kind of leads into the next question.

For those who are creating and are looking to branch out, what advice can you give them about turning a passion into a rewarding career?

Chad:

I think probably the number one piece of advice I would give people is, oftentimes the creatives don't want to focus on the money, because they feel like they're being greedy, or that it will take away from the creativity. But, what happens is, if you don't understand your business model, it doesn't make sense. Your creativity just takes you to a dead end.

I would encourage anyone to understand the revenue stream prior to moving forward. That way, when you've kind of got your head down and you're being creative, you're at least on a path that was predetermined as far as your revenue stream. The whole concept of, "Well, I'll just make great content and money will kind of come in," like, you might as well play the lottery, because the odds are the same.

Sometimes people can stumble into it, but that doesn't necessarily make it effective, right, or scalable. With Flite Test, I had determined up front that I was going to seek sponsors. YouTube ad revenue wasn't even a thing I was considering. I think a lot of people go into YouTube thinking, "Oh, I'll get YouTube ad revenue without doing any math, or having any knowledge of how that works."

Most people, when you do the math, just automatically assume, "I'm going to become a channel with millions of subscribers, and then I'll get rich."

If you are one person, and you have a million subscribers, YouTube ad revenue will be quite good for you. But first of all, is that even possible? If you plan for that, part of your business plan is essentially winning the lottery.

Some people do though. Some people win a certain amount of money, and then they use that to justify moving forward, but then they get hung up down the road. They then find out when they try to do it again. Some people will do additional channels, or they'll just do another version of what they're doing, and then it doesn't work. What they're not realizing is they kind of stumbled into something through their passion, and then they've used that success to justify all of their other decisions.

Which, I've done that as well. I had a channel in-between called RotorDR1, which was a community-collaborated development for a feature film. While it was a success on some fronts, it was not a financial success. That was because I was following my passion with some sensibility mixed in, and Flite Test was a success. I used that as a badge of honor to make whatever decisions I wanted next to be successful. But it didn't work that way.

SwankyBox:
Oftentimes in the gaming industry people have no idea what to charge for sponsorships, or how to secure sponsorships. When they do encounter a sponsor, that sponsor already has a set value in their head because multiple people came through who didn't know what they were doing, and undercharged severely. So that when they were approaching future sponsorships, that's their benchmark. They're like, "Well, so-and-so did it for this much."

When you were starting out, how did you secure those sponsors, and how did you break down what your value was and what you should charge them?

Chad:
This is an important topic. If I speak on anything, I think this is probably the most fruitful piece that

you can get from me. I came into this as a marketing video producer. My company produced videos. I would say our ballpark average was $20,000. We would produce high-end marketing videos for $20,000, $30,000, $50,000.

Quite frankly, those videos were not as effective as one episode of Flite Test. So, I came at it with that mindset. I was like, "Okay, we're creating this. Not only are we creating something around a specific topic, it's already going out to a specific audience, and it's from people that have built credibility and are trusted."

If a client came to me, and let's just go into a different zone, now. Let's just say it was motorcycles. And they wanted to sell a bunch of accessories to a motorcycle. What kind of video would we create? What kind of marketing video? Well, obviously you can do a commercial. You can do a marketing video that shows at trade shows, or online, or however it might be presented.

You have a number of costs there. You have to make the video, and then you also have to find a way to get it to the viewer. All of that is super expensive. Just our part of it, which would be the video, could be a $20,000 cost. Then, on top of that, the client would have to find a way to get it in front of their customer, which would be cable television, could be online advertising, could be like I said at a trade show. Whatever it might be. That was a process.

These clients are spending tens of thousands of dollars, where Flite Test, I was saying, "Okay, $2,500 and we will feature your logo down in the corner of our 12 minute video."

We would thank the sponsor, and we would feature their products on our show. In my eyes, it was a no-brainer. Why wouldn't somebody spend $2,500 to get exposure to even 5,000 people that are exactly their demographic. When you look at it from a marketing standpoint, it's a no-brainer.

The problem is, YouTube and a lot of YouTube advertising people, they try to automate everything. So what happens is, all of this becomes a commodity. People just whittle it down to how many subscribers, how many views. But then they severely undervalue those views. The more people they get to do that, the more it diminishes the value of the sponsorship.

It really comes down to what you can sell it for. Obviously the more demand, the more it's worth. I would encourage any YouTuber to just understand the dynamics of a marketing video, and why and how that works. Then, don't just use that as a justification to put a big price tag on a sponsorship. Also design your episodes to serve those needs and then educate your possible client on how this helps them.

As a YouTuber, if you're going to do that, it's also my advice to know that they are your client. That you shouldn't expect them to bend over backwards for you, but you should serve them. You should say, "Hey. I'm going to create results for your sponsorship."

Not just get their product involved, or their name out there, but, "Hey. Here's a plan and a call to action to get people interested in your product." It should be a relevant product too. You shouldn't be incorporating a product that doesn't quite match the content or the people that it's intended for, who's in your audience.

There is something I'd like to add, or maybe it's an answer to a question you haven't asked yet, but a lot of what I was speaking to so far is assuming you have a successful channel. If I'm speaking to anybody thinking about getting into creating content on YouTube is, the number one question I get is, "How do you get sponsored?" Or, next, "How do you get viewed?"

They're both the same answer. Create compelling content. That's a very simple answer, but it's a very important thing to pay attention to, because there's no shortcut. People think that if you create a channel, and you think that it's great, but it's not getting views because of some other reason, you're fooling yourself and you're going to waste time.

It's not like you turn a corner and all of a sudden your whole audience discovers you. If you can get 100 views on your video, that's enough to get people to share it. If they're not sharing, it's because they're not seeing enough value. That becomes, in my opinion, your litmus test. There's how you know if you have something successful. You're not just going to turn a corner one day and just get gobs of views.

You might continue building content, and then maybe you hit a nerve with your content, but you're not going to produce the same kind of content for 10 episodes and then the 11th one hits. It'll only hit if you've hit that nerve.

SwankyBox:
What's the future look like for you as a creator? Where do you see your channels going in this upcoming year?

Chad:
I think with Rotor Riot, it's a really interesting time to be in this industry. Our channel is evolving to include a little more content for people entering the hobby. Because when we started our channel, it was a very small, niche group of people. But now it's becoming a little more mainstream. So you're getting people that weren't hobbyists before.

They were just into whatever hobby, but now they see drone racing on TV or something, so they want to know what it's about and they want to get into it. So, we want to tailor more educational and inspirational content towards the newcomers, as well as continue to support and represent the high-end, I guess elite type of racers and freestylists.

Regarding my involvement in new media and YouTube, I do have a desire to create other channels. I had just a few months ago started my own vlog channel, which really is a completely different motive. Flite Test and Rotor Riot were anticipated to be brands, and to have products and stores and do all of that. And to be entities within themselves.

My vlog channel is more therapeutic. I have a lot of conversations, interesting debates and discussions with people. My vlog is kind of an opportunity to just talk those through, vent my thoughts, and share odd things that are interesting to me. It's a different thing. If nobody watched it I would still do it, because it's more therapeutic than anything.

One thing I learned through a vlog is, it is quite a bit different than a topic-based channel. If it's an individual-based channel, it can still be topical. Like you do SwankyBox. It's still you, and it's a topic, but people are going to tend to see it as you. If it's more of an ensemble, like something like Dude Perfect, where you have a bunch of guys and then it's a brand, an overarching brand, those are two different types of channels, and they grow differently, and they gain their following differently.

I'd like to continue exploring that, and understanding the differences between a single character-based channel and an ensemble brand-based channel. Not that a character can't have a brand, but people associate the personality of a single-character channel as it's just one singular personality, where a collective is always morphing and changing. Because if you change those people out, the overall personality changes. So, I want to explore that some more.

• • •

If first person high-speed flight is your thing, you should definitely give Rotor Riot a gander. The environments they fly in are truly breathtaking as are the skills of the pilots. If you're planning on branching out into a bigger business as a creator, looking into how they are setup could prove very helpful!

PUSHINGUPROSES

youtube.com/pushinguproses

Running a YouTube channel that has a focus in gaming nostalgia means you often live and breathe nostalgia. However, this means that nostalgia in a sense sort of becomes commonplace. It loses a bit of its power to some degree. PushingUpRoses was a channel I would visit often because it covered a category of games my channel did not. I have very fond memories of my early computer gaming experiences, and her channel was a place I could go to indulge in a different kind of nostalgia. I can't recommend her content enough!

• • •

SwankyBox:
Starting off, I was hoping you could tell me a little about what your gaming channel for those reading who may be unfamiliar.

Roses:

For the most part, my channel focuses on retro computer gaming. This includes videos on individual games, topic videos and video essays, and sometimes vlogs. I also have a new show that focuses on murder mystery content, and every now and then I'll discuss a retro TV show or movie. The majority of content does have to do with gaming, but mostly, the channel is just about me and my interests. I try to bring a lot of my personality into my videos.

SwankyBox:

Why YouTube in general? Was there a moment in your life when you knew you wanted to give it a shot? You've been creating content on YouTube for quite a while now.

Roses:

I started out just posting Let's Plays on YouTube. Shortly after that I joined an aggregate website called That Guy with the Glasses, where the majority of producers used Blip as their platform. I regret that in retrospect because Blip didn't have the exposure and ease of use as YouTube, but Blip felt safer at the time and for years, paid more. As Blip started to decline, I decided to leave TGWTG and focus more on YouTube. In 2013 I changed up my content and started focusing on scripted videos with Let's Plays uploaded every now and then to fill in the gaps between the retrospectives. I think the moment I wanted to try YouTube is when I realized that I didn't want to be on a collaborate website because it just didn't feel like my own. TGWTG was the Nostalgia Critic's train. I wanted to be on the PushingUpRoses train. So far it has worked out nicely.

SwankyBox:
So many people who start on YouTube struggle with choosing a direction to go in. Selecting one of our passions to focus on is difficult. How did you ultimately settle on nostalgic gaming? Side note here: I absolutely love it because I sort of run a nostalgic channel as well. Knowing a place I can go for a different kind of nostalgia-fix is pretty cool!

Roses:
I think it IS really hard. When I joined YouTube, there was a "type of creator" that became popular, especially in the gaming scene. When I revisited YouTube in 2013, I felt like I had to be everything that was popular. Had to be funny, AND informative, AND have tight editing, AND whacky sound effects, AND . . . the list goes on. But I realized that you can't get far trying to appease other people's expectations. I finally found my groove writing in my own voice and covering things I genuinely love and am knowledgeable about. Don't get me wrong, it does take skill to find your place, but working on that skill is much easier when you love the content. I settled on retro gaming as my primary focus because my personality shined the most when I talked about it and eventually I let go of that pressure to be like everyone else and just settled for myself.

SwankyBox:
What has been your biggest obstacle as a creator?

Roses:
I've struggled with mental illness all my life; I was diagnosed in childhood. My biggest obstacle is being a public figure with Body Dysmorphic Disorder. Things that come easier to other creators are difficult challenges

to me, like being on camera, going to conventions, and taking photos. I can barely do those things, and people don't know how bad it is for me behind the scenes. Sometimes I feel like I chose exactly the wrong thing for me to be doing. Especially for how hard these things are for a person who suffers with this disorder, but it's also extremely rewarding when I can push through my anxieties. In a way, I use my YouTube career to challenge myself and it's become effective exposure therapy for me.

SwankyBox:
It can be intimidating for women to get into the gaming spotlight because expectations are always so high and harassers are a dime a dozen. What kind of advice do you have for the next generation of female content creators who want to focus on gaming? Is there anything important you learned as a creator?

Roses:
I wish I had some really excellent advice regarding handling the gaming community as a female producer. It can be extremely taxing; I've been judged on everything from my appearance to my taste in video games to my clothing choices to my HAIR choices. It is truly asinine sometimes. I think an important thing to have that can be helpful is a support group, especially with other women going through the same things. You can help each other build confidence and offer support when it's needed. But I think the biggest piece of advice I can give is to be yourself, no matter what. You don't need to be anything other than who you are to impress people. The pressure is going to get challenging; sometimes you might feel like you need to be prettier, or talk about popular things you have no interest in as an attempt to please an audience, but you will not be happy that way.

It's important to distinguish the difference between doing something annoying to up the quality of your work versus doing something because you think other people might want it. I also think it's important to listen to your audience and see what people are interested in, but don't compromise your entire personality to fit a specific mold.

What helps me feel empowered is that I always confront my harassers, and I've always fought back. Not everyone is comfortable with that, but I like standing my ground and not taking anyone's crap. If you feel more comfortable not engaging with harassers, that is up to you. Do what YOU need to do to feel good in a situation where you feel like someone is putting you down. It's not about the trolls or the harassers, it's not about them winning, it's about YOU winning. I hope more people will feel encouraged to be a part of the solution so more women can feel confident and safe in this community.

SwankyBox:
Were there any other creators who inspired you to start creating yourself?

Roses:
I'm not really sure. It was mostly the community of producers I saw on TGWTG before I joined, but not one individual person inspired me. I think it's because I really started doing these videos for myself, to prove to myself that I could do it despite my mental illness. I saw the community of people on TGWTG and really wanted that sense of comradery as well. My biggest inspiration for creating, just in a general sense, is probably Frida Kahlo, who never compromised who she was and was never afraid of candor, and used that in her

work. I strive to be like that with art AND video. It's why I choose to be so personal and blunt.

SwankyBox:
What does the future look like for you as a creator? Are there any exciting things you want to share with those who may be reading this?

Roses:
Hah, I am not sure! I am not good at predicting the future. But I do hope my new series on all things Murder Mystery will take off and become something people love, and I hope to be finishing my own book, a memoir, sometime in the next year or so. We'll just have to see what the future holds.

● ● ●

Retro gaming for computers will always have a fond place in my heart. If you long for a great nostalgic gaming experience, or are interested in games you may have missed, PushingUpRoses is the channel for you!

SCOTT DW

youtube.com/scottdw

When I was sitting at my desk job dreaming of being a YouTuber, Scott DW was someone I followed closely. I discovered his work through another favorite content creator of mine, and I was hooked on both his cinematography and music. I would jam to his tunes at my desk while I daydreamed of a life I currently wasn't living. He was a catalyst in me deciding to change my life direction, and for that I will forever be thankful.

• • •

SwankyBox:
First and foremost, why don't you tell me a little bit about what you do on YouTube. Obviously I know what you do, but for those reading how would you describe what you do?

Scott:
When people used to ask what content I made it was always very hard for me to answer that question. There were so many types of content that I felt that I made or that I wanted to make. So, I always use a few descriptive words: Kind of musical, comedic, and epic. [laughs] I frame it as very high quality, cinematic, musical, comedic ridiculousness. So that's really the gist of my channel. I have a filmmaking background, a song writing background, and I never ever, ever planned on becoming a YouTuber. I just, through a series of crazy events in my life, sort of stumbled into YouTube. Before I knew it, it had been five years. It's been a surreal journey. It literally kind of changed overnight for me. It wasn't so much like, "I wanna be a YouTuber, I wanna see if I can do this." I was on a different life path.

SwankyBox:
How did you actually get into YouTube then?

Scott:
It's a bit of a long story, but I was trying to build a career as a cinematographer. Even though I was building this career as a cinematographer, I loved writing. I love writing characters and dialogue. I kept this notebook that was kind of just my creative-all notebook. It's where I would write lyrics for music and ideas for short films. All these different little quirky tidbits of things that were meant for nothing other than getting from my head to a piece of paper.

Anyways, I was working on a film project for a university that was a parody. It was a spoof of the Old Spice commercial that like changed the world. They ended up uploading the video to YouTube and sure enough it went viral soon after. Two or three million views in a week. Mind you, this was seven or eight years ago. Like, back then getting a million views just didn't happen. This is when a million views on YouTube was like discovering a gold mine. The crazy thing is at the top of the description they credited me as the writer and cinematographer or something. Something really bizarre, but it had my name and my email. Before I knew it I was just completely flooded with job opportunities. Like, commercial opportunities, and that was my very, very first experience with YouTube and what's funny is, as positive as that experience was, it wasn't enough to say, 'Hey, you know, maybe something on YouTube is worth looking at or pursuing." It was another two or three years before I would even start pursuing YouTube. However, this experience changed me. I became a go-getter from this point forward. If you dream it there's no reason why you can't accomplish it.

Fast forward and I'm working on the TV show Bones. I remember I was hanging out with the cinematographer for the show and I'm picking his brain. I'm asking him, you know, about success and what he attributes to his career and how he got to where he was today. He told me something so fascinating. This was right around the same year I ended up falling into YouTube, but he told me, "You know when you come to LA you're this fish in this pond with millions of other fish and you're kind of competing for the same thing." We've all heard the saying small fish in the big pond. He said honestly what did it for him was going somewhere with a small pond and becoming a big fish. I remember him telling me, "Make LA want you, make the people you wanna work with want you versus climbing the ladder for forty years and working your way into it." Now that stood out to me so strongly because here I am, in LA, thinking

that, you know, the key to success is to get in line and
wait my turn.

Anyways, fast forward again. I'm working and I have
this opportunity to go shoot a video with this group called
the Color Run. They were like, "We want this to be really
cinematic, something really, really cool, something shar-
able." I recommended that we should get a Phantom slow
mo cam. They were super supportive and agreed. Well,
long story short I find a Phantom and I go and I do this
event. While we're shooting this event, I'm talking to the
Phantom operator. He actually lets me do the filming on
the Phantom which was like a dream come true.

I've always loved to make people laugh. My mind
is always thinking of weird things and it can become
a goal of mine sometimes. So here I am with this like
sixty year old Phantom operator and I'm thinking,
"How can I make this guy laugh?" Like, how can I make
this Phantom owner think I'm a funny guy. Why that
matters to me, I have no idea. I start literally spewing
out all these things where I'm like, "Oh you know, I've
had ideas for years of things I wanted to shoot on the
Phantom," and he's like, "Really? Like what?" and I
just started spewing out ideas of things that, like, you
literally should never or would never think to shoot on
a Phantom. And the first thing that came out of my
mouth was, "Well for one, I'd like to take . . . uh . . .
little kittens and I'd put baby capes on them . . . I'd have
them fly in slow motion," and he was like, "What the
hell did you just say?" [laughs]

And I was like, "Yes! I got to him. I don't know if I'm
making him laugh, but I definitely got to this guy." He
turns to me and he goes, "That's such a ridiculous idea.
You know what? If you actually shoot that I'll let you
use my camera for free," and this camera is twenty-five
hundred bucks a day. He wasn't kidding either.

I took it as a challenge. It seemed pointless because I was trying to build a career as a cinematographer and focus on relationships. But I made the video anyways. I found a friend who had kittens. My wife and I made capes. I shot a few other videos while I had the camera too, but they never saw the light of day. This flying cat video sat on a hard drive for four months while I went and worked with Devinsupertramp on some other projects. Devin and I went to film school together and we worked on dozens and dozens of projects together. When I went and started working on the traditional career, Devin went to Hawaii to make a documentary where he full on, like, fell into YouTube by sheer accident. He had no plans of doing YouTube or becoming a YouTuber, but over the course of filming this documentary in Hawaii he started making YouTube videos.

When Devin and I would chat and catch up, I would start thinking about this cat footage that I had filmed. I was like, "You know what? YouTube is so funny. It's all about these funny cat videos," and so I went about YouTube in this really weird way. For the first video I decided to edit this footage together. I tried editing it to around ten different songs and nothing was working. I literally can't find a single song to click with this video. It just doesn't feel good and I'm sitting there, kinda just looping this forty-five second cut and an idea kinda pops into my head. How funny would it be to write an original song? Like to write a hip hop song about these flying cats. Something that was funny and witty? So that's what I did. I reached out to my friend Brendan and we collaborated on a song. Kitten Air was born.

I then edited the video to the song and dusted off my old YouTube channel. I uploaded the video and then Brendan and I actually had a job together the next day. I was filming and he was doing audio. We randomly checked the video at lunch because we were like, "I wonder how the video's doing," and the video had 30,000 views. And we were like, "What the hell? Like what?" and I have zero subscribers. We get done with the shoot and check it again. Now it's at 100,000. I go to bed that night and I wake up the next morning to my phone ringing. It's Devin and he says, "Scott, I knew that you wrote music, but how did I never know that you wrote music like this?" And I said, "Well for one, I've never put my music out there. That's the biggest reason that you had no idea that this is the type of music I wrote."

It was funny because all it took was Devin listening to Kitten Air and he goes, "I love this song so much, would you be willing to write a song for my next video that's coming out?" I'm like, "Holy hell man, I dunno. I just did it once for Kitten Air I don't know if I could do it again." And I called Brendan and I said, "You wanna try to do it again?" and he says, "Sure why not." So we wrote a song called Little Voices and that went on Devin's unicycle video. Everything started happening at that point. The Kitten Air video got a million views. What's so crazy is that within the first week, not only did the video get a million views, but the song went into the iTunes pop charts. It made it into the top 50 and now Devin's at the point where every time we write a song he's like, "Cool can you start the next one?", "Cool can you start the next one?", and like before we know it we're writing music every single week.

I'm building a fanbase all of a sudden. There's like six or seven thousand subscribers on the Scott DW channel just from the Kitten Air video and every single comment is like, "This channel has one video, what's the next video gonna be?" and I'm like, "You're asking me?" I have no idea what I just did. Like, what did I just do, you know? And um . . . yeah man. That's how I started. [laughs]

SwankyBox:
What made you decide to eventually focus on high-energy short films focused around dancing?

Scott:
I was just reminiscing about this like two days ago with my choreographer. So dance is interesting. Because I write music, I established early on that I wanted to write original music for all of my videos. That would be just another thing that would set me apart. It'll allow me to do so much more with my content because I could literally create custom music to the video. I could have lyrics about the video. Like, I can take things to a whole different level this way. As a creator on YouTube, you're constantly thinking about, "Am I creating the best ever content for my channel? For my audience? Should I be doing something better?" You're always trying to think of how to switch it up and how to make it better. It was just one of those times where I'm thinking about how do I elevate this stuff, and I started thinking about dance because dance was something I fell in love with in high school.

I have four younger sisters, several of which all dance and then my wife danced for our high school. We met in ninth grade German class and she went on to be the captain of the dance team. She was the one choreographing everything and I became music editor for our school's dance team. So there's like this other side of me that's so dance-centric that I've never ever acknowledged, you know? I'm making all of this content and one day it just dawns on me that I've never done anything with dance even though I love dance. I love watching it and

I have a huge appreciation for it. I feel like I'm good at seeing if a dance is good or not.

I then get a killer idea. I call up my buddy Jason and say, "We have to make a dance video. It has to be stormtroopers twerking." I pitch him the whole video and he says, "No. It's so stupid, it'll never work. It'll never work." I remember him being really against the idea. I then get a call from Devin to go film something in Colorado. We're sitting there at lunch and he's like "What're you working on?" and I'm like "Alright. Check this out." I pitched him Stormtrooper Twerk and he goes, "Nah man. That'll never work. That'll never work." And I was like, "Why? Why does everybody think this'll never work?" He's like, "For one, you're going to spend so much money on the costumes and you'll never make that money back." I said, "Look. I know we'll probably not make this money back, but like screw it. I don't care. I don't care if I don't make money back. I think this idea is gold. I think it's gold!" And it's funny because Devin and Jason tried to talk me out of it and they almost succeeded. Like they full on almost succeeded. I remember sitting in my office one night just thinking about the idea and I had the stormtrooper costumes in front of me. Like, ready to check out online. It was like $8,000 worth of costumes and I was like, "What do I do? What if I lose everything?" I then pulled the trigger and bought them. In my mind I was thinking I'll never know if I don't try. I filmed the video and it blew up online. The video I was told wouldn't work was a smash hit.

So "Stormtrooper Twerk" was the first experiment and I tried it again and again and again, until, you know, with each video I kinda figured out what works and doesn't work. I started introducing the battle element. I really, really wanted to see if I could tell stories and create characters. For two solid years I really wanted to do this high school dance battle and I tried to get a lot of different brands behind it. So I had like five or six different brands over the course of two years and I couldn't get a single person to believe in that idea. Like, that's the funniest part. I could not get anyone to believe in the high school dance battle and then I think it was HTC that finally came along one day and said, "Hey we want to make a video." They happened to be the perfect brand for it, and I made "High School Dance Battle" which now has around 75,000,000 views. That video changed my entire life once again. It's changed my career, it's changed everything.

SwankyBox:
If you could give one piece of advice to an aspiring content creator who is starting today, what would it be?

Scott:
I've thought about this one, because this is always the ending question to every panel. I used to always say, "just keep creating and never let anything stop you," but there's more than that. My piece of advice is really about finding your voice. Everybody has a voice. That could refer to anything from the types of stories you tell to the type of content you make. The fact that you do gaming things, the fact that I do dance things. Those are all part of our voice. Our voice doesn't have to be constrained to that one thing, but everyone has a voice and I feel like the thing that help us as creators on YouTube is finding our voice and running with it.

So many of us, even me as an early YouTuber were like, "I don't know what my voice is, I just know that I like this, this, and this. I'm gonna create it all," and that's great. Like if that's the way you're going to approach it, just do it and over and in time you're gonna find your voice. So my advice is work on finding your voice. Don't let time, pressure, or people's influence change the fact that you need to find your voice and then you need to shout as loud as you can. I think that's the key. A lot of times people give up because they never found their voice. They weren't confident with what they were doing and I think we become confident when we find our voice. Our audience resonates with it. We resonate with it. At that point it all starts making sense.

SwankyBox:
What's the future look like for you? What exciting things do you have coming on the horizon and what do you hope to accomplish next?

Scott:
There's a lot of things that excite me and that's a huge thing that YouTube has done for me. It just constantly ignites fires and gets me excited to pursue more and more things. What's also funny is that I come from this traditional filmmaking background. The young film-maker within me has dreamt of coming back full-circle to Hollywood and making feature films. I'm now in a place where it's possible. Very early on some of those opportunities came. I remember some movie offers came with "Fruit Ninja", but it was never anything that felt right. But for the first time in my career, this kind of childhood dream is being realized.

I'm currently working on a directorial debut studio film which I'm excited about. Like I said, it's that young filmmaker's dream and it's coming full-circle back to the traditional world and it's neat that things worked out that way.

• • •

I've always been super passionate about dance myself, so watching Scott find his home in dance-focused videos was like a double win for me. Great cinematography, music, and choreography are the three elements to his work. He creates some of the most high quality content I know on YouTube, and you should definitely check out his videos.

MR. CREEPYPASTA

youtube.com/MrCreepyPasta

I met Mr. CreepyPasta actually quite recently. I had known of his channel prior, but I had only watched a few of his videos. Not too long ago we were both booked as guests for a convention and we rode the shuttle from the airport to the convention together. During this time we had a brief exchange, but later on during the convention he called me out from the crowd to come over to this booth. He gave me a shirt and told me it was a pleasure meeting me. I was pretty moved by this gesture. I was a total stranger not too long ago, but this act of kindness really made me feel welcome. From that point forward I was super curious to hear his story.

• • •

SwankyBox:
So not everyone reading this will know what a Creepypasta is exactly. I was hoping you could share

a little insight about what you do on YouTube as a creator.

Mr. CreepyPasta:

To answer the first part of that, a Creepypasta is taken from the term "copypasta," which is taken from the term "copy paste." It's a story that goes from internet forum to internet forum. It's like an urban legend that ends up spreading in the real world. A Creepypasta spreads through the internet though. So what I do is I take these urban legends, these things that are copied and pasted without any kind of audio whatsoever, and I try to give them audio. I try to give them new life. I'm trying to catalog these stories with live recordings, but as they've grown and grown, it's become more and more about supporting smaller authors and helping them reach a wider audience. It also helps kids to actually start reading.

I have a lot of different ways I cover these tales, but usually what I do is I go through contacting the authors of the stories if they have one that's listed. A lot of these stories are anonymous, like you usually think of with an urban legend. If there's an author for it, I'll contact them and see if they're interested in me covering the story. Usually authors are really flattered that the story could be posted to the channel and they're usually on board for it.

I'll then go through a recording of it. Usually I'll read through the story once and try recording it in one take. Anywhere that I stumbled, I'll fix it up. I have another guy who helps me with editing. He's the one who usually goes through and fixes up the story after I'm done mastering the audio. Once the mastering is set, then we ship it off to the video editor. Sound effects, music, and all the other things are added in. The editor is the one who does all that. And then it gets like a very simple visual. So it's kinda weird I'm on YouTube at all cause the visuals are almost nonexistent. They're not as important as the audio is, but YouTube really took off, so here we are.

SwankyBox:
Why did you choose YouTube to be your main outlet for storytelling? I imagine other audio-based platforms may have been appealing as well.

Mr. CreepyPasta:
When I decided to start on YouTube six or seven years ago, it was a very different place. So right now if you go around on YouTube and you look for Creepypasta narrators, audiobooks, and things like that, you can find a bunch. They're readily available. There's tons of people who do stuff like that. They have like one static image or one word, the title of the story or whatever, and then it's got audio that plays for however long.

But back when I started, it really wasn't like that. Six or seven years ago, YouTube wasn't a big entertainment website like it is now. Like now, if you want to go watch a video online, it's like yeah, let's go to YouTube. There weren't a whole lot of big name creators. YouTube used to be a lot more personalized. People used to just upload videos of themselves or pets. YouTube was used mostly for contests and things like that from other companies.

I had this girlfriend at the time and she was really big into wanting to do films. She wanted to upload these videos to YouTube. So that's what she would do. She had her own channel where she would do student films and I was an actor in them. And then things went sour in our relationship and I was like you know, I'm going to go ahead and do the YouTube thing cause

I'm open to horror. I'll do a YouTube channel that's related to horror. So I would tell these stories that I would find on Creepypasta.com and see if she liked it. She thought they were really dumb. But I did like four or five of them, and I was really bad. My acting wasn't great and my equipment wasn't great. So that's when I stopped. Then I came back like a month or two later and I saw people were actually watching and commenting on them so I picked it up. Because I'm guessing at the time there really wasn't that many people that would do that, record audio and put it up on YouTube.

I tried other things like Podbean to do podcasts and things like that. Which now I do podcasts as well on YouTube, but at the time my major issue was that I didn't understand how to do it. It was far beyond me and I never learned. So I just kind of didn't try. YouTube appears to be fine and this isn't gonna be anything, so I'm just doing this as a little side hobby. That's why I did everything on YouTube. I really fell into it more than I tried to make a calculated jump into it. And it just worked in my favor because at the time it was okay to fall into YouTube. These days, YouTube is very hard to fall into because it's harder to get started on YouTube than it was six years ago.

SwankyBox:
I noticed you take on the role of a character in your videos. How did this come about? Even in your live performances you usually wear a mask. How is it balancing your persona with the real you?

Mr. CreepyPasta:
So the character idea is really dumb. I don't mean it's dumb to do, it's just, like I said, with my channel, I don't particularly have an interesting story. These aren't

calculated things that came about. These are all things that I was like "Yeah, that's cool, I'll do that." You know? This character was the same idea. I kinda just fell into it. A lot of the times, what I do is luck. It's not really anything I've decided.

The blue man character that I have on my channel is kind of a really funny and random character. It's very much based off of the CryptKeeper from Tales from the Crypt. The blue man has a mansion or crypt or whatever and he has a skeleton sidekick named Billy that doesn't speak. Billy is obviously dead, but he doesn't react to him being dead, and is kind of like his best friend. Billy is in the room with him all the time. My wife actually gets on me whenever I kind of just talk to him when I'm working. I'll just randomly talk back and forth to him and she laughs at that. I treat him like a real person because he's in videos with me all the time.

The persona I have actually wasn't a creation of my own. When I started YouTube I was actually in college. One of my friends was an artist and she was a sculpture major, I think. And when we were in college, I told her I started this YouTube channel and was like, "Hey, I wanted to have an icon that would be made up, can you draw me something to use on my channel?" She goes, "Yeah, sure I can do that. But we're in the middle of finals so I can't do it right now. I have to work, so use this." She gave me a painting that she did of me wearing a mask. It was actually of me, she took my bone structure, and she made that into the icon. Now her dad actually has it and he works over at one of the local news stations. Whenever kids come by doing tours they actually see it and they're like, "Oh, you know Mr. CreepyPasta." [laughs]

The blue man character is something I made that up on the fly. I needed something to help me be a little more personality-driven on the channel. So the way he acts on camera is not too different from the character I actually play. My actual person character. He talks in my voice and not a spooky narrator voice or anything like that. Because that's just kind of me being me on camera. And I mean, honestly, the real reason I made him with the mask and everything and not showing the real me on my channel was kind of just because I have this weird obsession and love for superheros.

I wanted to have a secret identity because I thought it was cool to have a secret identity. So I made it and it kind of worked in my favor. All of a sudden it became a big question. Who is Mr. CreepyPasta, what does he really look like? It became a really big thing and I just embraced it. When I saw people were getting into it and thought it was funny, then I made that a big part of the channel. If it became popular among my listeners, I definitely wanted that to be more of a thing.

That's the thing with Billy, actually. Billy was a joke in one opening. I had a skeleton that was playing video games with me and I said, "Get lost Billy," and I threw him off the table. And everybody started laughing about it. "Poor Billy, poor Billy." Everyone loved the fact that I brought Billy back and made him a thing. These characters are not anything that I've really thought about. They sort of just evolved.

SwankyBox:
When you first started creating on YouTube did you have any issues? What was the hardest thing to overcome?

Mr. CreepyPasta:
One thing was definitely having thick skin. Which is something that, I don't know if YouTube talks about it anymore. But they used to put a thing on the creator hub.

Thick skin is essentially being able to put up with the trolls and jerks on YouTube. I would just say, of course, constructive criticism is always one thing. Criticism as in, I couldn't hear this, this effect was too bright, the sound effect was too loud. Things like that are different. I mean everybody needs to take constructive criticism to be able to grow. But then there are people who just say mean, horrible things and then you know, like, it's just hurtful comments and there's no need for it. Nobody really needs it, it doesn't help you out, but people say it. And it's a well known fact that people online will do that because they're hidden behind a computer. You all of a sudden feel like nobody knows who you are, you can be whoever you want to be, and that means most of the time there are no consequences for your actions. So hate is spewed.

One of the hardest things for me to deal with is actually that. Just people who are trolling. And one of the things that I ended up learning about was having "thick skin." You kind of have to toughen yourself up for it. I do a couple panels about YouTube-building at conventions and I usually say everybody has a limited amount of time on earth. Whenever you get negative comments, the best way to deal with it, and the thing I usually live by even if it is toxic, is thinking that at least somebody has given you a small piece of that time that they have on earth. At least that helps you look at it in a more positive way. It gives at least anything negative, no matter how negative it is, a more positive spin. That way, you know, this is one thing that's difficult for me to deal with, but it's still something good. Something good still comes out of it. That's the way I look at it, within reason of course.

People also desensitize themselves to horror so easily just because they consume it all the time. Then they want to get mad because they're not scared anymore. Like man, you did this to yourself!

SwankyBox:
What I love about you as a creator is that you took your storytelling and built a business out of it. People come to you as their ideal narrator. Beyond merchandise and conventions, I know you have a book out as well. I was hoping you could talk about how you branched out as a creator to sustain yourself since advertisements aren't the most reliable.

Mr. CreepyPasta:
I actually learned this from CreepsMcPasta, another Creepypasta narrator. I was there when he first got started. He's a really great friend and we always talk about different things, different bits of horror, stuff like that. He actually has this Google document and every time he gets an idea for something he just writes it in there. A lot of them are just garbage. They're just really dumb things. A lot of them aren't even full ideas, they're just words and he laughs about them later. At one point we were reading through the thing and I think he wrote down sweaty hands and was like "I don't even remember what this was even about, but sweaty hands." He has this document that he writes ideas in. And one day, maybe, he might revisit the idea.

So whenever an idea popped up I started doing the exact same thing. And I started making it into something that I could potentially use. So I have different ideas that I'll just write down that are sometimes not even complete ideas, they're just words. But later on if I want to look at it, I can decide to do it. Sometimes they're just things I want to do. We have different things that I haven't even touched on that we've started and never completed.

Really, branching out or thinking about ways to branch out is just continuing your education. Learn to do new things, don't just become comfortable with what you do. Don't get me wrong, there are days I won't do anything. I'll just play video games all day because that's what I want to do. But other days, I mean, you can't spend your whole life playing video games. You've gotta find new things that are interesting and learn to do new things. Every time you want to learn to do something new, you can always bring that over and include your audience with it.

So I mean, that's what we're doing with the books. We've never touched on that before but a publisher said, "Hey, would you be interested in that?" They said would you be interested in writing a book and I went over to my idea list and was like no, I don't want to write a book because I work with all these other people. They want to write books. Can we get them in on it? If they can get in on it, then yeah, I want to work with you guys. The publisher was really cool with it so they were like, "Yeah, let's get them on and see what we do." So that's where the anthology came from. The comic book was another idea that I'd been working on for quite a while.

Everything else like shirts were actually a demand from the fans at the first convention I went to. They were like, "Can we get shirts?" I was like, "I don't have that." So I went ahead and put together some shirt stuff. I think a lot of it, like I said before, goes down to listening to people. Don't always make everything for you. I know a lot of YouTubers like to say that your YouTube channel is for you because it's yours and you can do what you want. Which is true.

But a lot of the time you can't forget that it's not all about you. This sort of goes in line with branching out, but having a YouTube channel about you and doing what makes you happy is really cool, but if you want to see big success, you can't just do what makes you happy because there's a lot of other people that you're trying to make happy. Making yourself happy is very important but making other people happy is more important for your brand and for your business. Listening to your audience is really importation because they're the ones who are gonna watch your stuff.

I'm just saying if you're a gaming channel and you want to play a puzzle game instead of always playing horror games, expect a different outcome. Playing that puzzle game may make you happy of course, but recognize that when people don't want to watch that as much as they want to watch you doing horror things, it's not because they lost interest in you as a person. It's because your core audience was there for something else and if you want to make them happy, you need to find a happy compromise between the both of you.

SwankyBox:
Obviously you moved forward with creepy storytelling for YouTube, but were there any other passions you considered pursuing?

Mr. CreepyPasta:
There's other things I've wanted to try later on besides just horror. Again, it's one of those things like listening to my audience, right? I don't want to do too much outside of horror. I even started playing games a little bit and they're not as popular. I still get a decent amount of hits on them but they're not as popular and I just kind of do them a little here and there.

One thing I really want to do, and this is so far in the other side of the spectrum that I've never touched on it, but I've considered starting a second channel. I really wanted to do more comic book stuff. Horror is my whole life and I'm never gonna leave it, but I've wrote scripts for sci-fi and comedy stories. All these other things that also deal with audio that I can't do because my name is Mr. CreepyPasta.

I wanted to break more into doing other genres. I wanted to become a full audio channel but it's just becoming really hard to do that. So I've not been able to do it. On my channel a couple of years ago, I used to do these comic book audio dramas and they got like no views. I'm passionate about all these superheroes. I've even got a tattoo of Superman on my arm. It's difficult because I don't know how I could even go about doing it without disrupting my audience.

SwankyBox:
If you had once piece of advice for the next generation of content creators, what would it be?

Mr. CreepyPasta:
Technically a piece of advice that I tell myself when I press that upload button is that everything is going to have exponential growth. You don't know if being the worst of something might end up being the best of something. So you have to stick with doing it and continually adapt. "Oh, I'm not getting anybody to watch." This is what I feel most people have a problem with. "I've been doing this for two months, I don't have very many people watching." That's fine because YouTube is hard and you have to be patient. But when things take off, they will take off big. So stick with it. You'll either be known as the best or the worst, but you'll still be known.

SwankyBox:
Were there any other creators who inspired you to start creating yourself?

Mr. CreepyPasta:
There were. It wasn't so much that it was like, "Oh this is the person I watched before I got started." But after I got started and began watching a lot more YouTubers. I think anybody you talk to has people who inspired them. Markiplier was one of them for me. His level of interaction with his fans was really amazing. I had the chance to meet him too. He was a fantastic guy and he went on far longer than he needed to because he wanted to make sure he got to meet everybody. There was huge line of people waiting to meet him. He inspired me greatly.

Another one was The Little Fears, technically the OG Creepypasta narrator. She would do like short three or four minute videos narrating things and stuff like that. Compared to what I was doing at the time, she was so much better at it than I was. So she kind of really inspired me to pick up my game with that!

• • •

If you thrive off getting the chills and being creeped out, let Mr. CreepyPasta be your guide. His wide variety of creepy storytelling videos will certainly make you shiver. Just be sure to not spook yourself too much if you're listening alone at night!

CHASE YOUR FUTURE

YouTube changed my life. Just a few years ago I was sitting at my office job daydreaming the days away. I had no real life plan because I was afraid to truly put my heart into something. I had wavering faith in a cookie-cutter life process that I blindly accepted. I hoped that luck would be on my side one day and it would all work out. I feel so fortunate to have been inspired enough to stray from that path. I felt like someone rewrote my life timeline and the entire direction of my life changed.

If you've ever considered giving YouTube a whirl, don't wait. Use everything in this book to pursue your dreams and make them a reality. When I first started on YouTube I honestly wish I had a guide of some kind. Something to outline the steps I needed to take so I would have the confidence to continue pushing on. Perhaps that was some strange foreshadowing that I needed to write this book!

I honestly can't wait to see what kinds of things you create. Knowing that I'm able to pass on the torch that was once given to me is kind of a surreal feeling. I feel like a YouTube historian or something. "Back in my day, YouTube didn't even have monetization!"

I digress. Go out and chase your future. Live the life you want to live, and when your time comes after you find success, pass that torch to the next generation of content creators with a smile on your face.

The world is yours.

ACKNOWLEDGEMENTS

Where does one start? My journey on YouTube has been quite a long time coming and there have been a ton of people who have supported me along the way.

First and foremost, my parents. You both never doubted me for a second when I told you I wanted to leave my job and carve out my own path. Of course you were worried since I had just found "success", but you believed in me regardless. You knew I became a go-getter and even though you had no idea what YouTube was, you believed in my choice. That has certainly meant the world to me.

To my brothers. Both of you were there from the beginning and even helped me write out my first videos. I'm still sitting on a stack of our first video concepts about top 10 anime battles, epic fights, and the cheapest characters in fighting games. Thanks for contributing your thoughts and for watching me grow on my journey. Our childhood gaming memories were really the foundation of all of this, which I think is pretty darn cool!

To my fiancée Stephanie. You were there every time I fell down to pick me right back up. We both deviated from our life paths to chase after a creative dream, and I wouldn't change it for the world. Thank you for being my partner and my hiking buddy on this long, crazy journey to our futures.

To my inspirations. Markiplier, Devinsupertramp, and MatPat. All of you played a role in me making the jump into the unknown. You're like the scarecrow, tin man, and lion to my Dorthy. I'm not sure if that even makes sense, but you are. Markiplier, you always instilled in me that anything was possible. I loved watching you grow as a creator because you gave me so much hope. Your accomplishments empowered me to seek out my own. Devinsupertramp, you truly defined turning a passion into a career. Watching your videos showcasing amazing talents in equally awesome locations took me to far away places while at my desk at work. For a moment I was free and taking on the world vicariously. MatPat, you kept my wit sharp and reminded me that knowledge was my greatest gift. Gaming would be my medium, but what I accomplished with it was truly up to me. You empowered me to stop waiting for something to happen when I could make it a reality with my own two hands. All three of you helped me out greatly, and for that I'll always be thankful.

To What's With Games, SnowKnowsShow, and Crispy Pixel for being there when I started. I was very fortunate to stumble upon our little chat group through Reddit. Having others to talk to about creating videos helped out a lot. I'll always remember our late night chats as they were definitely something that kept me going despite sometimes wanting to throw in the towel.

To Nullatrum and Shesez. Although both of you have never met, I've always cherished our talks. Both of you entered my life at different times during my journey on YouTube and I truly feel lucky to have gotten to know each of you.

To Jonathan "Duke" Williams. Thanks for being a voice of reason when it came to all things video. Your knowledge on the subject exceeds pretty much anyone I know, and that's truly an amazing gift.

To Zach, Louie, Stephanie, Diederik, and Mitch. Thanks for lending a hand with editing when I needed it most!

To Kevin and Stephanie for helping me with all the editing in this book. Many a "certainly," "however" and "highly recommend" died in the process.

To all of my friends who still supported me when I became a YouTube hermit and closed off from the world. You would pull me back into reality and it was greatly appreciated. That may sound a tad silly, but it means more than you'll ever know.

To Corey. You put up with my grand YouTube vision in the early days of SwankyBox and never questioned it. You honestly made making videos a blast, and I'm happy to have you as a friend.

To Steve. You're destined for great things, you just don't know it yet.

And last but certainly not least, to my pets. The pets I had growing up and the pets I care for today. Thank you for spending time with me during the darkest of days and for always being there for me no matter what.

ABOUT THE AUTHOR

SwankyBox (Bradley Burke) is a YouTuber who runs a video-game-focused channel with tens of millions of views. He speaks at conventions around the country about YouTube, storytelling, and pursuing your creative passions. By trade he is an animator, videographer, and writer. He took the YouTube plunge in 2015 and has been living in the world of online video ever since.

Brad quickly learned that teaching people through gaming was very effective. He constantly encourages those who are watching to think outside of the box and to contribute their own thoughts to the discussion.

Brad's attentiveness to each viewer's experience has allowed him to reach the front page of Reddit twice for videos he created. Beyond that, his channel gained over one hundred thousand subscribers within the first year of pursuing it full-time. He constantly analyzes trends to deliver optimized content for a search-heavy online world. He also is a YouTube consultant for other creators and businesses.

Connect with Brad at: SwankyBoxMedia.com

THE
YOUTUBER
JOURNEY

Bring Brad to your organization, convention, or event!

YouTuber / Author / Speaker

Brad has spoken around the country about YouTube, storytelling, and pursuing your creative passions. Whether it be at industry conferences or fan conventions, he offers a wide variety of programming and topics to choose from.

Beyond that, Brad has consulted for many organizations and creators about the power of online video.

Contact Brad Today:

SwankyBoxMedia.com

CPSIA information can be obtained
at www.ICGtesting.com
Printed in the USA
LVHW08s0057080918
589551LV00008B/145/P